ELECTRA AND OTHER PLAYS

EURIPIDES, the youngest of the three great Athenian playwrights, was born around 485 BC of a family of good standing. He first competed in the dramatic festivals in 455 BC, coming only third; his record of successes in the tragic competitions is lower than that of either Aeschylus or Sophocles. There is a tradition that he was unpopular, even a recluse; we are told that he composed poetry in a cave by the sea, near Salamis. What is clear from contemporary evidence, however, is that audiences were fascinated by his innovative and often disturbing dramas. His work was controversial already in his lifetime, and he himself was regarded as a 'clever' poet, associated with philosophers and other intellectuals. Towards the end of his life he went to live at the court of Archelaus, king of Macedon. It was during his time there that he wrote what many consider his greatest work, the *Bacchae*. When news of his death reached Athens in early 406 BC, Sophocles appeared publicly in mourning for him. Euripides is thought to have written about ninety-two plays, of which seventeen tragedies and one satyr-play known to be his survive; the other play which is attributed to him, the *Rhesus*, may in fact be by a later hand.

JOHN N. DAVIE was born in Glasgow in 1950, and was educated at the High School of Glasgow, Glasgow University and Balliol College, Oxford, where he wrote a thesis on Greek tragedy. From 1975 to 1984 he taught Classics at Harrow, before moving to St Paul's School to become Head of Classics. He is the author of two articles on the problems of writing favourably about monarchy in a democratic society such as fifth-century BC Athens.

DR RICHARD RUTHERFORD was born in Edinburgh in 1956, and was educated at Robert Gordon's College, Aberdeen, and at Worcester College, Oxford. Since 1982 he has been Tutor in Greek and Latin Literature at Christ Church, Oxford. He is the author of a number of books and articles on classical authors, including a commentary on books 19 and 20 of Homer's *Odyssey* (1992), and *The Art of Plato: Ten Essays in Platonic Interpretation* (1995).

EURIPIDES

ELECTRA AND OTHER PLAYS

Translated by JOHN DAVIE,
with an introduction and notes by
RICHARD RUTHERFORD

PENGUIN BOOKS

PENGUIN BOOKS

Published by the Penguin Group
Penguin Books Ltd, 27 Wrights Lane, London w8 5tz, England
Penguin Putnam Inc., 375 Hudson Street, New York, New York 10014, USA
Penguin Books Australia Ltd, Ringwood, Victoria, Australia
Penguin Books Canada Ltd, 10 Alcorn Avenue, Toronto, Ontario, Canada m4v 3b2
Penguin Books India (P) Ltd, 11, Community Centre, Panchsheel Park, New Delhi – 110 017, India
Penguin Books (NZ) Ltd, Private Bag 102902, NSMC, Auckland, New Zealand
Penguin Books (South Africa) (Pty) Ltd, 5 Watkins Street, Denver Ext 4, Johannesburg 2094, South Africa

Penguin Books Ltd, Registered Offices: Harmondsworth, Middlesex, England

This translation first published 1998

7

Translation copyright © John Davie, 1998
Introduction and notes copyright © Richard Rutherford, 1998
All rights reserved

The moral right of the translator and editor has been asserted

Set in 10/12.5 pt Postscript Monotype Bembo
Typeset by Rowland Phototypesetting Ltd, Bury St Edmunds, Suffolk
Printed in England by Clays Ltd, St Ives plc

CONTENTS

GENERAL INTRODUCTION

'I portray men as they should be, but Euripides portrays them as they are.'
(Sophocles, quoted by Aristotle, *Poetics*, ch. 25, 1460b33−4)

'Whatever other defects of organization he may have, Euripides is the most intensely tragic of all the poets.' (Aristotle, *Poetics*, ch. 14, 1453a28−30)

'I am really amazed that the scholarly nobility does not comprehend his virtues, that they rank him below his predecessors, in line with that high-toned tradition which the clown Aristophanes brought into currency . . . Has any nation ever produced a dramatist who would deserve to hand him his slippers?' (Goethe, *Diaries*, 22nd Nov. 1831)

'What were you thinking of, overweening Euripides, when you hoped to press myth, then in its last agony, into your service? It died under your violent hands . . . Though you hunted all the passions up from their couch and conjured them into your circle, though you pointed and burnished a sophistic dialectic for the speeches of your heroes, they have only counterfeit passions and speak counterfeit speeches.' (Nietzsche, *The Birth of Tragedy*, ch. 10)

I

Already in his own lifetime Euripides was a controversial figure. Daring in his theatrical innovations, superbly eloquent and articulate in the rhetoric which he gave to his characters, closely in touch with the intellectual life of his time, he has stimulated and shocked audiences

vii

and readers not only through the unexpected twists and turns of his plots, but also by the alarming immorality of many of his characters. But before exploring these and other aspects of his work in more detail, we must briefly put him in context, by giving an outline of the earlier history of the Athenian genre of tragedy, and the work of Aeschylus, his great predecessor, and of Sophocles, his older contemporary.

Unlike epic poetry, which was a traditional form familiar throughout the Greek world, tragedy was a relatively new invention in the fifth century BC, and one which was particularly Athenian. Its origins and early development are obscure: if, as Aristotle believed, it originated in a form of choral song, the 'dithyramb', a song in honour of the god Dionysus, then it has already been transformed before the time of Aeschylus. Ancient tradition held that contests between tragic playwrights had become an established part of the festival known as the City Dionysia (held in March) some time in the 530s, and that the key figure of these early days was a dramatist called Thespis. Our earliest surviving tragedy is Aeschylus' *Persians*, performed in 472, a full sixty years later. The dramas which have survived span the rest of the fifth century, a period of intense political activity and social and intellectual change. Hence generalizations even about the extant dramas will be dangerous, and we must always bear in mind that we have only the tip of the iceberg.

The Athenian tragedies were performed in the open air, in a theatre enormous by modern standards: some experts believe that it could have contained more than 14,000 people, as it certainly could after reconstruction in the fourth century.[1] This large audience was probably composed mainly of men (it is likely that women could attend, but probable that not many did so). Those attending paid for admission, but the price was low, probably less than half a labourer's daily wage; in the fourth century even this charge was paid for out of public subsidies. The stage-arrangements were sparse: a building set behind the main area where the actors moved would represent a palace or other such building according to the needs of the play. Perhaps on a lower level (though the layout is much disputed) was the open area called the *orchestra* ('dancing-space'), in which the chorus stood or danced. The events were presented as happening out of doors, theatrically necessary but also more natural in Mediterranean life. Entrances along passages on either side of the theatre were loosely conceived as leading to different destinations − country or city, army camp or seashore, depending on the plot. Actors were all male (even for female parts), normally Athenian citizens; all wore masks and dignified formal dress; speaking actors were almost invariably limited to three in number, but could take on different roles during the play by changing costume and mask offstage. Stage equipment and props were few; the action was largely stylized, even static, with the more violent action conceived as taking place offstage, then being reported to the actors, often in a long narrative speech. All plays were in verse, partly spoken and partly sung; although Euripides made several strides towards more 'realistic' drama, the effect of a Greek tragedy in his time would still have been to move the audience to a distant world, where great figures of the mythical past fought and disputed over momentous issues.

Every Greek tragedy had a chorus, a team of twelve or fifteen singers representing the community or some other body concerned with the events of the drama. It may be that originally tragedy consisted wholly of choral songs; if so, the key innovation, whether Thespis or another was responsible, must have been the introduction of an actor who engaged in dialogue with the chorus, who could withdraw and take part in events offstage, then return to inform them of developments. Aeschylus is said to have introduced a second actor, Sophocles a third. There the tragedians stopped, though as the century passed the three actors were often expected to play more roles, and 'mute' actors (domestic slaves, attendants or soldiers) were permitted. In general, the importance of the actors and the size of their role in the play increased, while that of the chorus declined; but in the work of the three great tragedians the chorus was never unimportant, and their songs or 'choral odes' do far more than fill in time or allow an interval: these odes comment on the action, react to it and ponder its significance, placing it in a larger perspective, chronological and religious. Some of the finest poetry in Greek tragedy comes in the choral odes.

We tend to think of the theatre as a recreation, and one which is available more or less any night of the year. The position in ancient Athens was quite different. Drama was part of a civic occasion, the festival of Dionysus. Although the city held many religious festivals, tragedies were performed only at a few, and at fixed points in the year. It was not possible for a dramatist to stage anything he liked at any time; he had to apply to the proper authorities and be 'granted a chorus', given permission to compete and financial support (it is true, however, that we also have evidence for theatrical activities in rural Attica, where procedure was perhaps less formal than at the great civic festivals). In the earliest times the dramatist would also play a part in his plays, though Sophocles is said to have given this up because his voice was weak. Still more important, the author was also the producer, working together with his actors and choruses and training them. At the City Dionysia three tragedians would compete for the prize every year; each of them would present three tragedies – sometimes but not necessarily a connected 'trilogy'. Aeschylus favoured these trilogies (as his master-piece, the *Oresteia*, illustrates), but they seem to have gone out of fashion after his death, and the overwhelming majority of surviving tragedies are self-contained dramas. After that each competing dramatist would also put on a 'satyr-play'. This last was a wild and fantastic tailpiece, usually shorter than a tragedy: it always had a chorus of satyrs, the bestial entourage of Dionysus, and usually treated mythological themes in a burlesque and bawdy way. The only complete example to survive is Euripides' *Cyclops*, an amusing take-off of the story told in Homer's *Odyssey* about the hero's encounter with the one-eyed monster.

What of the content of the tragedies? Perhaps the most significant fact is that the subjects are almost always mythological.[2] The only surviving exception is Aeschylus' *Persians*, though we know of a few others in the early period. The *Persians* commemorates the victory of the Greeks in the recent war against Xerxes, king of Persia, and in particular the battle of Salamis, which had taken place only eight years earlier. But this exception in a way proves the rule, for the play is not set in Greece, but at the Persian court, presenting the subject from the Persian viewpoint. Nor is it mere jingoism: the theme is almost mythologized, raised to a grander and more heroic plane. No individual Greek is named or singled out for praise: the emphasis falls rather on the arrogant folly of a deluded king, who has led his people to defeat. There is, as always in tragedy, a supernatural element: the ghost of

Xerxes' father, summoned back to earth, pronounces stern judgement on his son's rash ambition. In the rest of the tragic corpus, the dramatists use myth to distance their stories in time, and so give them universality. Instead of setting their actors the task of impersonating living generals or politicians confronting contemporary crises, the tragedians, like Homer, show us men and women who are remote from us in their circumstances, yet vividly like us and real in their hopes, fears and desires.

Secondly, Greek tragedy is civic in emphasis: its plots, that is, deal with kings and rulers, disputes and dilemmas which have vital implications for the state as a whole. If Oedipus cannot find the murderer of Laius, the plague which is already devastating Thebes will destroy it. If Odysseus and Neoptolemus cannot recover Philoctetes and his bow, Troy will not fall. Consequently tragedy normally deals with men and women of high status – monarchs and royal families, tyrants and mighty heroes. Characters of lower rank generally have smaller parts. As we shall see, however, this is one area in which Euripides showed himself an innovator: 'I made tragedy more democratic', he is made to say in the satirical treatment of tragedy in Aristophanes' *Frogs*, produced after his death.

Thirdly, complementing and often conflicting with the political dimension, the family is regularly the focus for tragic action. Part of the lasting power of Greek drama lies in the vividness with which it presents extreme love and (still more) intense hatred within the family: matricide, parricide, fratricide, adultery and jealousy, even incest and other forbidden passions. Duty to family and duty to the state may come into conflict: can Agamemnon bring himself to abandon the expedition against Troy, or must he take the terrible decision to sacrifice his daughter for a fair wind? Loyalty to kin is central to *Antigone*; conflicting obligations to different members of the family create many of the dilemmas in the *Oresteia*. The list could easily be extended.

Fourthly, there is the religious aspect. We know too little of early tragedy to confirm or deny the theory that it concentrated mainly on the myths of Dionysus, in whose honour the plays were performed; but by Aeschylus' time the scope has obviously broadened. But no Greek tragedy is secular. Although the dramatists normally focus on the actions and sufferings of human beings, the gods are always present in the background. In early tragedy they figure quite frequently on stage as characters (as in Aeschylus' *Eumenides*). Sophocles seems to have been much more restrained in this, while Euripides normally confines them to the prologue (where they do not usually meet any mortal characters), or to the conclusion of a play, where a god may appear on a higher level, above the stage-building. Sometimes this seems to be a matter of the god standing on the roof of the building, but more spectacular still was the use of a crane-like device to allow the divinity the power of flight. From this remote position of authority the god would declare his will, *ex machina* as the phrase has it, intervening to resolve or at least impose a conclusion upon the events on earth.

Even when gods do not appear, they are frequently invoked, addressed in prayer, called to witness an oath, sometimes questioned or challenged. With the awesome powers of Olympus watching and influencing events, human affairs gain a larger significance: these are not trivial wars or petty crimes, if they attract divine attention and even retribution. Yet because the humans often seem helpless pawns or puppets in the divine game, the greatness of the heroes can seem sadly insignificant, and their proud boasts or ambitions may often be ironically overturned or frustrated. The wiser players on the tragic stage sometimes draw this pessimistic conclusion. 'I see we are but phantoms, all we who live, or fleeting shadows,' says Odysseus in Sophocles' *Ajax* (125–6); or as the chorus sing in *Oedipus the King,* after the horrible truth is out: 'Alas ye generations of men, how close to nothingness do I count your life. Where in the world is the mortal who wins more of happiness than just the illusion, and after the semblance, the falling away? With your example, your fate before my eyes, yours, unhappy Oedipus, I count no man happy' (1186–96).

One last general point should be made. Greek tragedy was intended for performance: although texts undoubtedly circulated, the primary concern was production in the theatre.[3] It is important to try to reconstruct the stage movements, the points at which characters enter and exit, observe one another, come into physical contact, pass objects to another person, and so forth. Major questions of interpretation may hinge on these seemingly small-scale puzzles: to take an example from the plays in the first volume of this series, does Hippolytus ever address Phaedra or not? It all depends on how we envisage the staging, and relate it to the words, of a particular scene (*Hippolytus* 601–68, esp. 651ff.). In the present volume, the case of *Andromache* is particularly striking: in the original performance, the character Andromache either appeared in the final scene or she did not. Since she speaks no words in that scene, the text gives us no guidance; but her mute appearance, recalling to the audience her previous suffering and the miseries of Troy, would modify the effect of the end of the play, in which so much is made of the death of Neoptolemus, one of the sackers of Troy.

Moreover, the tragic performance involved music and dancing by the chorus, of which we can recover next to nothing – a few descriptions in ancient prose authors, a handful of papyri with musical annotation, and pictures of dramatic productions on vases do not get us very far. To compare our situation with that of an opera-lover confined to studying a libretto would be unfair to the tragedians, for the spoken dialogue of tragedy is far richer and more significant, demands far more attention from the audience, than the interludes between songs in opera. But we should not forget that, particularly in the choruses and the other lyrics, we have lost what the original cast and audience would have regarded as a vital part of the production.[4]

II

To try to sum up the work of Aeschylus and Sophocles in a few paragraphs is to risk pure banality.[5] The attempt must be made, however, if we are to see Euripides in relation to his great predecessors. Seven complete tragedies attributed to Aeschylus survive, including his monumental trilogy, the *Oresteia* (*Agamemnon*, *Libation-Bearers*, *Eumenides*). One of the others, *Prometheus Bound*, has recently been subject to close critical scrutiny, and on the basis of this analysis many authoritative judges think it spurious; but if so, its author shares something of Aeschylus' grandeur of conception and magnificence of language. As already explained, Aeschylus tended to use the trilogy form, which permitted him, as in the *Oresteia* and in the series of which the *Seven against Thebes* is the third, to trace the history of a family through several generations, showing how the sins of the elders are re-enacted or paid for by their descendants. Inherited guilt, ancestral curses, persecuting Furies, vendetta and religious pollution – concepts such as these permeate the world of Aeschylean tragedy, a world of dark powers and evil crimes, in which humans must pray and hope for justice and retribution from the gods, but may pray in vain, or find that the gods are slow to respond. Austere in its characterization, eloquent yet exotic in its polysyllabic style, dominated by long and complex choral songs, his drama often seems to belong to a much older world. Yet this is only one side of a complex artist; Aeschylus, born in the sixth century BC, is also the poet of democratic Athens, deeply concerned with its ideals of reasoned discussion and decision-making. By the end of the fifth century he was established as a classic (his plays were re-performed in recognition of this), though he could also be regarded as remote and difficult. Aristophanes' *Frogs*, which dramatizes Dionysus' quest in the underworld for a great poet to bring back to life, presents Aeschylus as a symbol of the good old days, but also as a composer of grandiose and incomprehensible lyrics. In the next century, Aristotle in the *Poetics* uses examples from Sophocles and Euripides far more than from Aeschylus.

To sum up Aeschylus as a poet of archaic grandeur would, however, be quite misleading. He is capable of much lighter and even humorous passages: particularly memorable are the sentimental reminiscences of Orestes' nurse in the *Libation-Bearers*, or the complaints of the herald in *Agamemnon* about the awful time the common soldiers had at Troy (it is significant that both of these are lower-class types; the great tragic figures are not allowed these more chatty interludes). More important, in his presentation of the doom-laden world of the heroic age he not only shows us horrific events and catastrophe, but also allows his characters to work towards a difficult resolution. In Aeschylean tragedy there is a strong emphasis on the power of the gods, particularly the will of Zeus, who oversees human lives and may bring blessings as well as destruction. Not all the dilemmas faced by Aeschylus' characters are insoluble, although the final outcome may be preceded by further hard choices or disasters. The city of Thebes is saved from invasion, but only through the death of Eteocles, its king. Above, all in the *Oresteia*, the one trilogy which we can study as a magnificently unified whole, Aeschylus dramatizes the contrast between a darker world of vendetta and savage intrafamilial conflict and a society in which the rule of law has an important place, where argument and persuasion may prove superior to hatred and violence. It is a society which mirrors or idealizes his own: the refugee Argive Orestes, pursued by the monstrous Furies, finds sanctuary in a mythical Athens where Athena presides over an archetypal lawcourt. In this trilogy, although the suffering and crimes of the past are not forgotten, the final emphasis is on the enlightened justice of the present, and the reconciliation of opposed factions among the gods promises prosperity in the future. Aeschylus as a boy had seen the overthrow of the Athenian tyrants; he had fought at Marathon, and in his later years saw the transformation of his city into a democracy and the centre of an empire. It is no surprise that ideals of political debate and civic harmony are prominent in his work; but in view of the darker side discussed above, it would be facile to label him an optimist, either about human nature or about human society. The tragic power of his dramas is not diminished by his central recognition that something positive may, in the end, emerge after or out of suffering.

Whereas Aeschylus' characters (*Prometheus* apart) are above all members of a family or of a larger community, Sophocles tends to focus on individuals set apart from their society or at odds with those who care for them: Ajax, Antigone, Electra, Philoctetes, the aged Oedipus. With him, more than with the other two tragedians, it makes sense to speak of tragic heroes and heroines. Again we have only seven plays, selected in late antiquity for school study, and we know that this represents less than a tenth of his output; moreover, those we have are mostly impossible to date. Obviously generalizations must be surrounded with cautious qualifications, but we can recognize a number of other differences from Aeschylus (to whom he nevertheless owed much). The abandonment of trilogy-form has already been mentioned. The role of the chorus is somewhat reduced, though some of the odes which reflect on human achievement and its smallness in relation to the timeless power of the gods have a poetic splendour to match almost anything in Aeschylus. The characters have more depth and subtlety:

as an anonymous ancient biographer said of Sophocles, 'He knows how to arrange the action with such a sense of timing that he creates an entire character out of a mere half-line or a single expression.' Partly because he makes more varied use of the third actor, Sophocles constructs scenes which involve more shifts of attention, more realistic and sophisticated interplay between characters, than we can easily find in Aeschylus. Another difference is in the religious atmosphere. Aeschylus regularly brought the gods on stage and allowed them to converse with humans (the Furies, Athena and Apollo in *Eumenides*, Aphrodite in the lost third play of the *Suppliant Women* trilogy); Sophocles does so only rarely, and even then the gap between man and god is emphasized: Athena is remote and haughty with Odysseus in *Ajax*, Heracles commanding and superhuman in *Philoctetes*; both are probably out of reach, above the human level. In general, the gods do not communicate plainly or unambiguously with mortals: oracles and prophecies offer mysterious and misleading insights, and even Oedipus, the most intelligent of men, can find that his whole life has been lived on completely false assumptions. The limitations of human knowledge allow ample scope for dramatic irony, where the audience understand the double meanings or the deeper truths behind the superficial sense of the words. Central to Sophoclean tragedy is the gap between reality and appearance, understanding and illusion; his characters often discern the truth about their circumstances, or themselves, only when it is too late to avert disaster.

Sophocles has sometimes been seen as a particularly 'pious' writer or thinker. In part this results from a very partial reading of certain selected passages which have been taken to express the poet's own opinions (always a dangerous method); in part it derives from information about his involvement in Athenian religious life, for instance the cult of Asclepius. But within his plays, although the power of the gods is beyond question, and those who doubt that power or reject their oracles are swiftly refuted, it is hard to see any straightforward scheme of divine *justice* at work. Divine action is characterized as enigmatic and obscure. There is an order in the world, as is shown by the fulfilment of oracles; but the pattern is often too elusive for men to grasp. The gods are not indifferent to humanity: they punish Creon in *Antigone*, they grant a home and honour to Oedipus at the end of his life (*Oedipus at Colonus*). But there are also mysteries which remain unanswered: why does Antigone have to die? Why did Philoctetes suffer agonies in isolation on Lemnos for nine years? Any open-minded reader of these plays will acknowledge that Sophocles does not give us a simple or uniform account of human life or of mankind's relation to the gods and fate. Had he done so, the plays would probably not have remained so hauntingly powerful over two and a half millennia.

Sophocles is justly regarded as the greatest master of formal structure – no mere mechanical technique, but a vital aspect of his art. The development of each scene, in each play, is beautifully paced; the contrasts of style and mood between successive scenes, or between one scene and the choral song which follows, are achieved with seemingly effortless brilliance. These skills are combined with deep understanding of character in the scenes between Neoptolemus and Philoctetes, with mastery of tension and irony in the advancing quest which will lead Oedipus to self-discovery. On a more minute level of style, *Oedipus the King* also shows his subtlety of technique in the exchange which culminates in the revelation of the hero's identity (1173–6): here each line is divided between Oedipus and the herdsman whom he is questioning, and as the truth becomes plainer Oedipus' questions become shorter and more faltering, the servant's responses fuller and more desperate. This flexible handling of dialogue form is only one small example of the complete command Sophocles has over his medium. Appalling hatred and unbearable loss are expressed in formal verse of wonderful lucidity and sharpness; only rarely do the eloquent lines dissolve into incoherent cries of pain, as they do when Philoctetes is overcome by his repulsive wound.

III

We turn now to our main subject, the third of the great tragedians. It is far too commonly supposed that Euripides comes 'after' Sophocles, and this can easily lead to a simplifying formula which sees Aeschylus as primitive, Euripides as decadent, and Sophocles as the apex of perfection in between. In fact although Euripides was clearly younger, he and Sophocles were competing together, often against one another, for most of their lives, and Sophocles died within a year of his rival. Both were very much younger than Aeschylus, though they will certainly have seen some of his later productions. Sophocles in fact competed against Aeschylus with his first production, in 468 BC, and won; Euripides first put on a tetralogy in 455 with a less satisfactory result, coming third. We do not know his competitors on that occasion. From that point on Euripides was constantly in the public eye, putting on a total of around ninety plays up to his death in 406 (his last plays, including the *Bacchae*, were produced posthumously).

We know very little about his life, and what comes down from antiquity is often unreliable (a great deal seems to be derived from the comic treatment of the dramatist by Aristophanes). There is a long-standing tradition that he was unpopular and unsuccessful in his career. We are told that he was melancholy, thoughtful and severe, that he hated laughter and women, that he lived in a cave looking out to the sea from Salamis, that he had a substantial library. None of this amounts to much more than doubtful anecdote. A more concrete statement, which probably rests on inscriptional evidence, is that he won the first prize four times (once posthumously) in his whole career. This sounds more dramatic than it is, since prizes would be awarded to the tetralogy of plays as a whole: in other words, sixteen out of about ninety plays were winners. Even with this reservation, however, there remains a contrast with the other two tragedians: Aeschylus and Sophocles were each victorious with over half their plays. In the end Euripides is said to have emigrated to Macedonia, where King Archelaus was gathering a circle of poets and intellectuals to give tone to his court. It may be doubted whether he left Athens purely because he felt unappreciated; the hardships of life in a city engaged in a long war which she now looked likely to lose might be a more pragmatic explanation. He died in Macedonia, an event again elaborated in wild anecdotes (he was allegedly torn to pieces, like Actaeon in myth, by a pack of hunting-dogs). We should not attach too much importance to the figure about his victories, for it is clear that he was repeatedly granted a chorus, and that the Athenians enjoyed and were fascinated by his work. The constant parodies and references to his plays in

Aristophanes' comedies are not only satirical criticism but a kind of tribute to a playwright whose work he obviously knew intimately and whose significance was beyond question.

We happen to have more plays by Euripides than by the other two tragedians put together: the complete total is nineteen, but that includes the satyr-play *Cyclops* and also *Rhesus*, a play widely thought to be a fourth-century imitation. This larger figure is partly accidental, the results of the hazards of transmission through the ages, but partly reflects the popularity of Euripides in the educational tradition – his language is easier, his speeches were more suitable for aspiring orators to study, and his plays, with their heady mixture of intellectual and emotional appeal, might be found more immediately accessible.[6] We can also put fairly firm dates on a good many of the plays, because of information which survives in copies of the original inscriptions recording victories in the contests and citing the names of annual magistrates of Athens. Where external evidence for dating is lacking, the date of a play can be determined within limits by 'stylometry', that is, the statistical analysis of the poet's changing linguistic and metrical habits, using the firmly dated plays as a framework.[7] This means not only that we can say something about Euripides' development as a poet, but also that it is possible to identify, or at least speculate about, passages which touch on or allude to Athenian politics and other contemporary events. This is naturally most tempting with plays such as the *Children of Heracles* and the *Suppliant Women*, which are set in Athens and present a mythological image of the Athenians as benefactors of others. But there are many other passages which, without naming Athens, use the language of contemporary politics or ideology. A good example comes in *Orestes*, in which a detailed account of a meeting of the assembly of Argive citizens includes lines which remind the reader of historical and rhetorical texts of the period – of the historian Thucydides' portrayal of Athenian demagogues, for example (*Orestes* 866–952, esp. 902–16). Although the importance of this approach has sometimes been exaggerated, and the tragedies are not allegories of history, it is a mistake to rule out such allusions on principle.[8]

None of the plays we possess in entirety is from the earliest stage of Euripides' career; the first, *Alcestis*, was produced in 438 BC, when he was already in his forties. The great majority of surviving plays come from the last three decades of the fifth century, the period of the great war between Athens and Sparta, a time in which the cultural and political prominence of Athens was still conspicuous but no longer unchallenged, and by the end of the period increasingly under threat. Euripides did not live to see the defeat of Athens, but several of his later plays suggest growing pessimism about political and military leadership, about civic deliberation, and about the conduct of the victors in wartime. These are not novel themes, in poetry or in life, but they have an added resonance in the light of fifth-century history.

The sheer range and variety of Euripides' plays is extraordinary. Perhaps if we had as many of Aeschylus' or Sophocles' plays they would seem equally difficult to categorize; but it is tempting to see Euripides as particularly innovative and trend-setting. Like Sophocles, he seems to have worked mainly on sequences of self-contained plays, though it looks as if the *Trojan Women* was the third of a trilogy concerning the Trojan war from its origins to its conclusion. Unlike Sophocles, he does not generally take a single heroic figure to form the focus of a play – only *Medea* easily fits this pattern. There is a strong tendency to divide the play between major characters: thus in *Alcestis* the heroine gives way to Heracles, the sufferer to the doer; in *Hippolytus* Phaedra dominates the first half of the play, Hippolytus the second; in the *Bacchae* the action is polarized, with the mortal Pentheus and the disguised god Dionysus in conflict throughout. Other plays extend this experimentation to the overall structure. Thus in *Andromache* we begin, as we might expect, with the widow of Hector in difficulties, but as the action advances Andromache is forgotten and other events follow, with different characters taking the limelight. In the *Trojan Women* the continuous presence of Hecabe, the grieving queen of Troy, seems to mark her out as the 'heroine', or at least the principal sufferer, but she is a figure who can achieve nothing. As the play unfolds we are shown a series of scenes which embody the suffering and ruin accompanying the fall of Troy, a sequence which adds up only to further misery. Other plays multiply characters and divide our attention still more: *Helen* has eight human characters with full speaking parts, *Orestes* nine, the *Phoenician Women* eleven.

The plays of Euripides, although they still work within the traditional range of myths, do not generally dramatize heroic initiatives and triumphant achievements. His are tragedies of suffering rather than of action (*Medea* again is a special case, a partial exception). Phaedra, Andromache, Hecabe, the Trojan women, the chorus of mothers in the *Suppliant Women*, the guilt-ravaged Orestes, are all presented as victims, whether of war or other persecution, human folly or divine antagonism. Even when they do attempt to take the initiative, to assert themselves through action, the consequences are rarely presented positively. Phaedra's efforts to preserve her good name bring about Hippolytus' death without achieving her objective; Electra and Orestes in *Electra* destroy their mother, but with psychologically devastating results for themselves; in *Orestes*, the young man's matricide makes him an outcast, and his efforts to take revenge on his mother's sister Helen are first frustrated, then turned to near-farce. Even when Euripides is reworking material which had been treated grimly enough by Aeschylus, he regularly gives his own version a new twist. The brutal sacrifice of Iphigenia at Aulis, so that the Greek fleet may sail for Troy, was presented by Aeschylus in an unforgettable choral song as a terrible necessity, an agonizing decision reluctantly taken by Agamemnon, and one which will have momentous consequences. In Euripides' version, *Iphigenia at Aulis*, Agamemnon and Menelaus chop and change, other members of the expedition seem to have more authority than the leaders have, Iphigenia herself changes her mind, and, most disturbing of all, there is the off-stage presence of the army, an uncontrollable mob of soldiers panting for blood. *Iphigenia at Aulis* is a fast-moving and constantly attention-grabbing play, but one in which the high seriousness of the Aeschylean ode is dissipated, and the tragic sacrifice becomes wasteful self-deception. As A. P. Burnett put it: 'In these plays the poet shows men scaled for comedy trying to live in a world still ruled by the gods of tragedy.'[9]

Some of the ways in which Euripides made old subjects new have already been mentioned. This practice was not simply a perverse desire on his part to alter tradition. Between 480 and 430 BC some 500 tragedies would have been staged; a middle-aged man in his audience might have seen over two hundred.[10] The Athenians, like any audience, enjoyed innovation: indeed, originality and novelty were at a premium in the second half of the fifth century, as new ideas and new literary styles made their appearance in Athens. Euripides was in part responding to audience demand (though it is only fair to add that a sizeable portion of his audience would be more conservative, and that Sophocles clearly did not feel the need to innovate so ostentatiously). By the middle stage of Euripides' career Aeschylus looked archaic: in his *Electra*, the younger tragedian unmistakably parodies a recognition-scene from Aeschylus' *Libation-Bearers*, in which the discovery of a lock of hair at Aga-memnon's tomb was taken as evidence of Orestes' return (513ff.). It is interesting to note that the grounds for criticism are improbability, lack of realism, violation of common sense. Aeschylus and his audience had been above such concerns; by Euripides' time it was more natural to apply to tragedy at least some of the standards of everyday life.[11] Nevertheless, the parody is two-edged: it turns out that the Euripidean Electra's scepticism is misguided, and the deduction from the Aeschylean token remains valid. The allusion to Aeschylus need not be merely dismissive.

Innovation can also be observed in the composition of Euripides' plots. It is natural for us to think of the myths as fixed and organized, as they are in the modern summaries which we find in handbooks; but in fact the fluidity of the legends is surprising, and the tragedians already found variations in the epic and lyric accounts which they inherited. Euripides often uses less familiar versions of myths, or com-bines stories normally kept apart. Although the loss of so much earlier literature makes firm assertions dangerous, it seems likely that he is modifying the legend in making Medea kill her own children deliber-ately (in an earlier version it was the Corinthians who took their revenge upon her offspring). In the legends of Heracles it was normally held that the hero's labours were a kind of penance for killing his children in a fit of insanity. Euripides reverses the sequence, making Heracles return home to his family triumphant after his labours are ended – then, the crowning horror, madness and slaughter follow. In his *Helen* he adopts the bizarre version of the lyric poet Stesichorus, which made Helen a prisoner in Egypt throughout the Trojan war, while Greek and Trojan armies fought for ten years over a phantom. The unexpected becomes the rule, in both plot and characterization: women behave manfully, slaves show nobility and virtue, barbarians express civilized sentiments.

Even when he is closer to the traditional versions, he often introduces new characters or explores the implications of legends with a fresh eye: thus in *Orestes* Menelaus, Tyndareus, Hermione and Orestes' friend Pylades all have prominent roles, and the effect is quite different from earlier versions of this myth. Characterization can also be modified: in Aeschylus' *Seven against Thebes*, Eteocles, king of Thebes, is a noble figure, though labouring under a curse; in Euripides' *Phoenician Women*, he becomes a power-crazed tyrant. In the *Electra* of Euripides it is even possible to sympathize with Clytemnestra and Aegisthus, the murderers of Agamemnon. Sharp changes of direction and unexpected shifts of personality are also common: in *Andromache*, Hermione at first seems a cruel and malicious princess, but later becomes a sympathetic victim. In *Medea*, the heroine vacillates throughout much of the play: loving mother or merciless avenger, which side of her character is to prevail? Aristotle in his *Poetics* (ch. 15) found fault with these startling reversals of character, singling out *Iphigenia at Aulis* for criticism: 'the girl who pleads for her life is quite different from the later one', he complains, referring to the scene where Iphigenia, after earlier begging for mercy, resolves to sacrifice herself in the name of Greece. Euripides also plays variations on his own earlier work: our extant *Hippolytus* is a second version, in which the portrayal of Phaedra is made more sympathetic and her character more complex.

In some ways Euripides can be seen as a more self-consciously literary dramatist than his fellow-tragedians. It is not accidental that it was he who was said to have a large library. He seems regularly to modify the conventions of his genre and adapt the work of his predecessors, sometimes even drawing attention to the changes he has made. The parody of the Aeschylean recognition-scene has already been cited; similarly, later in *Electra*, the trapping and killing of Clytemnestra within the hovel in which Electra and her husband have their home is a re-enactment of the killing-scenes within the palace of Agamemnon in Aeschylus' trilogy: humbler setting, unheroic characters, dubious morality all work together. In *Helen*, the heroine proposes that they contrive an escape by pretending Menelaus is dead and mourning him. Is that the best you can do?, asks Menelaus; 'there's a certain old-hat quality in the proposal' (1056). The point is that the trick has been tried often before in tragedy: the character is given the critic's fastidiousness. Aeschylus and Sophocles are also experienced in reshaping and adapting traditional motifs, but Euripides goes far beyond them in playing with conventions and exploiting the spectator's awareness of the dramatic situation. While shocked and moved by the events on stage, we are nevertheless frequently reminded that this is 'only' a play.[12]

As the example from *Helen* just quoted suggests, Euripides' plays are not devoid of lighter, humorous touches. Indeed, his wide repertoire includes not only starkly 'tragic' plays in the stricter sense, such as *Medea*, but also dramas which are harder to categorize. *Alcestis*, with its fairy-tale plot and happy resolution, seems to belong to a kinder and less threatening world than most tragedies. Later plays, notably *Iphigenia among the Taurians* and especially *Helen*, have often been classed as tragi-comedies. In both plays, after many misfortunes, the principal characters are reunited in a far-off setting (Helen is held captive in Egypt, Iphigenia in the Crimea), recognize one another after many false steps, and plan a successful escape back to Greece, outwitting their barbarian opponents. Hair-breadth escapes and cliff-hanging moments are common, as when Iphigenia is about to sacrifice her unrecognized brother to the goddess Artemis. We know that similar scenes occurred in lost plays by Euripides: in *Cresphontes*, a mother is on the point of killing her son with an axe, but the danger is averted, the potential tragedy dissipated.

There is much here which looks back to the *Odyssey*, with its complex plot full of deceptions and recognitions. Moroever, plays of this kind also look forward to later comedy, the types of plot favoured by Menander, Terence and eventually Shakespeare (not to mention Oscar Wilde).[13] These plays are sometimes called escapist, misguidedly; there remains a strong sense of suffering and waste in the past, and they undoubtedly still qualify as tragedies. But they do show the versatile Euripides experimenting with new types of play, and these experiments are accompanied by a lighter and more ironic tone, providing a very different kind of pleasure from the cathartic experience provided by the *Oresteia* or *Oedipus*. Euripides is plainly interested in variations of tone, juxtaposing scenes of very different emotional intensity. A 'comic' element may be found even in much grimmer plays, but there it is often used to reinforce the seriousness of the rest of the action. The self-pity and bad temper of the downtrodden Electra, for example, provide some humour as we sympathize with her husband, the long-suffering farmer; but their conversation also contributes to our understanding of Electra's tortured psyche. Far more macabre is the delusion of Heracles, who believes he is journeying to Mycenae, arriving there, punishing Eurystheus – when all the time he is in his own home, slaughtering his sons. The effect is intensely powerful: this madness would be funny if it were not so horrible.

In reading a plain text, and still more a translation, of Euripides it is easy to overlook the formal and musical aspects of the dramas. Here too we can see that he went beyond the earlier conventions of the genre, in ways which were exciting to the audiences, but also often controversial. Greek tragedy is broadly divisible into spoken verse and sung verse: the former is the medium in which the actors converse with one another or with the chorus-leader, the latter is most commonly found in the songs of the chorus. Already in Aeschylus there are plenty of exceptions: actors can sing solo parts or participate in lyric dialogue. In *Agamemnon*, the prophetess Cassandra voices her god-given insight in emotional song, to the bewilderment of the chorus; still more wild and agitated are the lyric utterances of Io, tormented by pain, in *Prometheus*. But Euripides seems to go further in giving his actors lyric passages, often highly emotional and linguistically rich (no doubt these were also striking in their musical accompaniment). The solo passages, arias or 'monodies', are often virtuoso pieces, and must have made huge demands on an actor: examples are rarer in the earlier plays, but there are several in *Hippolytus*. From the later plays the most memorable examples include Creusa's lament for the child she exposed years ago and now believes dead, the ecstatic suicide-song of Evadne, and (as in Aeschylus) the prophetic raving of Cassandra (*Ion* 859–922, *Suppliant Women* 990ff., and *Trojan Women* 308ff.). In the *Orestes* of 408 BC we find the prize example, a *tour-de-force* narrative of the attempt on Helen's life, sung by a Phrygian eunuch in a state of extreme panic, exotically foreign in its linguistic and rhythmical looseness, and no doubt accompanied by violent gestures and mime. The brilliant lyric parody in Aristophanes' *Frogs* (1309–63), which lifts lines from *Orestes* and elsewhere, shows how extraordinary audiences found his style in these arias. Other formal features of the drama would take too long to illustrate, but the general impression is of sharper and more prosaic or argumentative dialogue style combined with a more self-consciously 'poetic', decorative, image-laden, almost romantic style in lyrics.[14]

Several other aspects of Euripides' work can be illuminated by Aristophanes' *Frogs*, in which Aeschylus and Euripides compete against one another in the underworld. Although it is unsafe to use this play to establish Aristophanes' own aesthetic position, it is first-rate evidence for at least some of the things in Euripidean drama which made most impression on contemporary audiences. In the *Frogs*, Euripides is made to boast that

as soon as the play began I had everyone hard at work: no one standing idle. Women and slaves, master, young woman, aged crone – they all talked . . . It was Democracy in action . . . I taught them subtle rules they could apply; how to turn a phrase neatly. I taught them to see, to observe, to interpret; to twist, to contrive; to suspect the worst, take nothing at its face value . . . I wrote about familiar things, things the audience knew about . . . The public have learnt from me how to think, how to run their own households, to ask 'Why is this so? What do we mean by that?'   (*Frogs* 948–979, tr. D. Barrett)

In Euripidean drama others besides kings and heroes play major roles; a large number of plays are named after, and focused on, female characters. Indeed, it has been pointed out that most of Euripides' *thinkers* are women: certainly Creon, Jason and Aegeus are easily outclassed by Medea, and in both the *Trojan Women* and *Helen* Menelaus is inferior to his quick-witted wife.[15] Lower-class characters are more prominent and more influential: the Nurse in *Hippolytus* is a perfect example. In *Electra*, the downtrodden princess is married to a mere farmer, who respects her in her adversity, and has not slept with her. The farmer comes from a noble family now impoverished; his low status is contrasted with his honourable behaviour, but the latter still has to be explained by his noble birth. In both *Hecabe* and the *Trojan Women*, the decent herald Talthybius is sympathetic to the captive women, and shocked at the misdeeds of his social superiors. Mention should also be made of the many messengers in Euripides, several of whom are vividly and sympathetically characterized.

The other point which the passage in the *Frogs* emphasizes is the way these characters talk. Here we come close to one of the central aspects of Euripides' work, his fascination with argument, ideas and rhetoric. In the later fifth century BC professional teachers were instructing young men, in Athens and elsewhere, in the art of rhetoric, which in a small-scale democratic society could justly be seen as the key to political success. Types of argument were collected, methods of refutation categorized. It was possible, one of these experts claimed, 'to make the worse case defeat the better'. Euripides gives his characters the inventiveness and articulacy which these teachers sought to impart. This is particularly clear in the so-called *agon* ('contest' or 'debate'), at least one example of which can be found in most of his plays. The *agon* is a scene in which two (occasionally more) characters express their antagonism in long, highly argumentative and sometimes ingenious speeches: rhetorical skill is combined with energetic emotion. Examples are Jason versus Medea, Theseus versus Hippolytus, Helen versus Hecabe (*Medea*, *Hippolytus*, *Trojan Women* respectively). These scenes sharpen our understanding of the issues, and often challenge us to adjudicate between the parties involved. There is rarely a clear winner, either on the arguments or under the prevailing circumstances in the play: often considerations of power and self-interest matter more than who is in the right. As a result, tragic conflict-scenes seldom lead to a resolution, but tend rather to heighten the antagonism of those involved.[16]

Perhaps all drama suggests larger issues beyond the particular experiences enacted on stage, but Euripides' plays articulate these more abstract and universal concerns to an unusual degree. Although the characters on stage are not mere types – what could be called typical about Medea or Heracles? – their situations and dilemmas often suggest larger questions, more general themes and problems inherent in human life and society. When does justice become revenge, even savagery? Can human reason overcome passion? Should right and wrong be invoked in inter-state politics, or is expediency the only realistic criterion? These questions are not left implicit: the characters themselves raise them, in generalizing comments which are often given special prominence at the opening of a speech. The audience, like the characters, must often have been uncertain which side was in the right, and their attitude would naturally change as the drama unfolded. Many, perhaps most, Athenian theatre-goers would also have served as jurors in the law-courts (Athenian juries were often very large, 500 or more); many would also have voted on proposals in the democratic assembly. They were used to moral and verbal contests, real and fictional, public and private, forensic and literary. Indeed, Athenians were notorious for their addiction to debate: the contemporary historian Thucydides makes a politician call them 'spectators at speeches', a telling paradox.[17] It is no coincidence that this 'agonistic' aspect of Athenian society is so vividly reflected in the dramas. Euripides may have taught the audience to be glib and clever, but he was responding to a development already well advanced.

Perhaps no question has been as prominent in criticism as the nature of Euripides' beliefs, his philosophy. This may seem strange: why should we expect a dramatist to adopt a philosophic position, still less to maintain it from play to play? The reason that this issue seems to many people particularly important is that Euripides frequently introduces abstract ideas or theoretical arguments, sometimes drawing attention to the oddity of his character's language or thought. In the *Suppliant Women*, the Athenian Theseus and the Theban herald argue at length about the relative merits of democratic and monarchic government (399–456). Even if we allow that Theseus, the favourite hero of Athens, is no ordinary monarch, the anachronism involved in placing such a debate in the heroic age is obvious. In *Hippolytus*, Phaedra discourses on the power of passion and how it can overwhelm the mind's good resolutions: her calmness and the abstract tone of her words seem strange after her earlier frenzy. More striking still are the many passages in which characters question the nature, or the very existence, of the Olympian gods. In the *Trojan Women*, Hecabe, in need of inspiration in the *agon*, prays as follows:

O you who give the earth support and are by it supported, whoever you are, power beyond our knowledge, Zeus, be you stern law of nature or intelligence in man, to you I make my prayers; for you direct in the way of justice all mortal affairs, moving with noiseless tread.   (884–8)

These lines echo both traditional prayer-formulae and contemporary science; they involve contradictory conceptions of the supreme deity; they even hint at the theory that gods are merely externalizations of human impulses. Little wonder that Menelaus remarks in response 'What's this? You have a novel way of praying to the gods!'

In passages of this kind Euripides plainly shows his familiarity with the philosophic or metaphysical teachings of a number of thinkers: Anaxagoras, Protagoras, Gorgias and other figures known to us particularly through the writings of Plato and Aristotle. Influence from philosophy or abstract prose has occasionally been detected in Aeschylus and Sophocles, but any such cases in their work are rare and unobtrusive; with Euripides we are dealing with something new. This introduction of modern ideas coheres with his general tendency to make the characters of myth less remote and majestic, more like ordinary mortals with human weaknesses. Unsettling and bizarre these passages may seem, but they are clearly meant (as in the plays of Ibsen and Shaw) to surprise and stimulate: it would be absurd to suppose that Euripides did not realize what he was doing, or that he was incapable of keeping his intellectual interests out of his tragedies.[18]

Ancient anecdote claimed that Protagoras, an agnostic thinker, gave readings from his work in Euripides' house, and that Socrates helped him write his plays. Although these stories are rightly now recognized as fictions, the frequency with which Euripides introduces philosophic or religious reflections still needs explanation. An influential tradition of criticism has maintained that Euripides was a disciple of one or other of these thinkers, and that his dramas represent a concerted endeavour to open his countrymen's eyes to the moral defects of men and gods as represented in the traditional myths. In the earlier part of the fifth century BC, the lyric poet Pindar had questioned a myth which told of divine cannibalism, and in the fourth century Plato was to censor epic and tragedy in the name of morality. The myths were also criticized by Euripides' contemporaries on grounds of rationality and probability: how could sensible people take seriously stories of three-headed hounds of Hades, or other monstrous creatures? There is, then, no reason to doubt that Euripides could have seen reasons to be sceptical about some of the myths: he makes Helen doubt whether she was really born from a swan's egg, and Iphigenia question whether any deity could conceivably demand human sacrifice (*Helen* 18, 259, *Iphigenia among the Taurians* 380–91).

It is much less plausible to suppose that he was urging total scepticism about the gods or the supernatural, and proposing some alternative philosophical or humanist view in their place. It is difficult for the modern student to appreciate how different Greek religious thought and practice were from the Judaeo-Christian tradition.[19] There was no creed, no sacred books, no central priestly establishment. The city performed its sacrifices and paid honour to the gods, as had always been done; sometimes new gods were admitted to the pantheon; but cult was not the same as myth, and it was well known that myths contradicted one another and that poets made up many stories – many lies, as the Athenian Solon once said. To express doubts about one particular myth did not shake the foundations of religion. Outright atheism was rare and freakish. The more open-minded attitude of the great traveller Herodotus may have been commoner: he declared that all men were equally knowledgeable about the divine. [20]

Certainly there are serious difficulties in treating Euripides as an unbeliever on the evidence of his plays. This is not simply because, alongside the more questioning attitudes in the passages quoted, we find many speakers expressing profound faith and devotion, and choral odes which invoke the Olympians in magnificent poetry: one could always argue (though with some circularity) that these characters possessed only partial or erroneous insights into religion. More important is the fact that without the existence of the gods the plays simply do not work. How is Medea to escape if the sun-god, her grandfather, does not send his chariot to rescue her? How will Theseus' curse destroy his son if Poseidon is a mere fiction? How will the plot of *Alcestis* even begin to work unless death is something more than natural, unless there is a personified being against whom Heracles can do battle? A full discussion would also have to consider the numerous scenes in which gods appear at the end of plays to bring events under control: here, rationalizing interpretations truncate the dramas.

But if Euripides the 'anti-clerical' atheist cannot stand, neither can he simply be forced into the straitjacket of 'traditional' piety, even if that piety is defined in terms flexible and sophisticated enough to include Aeschylus and Sophocles. There remains overwhelming evidence that Euripides, in this as in other respects, was an innovator: just as he introduces new and often unfamiliar characters into traditional myths, or views familiar tragic situations from unexpected angles, so he combines traditional mythical and theatrical conventions about the gods with disturbing new conceptions and challenging ideas. Sometimes the contradictions become acute and paradoxical, as in a notoriously baffling passage of *Heracles*. In this play Heracles, son of Zeus by the mortal woman Alcmena, has been brought to his knees by the goddess Hera, who persecutes him because she resents Zeus' adulteries. Theseus, befriending Heracles and seeking to comfort him, refers at one point to the immorality of the gods, whereupon Heracles bursts into a passionate rejection of this concept:

I do not believe that the gods love where it is wrong for them to do so, or that they bind one another – I have never thought it right to believe this, nor shall I ever believe that one has been master of another. For god, if he is truly a god, needs nothing. These are merely the wretched tales of bards.

(*Heracles* 1340–46)

This outburst comes near to rejecting the very premisses that underlie the play and Heracles' own experiences within it. Is Euripides showing us something about Heracles' psychology? Insisting, in Plato's manner, on the moral inadequacy of the myths? Alluding to the poetic and fictional quality of his own play? Or all of these at once, and more? The passage, and the issues it raises, is likely to remain controversial.[21]

Although all such labels are bound to oversimplify a many-sided artist like Euripides, we may find more valuable than 'atheist' the term proposed by E. R. Dodds, one of the most gifted interpreters of Greek literature this century, who dubbed Euripides 'the irrationalist'.[22] By this Dodds meant that Euripides was interested and impressed by the achievements of human reason, not least in the fields of rhetorical argument and philosophic theory, but in the end felt that they were inadequate both as explanatory tools and as instruments to enable mankind to deal with the world. Reason versus passion, order versus chaos, persuasion versus violence – these antitheses are present in all Greek tragedy, but Euripides seems more pessimistic about the limits of man's capacity to control either himself or society.[23] The demoralizing and brutalizing effects of a prolonged war surely play a part in the development of his outlook: the *Suppliant Women*, *Hecabe* and the *Trojan Women*, or a decade later the *Phoenician Women* and *Iphigenia at Aulis*, all dramatize the suffering and callousness which war makes possible or inevitable. Even *Helen*, for all its playful irony and lightness of touch, implies a bleak and pessimistic view of human action: the Trojan war, far from being a glorious achievement, was fought for a phantom; and although Menelaus and Helen are finally reunited, that partial success cannot compensate for the countless lives thrown away on the plains of Troy.

On this reading, Euripides does not assert the independence of man from divine authority; he is neither an agnostic nor a humanist. Rather, he acknowledges that there are forces in the world which mankind cannot understand or control. They may sometimes be described in the language of traditional religion, or referred to by the names and titles of the Olympians, though even then he often suggests some new dimension: 'she's no goddess, then, the Cyprian, but something greater', cries the nurse when she learns of Phaedra's desire (*Hippolytus* 310). At other times he will make his characters speak of nature, or necessity, or chance: as Talthybius asks in *Hecabe*, 'O Zeus, what am I to say? Do you watch over men or are we fools, blind fools to believe this, and is it chance that oversees all man's endeavours?' (489–91). Or again, a speaker may throw out the suggestion that 'it is all in the mind': 'when you saw him your mind *became* the goddess. All the indiscretions of mortals pass for Aphrodite . . .' (*Trojan Women* 988–9). The supernatural, however it is defined, embraces those things which are beyond human grasp. The author of the following speech, again from *Hippolytus*, may not have been a conventional Greek thinker, but he understood how to communicate religious longing.

It's nothing but pain, this life of ours; we're born to suffer and there's no end to it. If anything more precious than life does exist, it's wrapped in darkness, hidden behind clouds. We're fools in love – it's plain enough – clinging to this glitter here on earth because we don't know any other life and haven't seen what lies below. *(Hippolytus* 189–96)

No play of Euripides raises these questions more acutely than the *Bacchae*, almost his last and surely his greatest tragedy. It is also his most controversial work: it has been read as evidence of a change of heart, a conversion of the ageing playwright to the truths of religion, while others have preferred to see it as a denunciation of ecstatic cult, expressing the tragedian's deep distrust of irrational action.[24] It would be quite impossible to do justice to the play here; what can be done is to sketch a few of the ways in which, for all its special qualities, it is quintessentially Euripidean.

The *Bacchae* describes the coming of Dionysus, still a new god in the mythical world of the play, to his native city of Thebes, accompanied by a chorus of loyal bacchantes. The god seeks recognition in his own land, but comes in disguise, as gods often do, to test the citizens; even the chorus suppose him to be a human priest. The youthful king Pentheus, ignoring good advice from older heads, proceeds to defy the god, little knowing the power he is confronting. At first Dionysus plays the part of an innocent captive in Pentheus' power, answering his questions and leading him on; but he soon escapes from captivity and in a series of scenes gradually gains an ascendancy over the king. In the end Pentheus is completely in his power (magic? hypnosis? or something in Pentheus' own heart that answers the Dionysiac summons?). The god, still not revealing his identity, leads him to the mountains where the Theban women are running wild in bacchic frenzy. A messenger reports the horrifying outcome: Pentheus is dead, literally torn to pieces by the women, with his own mother Agave in the lead; in her madness she believes she has slain a wild beast. The bacchic chorus rejoice that their divine master has been vindicated; but even they feel some pity and distress when Pentheus' mother brings on the head of her son and is slowly coaxed back to sanity and misery by her father Cadmus. The whole royal house is to be punished for their unbelief; Dionysus, appearing finally without disguise, *ex machina*, drives Cadmus and Agave into exile, and his pitiless speech contrasts with the tender parting of father and daughter. The cult of Dionysus will now be celebrated in Thebes, but its inauguration has been achieved through the slaughter of the opposing king.

The theme is traditional. Tragedy may have originally focused on Dionysiac subjects; in any case, we know that Aeschylus wrote a trilogy on how the god overcame his early opponents, which Euripides seems to have imitated. In this play Euripides to some extent abandons many of the stylistic and rhetorical features which made his late work so striking: there is no *agon*, for example, and the choral odes are more directly relevant to the play as a whole. Other aspects discussed above are well represented, however: the touches of sophistic argumentation (especially in the pompous lecture by the prophet Tiresias, who claims to know the 'true' nature of Dionysus); the brilliantly vivid and often gruesome narrative of the messenger; the macabre black humour of the scene in which Dionysus clothes Pentheus in female bacchic dress, and in which the king preens himself in his new outfit, unaware that he is being attired as a ritual victim.

Furthermore, the overall treatment of the theme is very different from anything we can imagine from Aeschylus' hand. The play could have been a straightforward tale of *hubris* punished, an evil man struck down by a proud but just god. What is different in the *Bacchae* is the presentation of Pentheus as a weak and unstable young man, psychologically more interesting than the standard tyrant-figure. As already mentioned, the scenes between him and Dionysus are hard to interpret: on the one hand the god is playing with the foolish king like a cat with a mouse, but on the other Pentheus seems eager to fall in with Dionysus' suggestions, pruriently keen to visit the maenads, perhaps even sexually attracted by the almost feminine beauty of the stranger. Euripides, as we have seen, is interested not only in the decisions and actions of his characters, but also in their inner psychology. As for the god himself, unusually present on stage throughout, he too is hard to evaluate. The chorus sing beautifully of the delights of Dionysiac worship: 'O blessed he who in happiness knowing the rituals of the gods makes holy his way of life and mingles his spirit with the sacred band, in the mountains serving Bacchus with reverent purifications' (73–7). We recognize here the playwright's understanding of religious devotion, just as we do in the lines in which Hippolytus prays to his beloved Artemis (73–87), or in the fragments of choral ecstasy from the lost *Cretans* (fragment 472). But the joy of union with nature is the inverse side of the madness that leads a mother to slay her own son – this, too, at Dionysus' bidding. Dionysus values honour from mankind, and relishes his revenge: is this what a god is truly like? The broken Cadmus entreats the god for mercy at the end of the play, in terms which echo the words of earlier plays.[25]

CADMUS: Dionysus, we beseech you. We have done wrong!
DIONYSUS: You were late to understand us. When you should have, you did not know us.
CADMUS: This we have come to recognize; but your reprisals are too severe!
DIONYSUS: Yes, because I am a god, and you insulted me.
CADMUS: Gods should not resemble men in their anger!
DIONYSUS: Long ago Zeus my father approved these things.

(1344–9, tr. G. S. Kirk)

It is not the business of a tragedian to solve the riddles of the universe, but to dramatize human experience in such a way as to arouse his audience's compassion and extend their imaginative understanding. This, and much else, is what Euripides offers to spectator and reader alike.

IV*

The five plays translated in this volume span a period from approximately 426 to 415; all are overshadowed by the Peloponnesian war, although from 421 until 415 hostilities were suspended. War is prominent in the

---

* Sections I–III of this introduction are reproduced, with minor modifications, from the corresponding General Introduction in the first volume of this series. We are grateful to Professor Stephen Halliwell for a number of corrections. Section IV adds a few more specific comments on the plays which figure in this volume, supplemented by the prefaces to each play.

background of all of the plays, and in one of them, the *Suppliant Women*, the main subject is a war undertaken by Athens to resolve injustices. That play does at least seem to allow that war may be conducted cleanly and in a good cause. Much less favourable is the presentation of the Greek victory over Troy: brutality and excess are evident in *Hecabe*, still more in the *Trojan Women*. We do not have to read the plays allegorically to see that the experience of Athens' conflict with Sparta and the discontent of her imperial subjects may have had some bearing on Euripides' treatment of the Trojan war. Although some individuals may stress the glory of the Greek achievement, the general tendency is to stress the sufferings of the defeated, and the women of Troy, particularly the young women robbed of husbands and children, are treated with deep sympathy. By contrast with the youthful nobility of Polyxena, the cynical realism of Odysseus in *Hecabe* seems hateful.

As three of the plays deal with the subjugation and enslavement of foreigners ('barbarians') by the Greek victors, much is made of the contrast between Greek and barbarian, freedom and slavery. As often, Euripides seems to break down the obvious oppositions: it is the Greek leaders at Troy who show 'barbaric' behaviour, and even their womenfolk, such as Hermione and Clytemnestra, readily adopt the luxurious dress and extravagant entourage that Greek writers affected to despise in foreigners. As for slavery, Hecabe's comments on Agamemnon's situation are more widely applicable: 'In all the world there is no person who is free; either he is the slave of money or circumstance, or else the majority of his fellow-citizens or code of laws prevents him from acting as his better judgement dictates' (*Hecabe* 864ff.). Similarly, Hermione has greater wealth and support than Andromache but cannot please her husband and in the end lives in fear of his retaliation. Apparently straightforward power-relations are shown to be ambiguous, apparent certainties turn out illusions.

Revenge and retaliation are prominent in several of these plays: Orestes' plot to bring about Neoptolemus' death, Hecabe's vindictive punishment of Polymestor, the matricide executed jointly by Electra and Orestes. Each of these schemes for revenge is successful, but in none of these cases is the audience expected simply to endorse the deed: moreover, in Hecabe's case the satisfaction is short lived, while in that of Electra and Orestes their triumph is dispelled by their belated consciousness of the horror of what they have done. Other actions, such as the slaying of the infant Astyanax or the sacrifice of Polyxena, seem to have still less justification. Again the *Suppliant Women* stands apart as an exception: there the punishment of the arrogant Thebans goes no further than defeating them in battle, and the virtuous King Theseus refrains from sacking or looting their city, concentrating instead on performing the proper rites of burial with his own hands. In the *Suppliant Women* and elsewhere (*Hecabe* 466–74, *Trojan Women* 208–9, *Electra* 1254–72, 1319–20), the poet's own city still seems to preserve a halo of nobility, although in general there is little to cheer the soul in these dramas.

The poetic range of the plays shows the poet's customary versatility. For obvious reasons, with such a harrowing series of subjects, lamentation and grief-stricken song are prominent in all five of the plays. Impassioned mourning of those who have died in war, painful recollection of the joys of peace and the illusions of safety, are recurrent themes in the choral songs. Among the high points of creative imagination must be mentioned the odes in which the Trojan captives remember the night on which Troy was taken (*Hecabe* 905–51, *Trojan Women* 511–67); the melancholy retellings of the fateful 'Judgement of Paris', the origin of Trojan woe (*Andromache* 274–92, *Hecabe* 630–56); or the baroque reminiscence of the panoply of armour worn by Achilles when he set out with the Greek fleet from Aulis (*Electra* 432–86). At the other extreme is the vivid presentation of Electra's life of poverty and self-degradation. The more cerebral techniques of rhetoric also remain prominent: each of the plays has at least one *agon*, and in *Andromache*, *Hecabe* and the *Suppliant Women* there are two. As already in *Medea* and *Hippolytus*, violent emotion is channelled into formal argumentation: these interludes provide a sharper and sometimes chilling intellectual pleasure as callous acts are justified with alarming articulacy. Scenes of spectacle and daring stage-management are equally numerous: the ecstatic, maddened suicide of Evadne, who leaps to her death upon her husband's pyre (*Suppliant Women* 1069–71); the prophetic declarations of another distraught woman, the priestess Cassandra (*Trojan Women* 308–40); the agony of the blinded Polymestor, stumbling on hands and knees out of the stage-building, screaming aloud in pain and fury (*Hecabe* 1056–1106). Even in translation and in inert form on the printed page, these plays still have the power to arouse a sympathetic reader's astonishment and awe.

NOTES

1 On the festivals and theatrical conditions, see above all Pickard-Cambridge, *Dramatic Festivals of Athens* (2nd edn, Oxford 1968); E. Csapo and W. J. Slater, *The Context of Ancient Drama* (Michigan 1995); more briefly E. Simon, *The Ancient Theatre* (Eng. tr., London and New York 1981), pp. 1–33; O. Taplin, *Greek Tragedy in Action* (London 1978), ch. 2. A readable account of the theatrical context is provided by R. Rehm, *Greek Tragic Theatre* (London 1992). See also J. R. Green, *Theatre in Ancient Greek Society* (London 1994).

2 For an excellent discussion of the types of myths favoured, see B. M. W. Knox, *Word and Action* (Baltimore 1979), ch. 1.

3 O. Taplin, *The Stagecraft of Aeschylus* (Oxford 1977); D. Bain, *Actors and Audience* (Oxford 1977); D. Mastronarde, *Contact and Discontinuity* (London 1979); M. Halleran, *Stagecraft in Euripides* (London and Sydney 1985); R. Rehm, op. cit.

4 See M. L. West, *Ancient Greek Music* (Oxford 1992). On dance, see Pickard-Cambridge, op. cit., ch. 5.

5 For fuller essays, see R. P. Winnington-Ingram and P. E. Easterling in *The Cambridge History of Classical Literature*, vol. 1, ed. P. E. Easterling and B. M. W. Knox (Cambridge 1985; paperback 1989); also the pamphlets by S. Ireland and R. Buxton in the *Greece & Rome New Surveys* series (Oxford).

6 Revivals of older tragedies became a regular feature at the festivals from 386 BC onwards: see Pickard-Cambridge, op. cit., pp. 99–100. Euripides' plays were frequently chosen. For the possibility of performances outside Athens already in the fifth century BC, see P. E. Easterling, *Illinois Classical Studies* 19 (1994), pp. 1–8.

7 This work is highly technical, but the essentials can be gleaned from A. M. Dale's introduction to her commentary on *Helen* (Oxford 1967), pp. xxiv–xxviii.

8 See further G. Zuntz, *The Political Plays of Euripides* (Manchester 1955), chs. 1–3, esp. pp. 78–81. Some more recent approaches, which all seek in different ways to put tragedy in an Athenian context, can be found in the collection *Nothing to do with Dionysos?*, ed. J. Winkler and F. Zeitlin (Princeton 1990), and *Greek Tragedy and the Historian*, ed. C. B. R. Pelling (Oxford 1997).

9 From the jacket blurb of *Catastrophe Survived* (Oxford 1973).

10 I draw here on R. P. Winnington-Ingram, 'Euripides, *poietes sophos* [intellectual poet]', *Arethusa* 2 (1969), pp. 127–42. His points are further developed by W. G. Arnott, 'Euripides and the Unexpected', in I. McAuslan and P. Walcot (eds.) *Greek Tragedy* (*Greece & Rome Studies* 2, Oxford 1993), pp. 138–52.

11 In Aristophanes' *Clouds*, originally produced in 423 BC, the rebellious Pheidippides is asked by his father to sing a passage of Aeschylus, and scoffs at the idea, dismissing the older poet as a bombastic and incoherent ranter. When asked to produce a modern alternative, he shocks his father by reciting a passage from Euripides' *Aeolus* defending the merits of incest!

12 This aspect of Euripides has been emphasized in recent years, sometimes to excess: see e.g. S. Goldhill, *Reading Greek Tragedy* (Cambridge 1986), esp. ch. 10.

13 B. M. W. Knox, *Word and Action*, op. cit., pp. 250–74 ('Euripidean comedy').

14 Good summary, with further references, in C. Collard, *Euripides* (*Greece & Rome New Surveys* 14, Oxford 1981), pp. 20–29.

15 The reference to Euripides' thinkers comes from E. R. Dodds' essay 'Euripides the Irrationalist', *Classical Review* 43 (1929), pp. 87–104, reprinted in his collection *The Ancient Concept of Progress and Other Essays* (Oxford 1973), pp. 78–91. On women in Athenian literature and society, see further J. Gould, 'Law, custom and myth: aspects of the social position of women in classical Athens', *Journal of Hellenic Studies* 100 (1980), pp. 38–59; S. Goldhill, op. cit., ch. 5; and the essays in A. Powell (ed.), *Euripides, Women and Sexuality* (London 1990).

16 For a very helpful essay on this side of Euripides, see C. Collard, 'Formal Debates in Euripidean Drama', in I. McAuslan and P. Walcot, op. cit., pp. 153–66; also M. Lloyd, *The Agon in Euripides* (Oxford 1992).

17 Thucydides iii, 38, 4. It is particularly striking that the word translated as 'spectator' is the regular term for a member of the theatrical audience.

18 A. N. Michelini, *Euripides and the Tragic Tradition* (Madison, Wis. and London 1987), part 1, gives a well-documented history of the debate over Euripides' views. A seminal work, still enjoyable and stimulating, is G. Murray's short book *Euripides and his Age* (London 1913).

19 See the useful collection of essays edited by P. E. Easterling and J. V. Muir, *Greek Religion and Society* (Cambridge 1985), esp. J. Gould's contribution, 'On making sense of Greek religion'.

20 Herodotus ii, 3, 2. On this subject in general, J. Mikalson, *Athenian Popular Religion* (Chapel Hill 1983) and *Honor thy Gods* (Chapel Hill and London 1991) are valuable collections of material, but tend to draw too firm a line between what happens in life and what appears in literature.

21 T. C. W. Stinton, *Proceedings of the Cambridge Philological Society,* new series 22 (1976), pp. 60–89; reprinted in Stinton, *Collected Papers on Greek Tragedy* (Oxford 1990), pp. 236–64; H. Yunis, *A New Creed: Fundamental Religious Beliefs in the Athenian Polis and Euripidean Drama* (Göttingen 1988), esp. pp. 155–71.

22 E. R. Dodds, op. cit.

23 Classic (over-) statement in K. Reinhardt, 'Die Sinneskreise bei Euripides', in *Tradition und Geist* (Göttingen 1960); also available in a French translation (K. Reinhardt, *Éschyle; Euripide*, Paris 1972).

24 E. R. Dodds' commentary on the Greek text of this play, *Euripides. Bacchae* (2nd edn, Oxford 1960) remains essential for serious study; see also R. P. Winnington-Ingram, *Euripides and Dionysus* (Cambridge 1948).

25 See esp. *Hippolytus* 114–20.

NOTE ON THE TEXT

We have no manuscripts in Euripides' hand, or going back anywhere near his own time. If we had, they would be difficult to decipher, and would lack many aids which the modern reader takes for granted: stage directions, punctuation, clear indications of change of speaker, regular divisions between lines and even between words. In fact, although some parts of his plays, mostly short extracts, survive in papyri from the earliest centuries AD, our complete manuscripts of the plays translated in this volume go back no further than the tenth century. Moreover, the textual evidence for the various plays differs greatly in quantity. Three plays were especially popular in later antiquity, namely *Hecabe*, the *Phoenician Women* and *Orestes* (the so-called 'Byzantine triad'). These survive in more than 200 manuscripts. Others, including the *Suppliant Women* and *Electra*, are represented in only one manuscript and its derivatives. *Andromache* and the *Trojan Women* fall in between, each surviving in a number of manuscripts of varying date. In a different category come the many quotations from Euripides in other classical authors, which sometimes preserve different readings from those in the direct tradition of Euripidean manuscripts.

This situation is not unusual in the history of classical authors. No ancient dramatist's work survives in his own hand: in all cases we are dealing with a text transmitted by one route or several, and copied many times over. In an age which knew nothing of the printing-press, far less the Xerox machine, all copying had to be done by hand, every copy in a sense a new version. The opportunities for corruption of the text – that is, the introduction of error – were numerous. The reasons for such corruption include simple miscopying or misunderstanding by the scribe, omission or addition of passages by actors in later productions, efforts to improve the text by readers who felt, rightly or wrongly, that it must be corrupt, accidental inclusion of marginal notes or quotations from other plays, and very occasionally bowdlerization of 'unsuitable' passages. Problems of this kind were already recognized in antiquity: efforts were made to stabilize the texts of the tragedians in fourth-century BC Athens, and the ancient commentaries or 'scholia' to some of Euripides' plays make frequent comments on textual matters, for instance remarking that a line is 'not to be found' in some of their early manuscripts, now lost to us. In the same way, when a modern scholar produces an edition of a Euripidean play, there are many places where he or she must decide between different versions given in different manuscripts. Sometimes the choice will be easy: one version may be unmetrical, ungrammatical or meaningless. But often the decision may be more difficult, and in many cases it is clear that no manuscript preserves the lines in question in the correct form. Hence the editor must either reconstruct Euripides' authentic text by 'conjecture', or indicate that the passage is insolubly corrupt, a conclusion normally signalled by printing daggers ('obeli') on either side of the perplexing passage.

A translator is in a slightly more fortunate position than an editor. The editor must make a decision what to print at every point, and uncertainty may prevail as to the exact wording even when the overall sense is fairly clear. In this translation James Diggle's excellent Oxford Classical Text has normally been followed: when he has marked a word or phrase as probably or certainly corrupt, we have usually adopted a conjectural reading, whether made by him or by a previous editor, even though we often agree that there can be no certainty that this is what Euripides actually wrote. In cases where the corruption is more extensive, we have tried to give a probable idea of the train of thought. These problems arise particularly in choral and other lyric passages, where the language is less close to everyday speech, and where unusual metre and dialect often misled copyists.

Many of the smaller problems involving variations of words or uncertainty over phrasing will be unlikely to cause difficulties to readers of this translation. More noticeable are the occasional places where it seems that something has dropped out of the text; usually this can be explained by the accidents of miscopying or by damage to some of the manuscripts from which our texts descend. The problem is not acute in the plays in this volume.

A much more serious problem which affects criticism of Euripides is that of interpolation. This is the term used to describe the inclusion of alien material in the original text, expanding and elaborating on the author's words. Sometimes the new material betrays itself by its very unsuitability to the context, and we may suppose that it has been included by accident (for instance, parallels from other plays were sometimes copied out in the margin, then found their way into the text in subsequent copies). Sometimes lines may be present in one manuscript but omitted in others: if they seem superfluous in themselves, they may well be a later addition. Sometimes a speech may seem unnecessarily wordy, and we may suspect without feeling certain that it has been expanded; here textual criticism merges with literary judgement. It has often been suggested that some passages in the plays have been 'padded out' by actors seeking to improve their parts: although this phenomenon has probably been exaggerated, it would be a mistake to rule it out altogether. One speech which has fallen under suspicion on these grounds is Medea's famous soliloquy as she wavers over the killing of her children (*Medea* 1019–80: the boldest critics would excise all of 1056–80). In the present volume there is no case of such central importance for the interpretation of a play, but interpolation has certainly been diagnosed in many places. One interesting case is Orestes' meditative speech at *Electra* 367–400, in which the young man expresses his admiration for virtuous poverty as represented by Electra's husband, and expands on this theme in extensive generalization. Too extensive, many readers have thought; hence the suggestions of various editors that parts of the speech are irrelevant interpolations. The standard text by Diggle cuts the speech down from 34 lines to 22, and if we accepted all the other deletions suggested by other scholars but not by Diggle, Orestes' speech would end up as a mere ten lines! In the translation our normal policy is to follow Diggle's text, and consequently the 22-line version of this speech is given; but for the interest of the reader the deleted passages from this speech are given in the Explanatory Notes (see *Electra* n. 20). The article by Goldhill cited below is a polemical discussion of the questionable assumptions which underlie many deletions of this kind. As with many such questions, there remains much room for argument; but Diggle's intimate familiarity with the author and clear-headed judgement demand respect, and our high opinion of his text has only been enhanced by closer study.

FURTHER READING

W. S. Barrett, *Euripides: Hippolytus* (Oxford 1964), pp. 45–84: a detailed account, requiring some knowledge of Greek and technical terms.

C. Collard, *Euripides* (*Greece & Rome New Surveys* 14, 1981), p. 3: a good one-page summary with bibliography.

S. Goldhill, 'Rhetoric and relevance: interpolation at Euripides' *Electra* 367–400' in *Greek, Roman & Byzantine Studies* 27 (1986), pp. 157–71.

L. D. Reynolds and N. G. Wilson, *Scribes and Scholars: A Guide to the Transmission of Greek and Latin Literature* (3rd edn, Oxford 1991).

M. L. West, *Textual Criticism and Editorial Technique* (Stuttgart 1973), part 1.

CHRONOLOGICAL TABLE

As we explained in the Introduction, not all of the plays of Euripides (and fewer still of Sophocles) can be firmly dated. This table shows all of the extant Greek tragedies for which we have fairly certain dates, and also lists most of Aristophanes' surviving comedies and some major historical events to put them in context. Conjectural dates are given with question-marks, and are usually fixed by analysis of metrical technique: they may well be three or four years out either way.

Year BC

c. 535–2	Thespis competes in first tragic competition		
		490	Darius' invasion of Greece
		480–79	Xerxes' invasion
472	Aeschylus *Persians*		
468	Sophocles' first victory, on his first attempt		
467	Aesch. *Laius, Oedipus, Seven against Thebes, Sphinx*		
463?	Aesch. *Suppliant Women, Aigyptioi, Danaids, Amymone*	c. 462	Radical democracy established at Athens

458 Aesch. *Agamemnon, Libation-Bearers, Eumenides, Proteus*	
456 Death of Aeschylus	
455 Euripides' first competition: third prize	
438 Eur. *Alcestis*	
431 Eur. *Medea*	431 War begins between Athens and Sparta
c. 430? Eur. *The Children of Heracles*	430 Great plague at Athens
	429 Death of Pericles
428 Eur. *Hippolytus* (surviving version)	
	427 Aristophanes' first play (now lost)
425? Eur. *Andromache*	425 Arist. *Acharnians*
	424 Arist. *Knights*
pre-423? Eur. *Hecabe*	
423? Eur. *Suppliant Women*	423 Arist. *Clouds* (original version)
	422 Arist. *Wasps*
	421 Arist. *Peace* Death of Cleon; peace of Nicias
c. 417? Eur. *Heracles, Electra*	
	416 Athenian massacre on Melos

TRANSLATOR'S NOTE

A new translation of an author as great as Euripides needs little justification, perhaps, but it may be useful to point out certain respects in which
this translation differs from those of the late Philip Vellacott which
Penguin published in four volumes between 1953 and 1972. In these,
for the most part, the translation was deliberately broken up into
verse-like lines, which created a certain stateliness that reflected the
dignity of the original but often resulted in the kind of English that
could only exist on the printed page. My aim has been to produce a
version that conforms far more to how people speak, and for this the
medium of continuous prose was essential.

A further consequence of the earlier approach is that all the characters speak the same form of stylized English, whether they are princes
or slaves. In adopting continuous prose I have tried to achieve a tone
that is more relaxed, less stylized and less close to the Greek word-order,
while remaining true to the original. There is a wider range of tones
and moods in recognition of the fact that, for all the uniformity of the
Greek, not every character maintains a wholly dignified tone. Some
speak in a more colloquial and fast-moving style, even verging on the
humorous (for example the Nurse in *Hippolytus*), while others require
a more dignified style because they are arrogant or demented or divine.

In the lyric passages, especially the choral odes, I have aimed at a
certain archaic formality of language in recognition of their emotional
or religious content, but the overriding concern has been to let the
freshness and beauty of the poetry come through to the reader as directly
as possible. These elements of song in Euripides' work were much
admired by his contemporaries and by later generations, and here, if
anywhere, the translator's responsibility weighs particularly heavily.

There is a change of presentation from the first volume (*Alcestis and Other Plays*, Penguin 1996). In order to mark more clearly the distinction between spoken and sung parts in the play, all lyric sections, where lines were sung because of their emotional intensity, have been put in italics. These are all the choral odes and passages of lamentation or intense emotion where a character sings his or her lines.

Euripides is intensely interested in human nature in all its different forms, and a modern translation must therefore try to take some account of the richness of his character portrayal and psychological insight. It is this belief that underpins my attempt throughout these plays to find and express variety of tone; I have tried to think of the words as being spoken by real persons rather than literary creations, remembering the remark attributed to Sophocles that, whereas in his own plays Sophocles showed men as they should be, Euripides drew them as they are.

This said, it remains true that the language of Attic tragedy, even in the case of Euripides, was never that spoken in the streets of Athens in the poet's day. As in Homeric epic, it is essentially a literary creation that aims predominantly at a certain grandeur in keeping with the dignity of its subject-matter. This inevitably imposes limits on how 'natural' a style should be attempted by a translator. However 'modern' Euripidean tragedy may seem compared with that of Aeschylus and Sophocles, its language was still sufficiently grand for Aristophanes to parody it relentlessly in his comedies as high flown and pompous.

As with the first volume, I have not attempted to produce an entirely modern idiom in these translations; the overall tone remains, I hope, essentially dignified, as Greek tragedy demands, and I have tried hard to be faithful to the original both in letter and in spirit, taking heart from the excellent prose translation of Virgil's *Aeneid* by Professor David West for Penguin, and the sensible remarks he makes on translation in his own introduction to that book.

No dramatist of any age can be content to live solely within the confines of the printed page, and naturally it would be very satisfying if theatrical companies or performers of any kind thought this version a suitable basis for a production of one or more of these masterpieces of the stage. I hope that the reader who comes fresh to Euripides in this volume may feel that his voice deserves to be heard more in the modern theatre.

My thanks go, once again, to my collaborator Dr Richard Rutherford of Christ Church, Oxford, for his introductory essay, prefaces and notes. His scholarly eye rescued me several times from 'translationese'. Any remaining infelicities are my responsibility. I am also grateful to Professor David Kovacs, translator of Euripides for the Loeb Classical Library, for sharing his thoughts with me on the problems and pleasures of translating this great dramatist; to Professor Robert Fagles, translator of Aeschylus and Sophocles for Penguin Classics, whose generous remarks on the first volume were much appreciated by a comparative novice in the art of translation; and to Pat Easterling, Regius Professor of Greek at Cambridge, for her encouragement and advice in the early stages. My thanks go also to the High Master and Governors of St Paul's School for enabling me to take a sabbatical from teaching in the summer term of 1996, so creating space for working on this project. My students at St Paul's have played their part in sharpening my focus on the plays and I am grateful to them. Above all, I want to thank my wife Philippa for her patience and support since I began working on these translations six years ago. Ten plays remain to be translated and I will need to trespass further on her good nature. My children, Lorna and Andrew, have moved from an attitude of puzzlement to one of amused tolerance of this strange activity of their father; I would like to dedicate this book to them and their mother.

J. N. D.

ANDROMACHE

PREFACE TO *ANDROMACHE*

Andromache was probably first produced in the mid-420s BC, in the middle of the 'Archidamian war', the first phase of the great Peloponnesian war between Athens and Sparta. Like *Hecabe* and the *Trojan Women*, *Andromache* deals with the aftermath of the Greek victory at Troy, mainly from the viewpoint of the vanquished. But unlike the other two, this play begins years after that victory, and back in Greece, in Phthia (part of Thessaly), where Hector's widow has been living as a concubine in the house of Achilles' son Neoptolemus. Persecuted by her mistress Hermione, Andromache and her child by Neoptolemus seek refuge at an altar, but the treacherous malice of Hermione, backed by her father Menelaus, lures them into captivity. In the nick of time old Peleus, Neoptolemus' grandfather, arrives to save them. In the rest of the play the plot takes a different turn: Orestes of Argos, notorious for the murder of his mother, appears and offers refuge to Hermione, who now fears the retribution of Neoptolemus. But further surprise follows: after Orestes and Hermione have escaped, it turns out that Neoptolemus is already dead, treacherously assassinated at Delphi by a mob recruited and inflamed by Orestes. The god Apollo himself, whom Neoptolemus had once offended, has taken his revenge. Peleus is devastated: he has lost first his son Achilles at Troy, now his grandson Neoptolemus at home in Greece. Yet consolation comes at last, with the final appearance of the sea-nymph Thetis, Peleus' former wife, now returned to her home in the sea: she foretells the fate of the survivors and promises that they will both be reunited with Achilles after Peleus' death.

As this summary shows, one key difference between *Andromache* and the other two plays mentioned is that the focus is not entirely on the misfortunes of the Trojan captives: although Andromache is the central figure of the first half, and presented in a highly sympathetic light, she fades out thereafter, and the spotlight shifts to her tormentor Hermione, whose initial cruelty and arrogance are modified in adversity. This shift of focus, though not uncommon in Euripides, is disconcerting for readers who expect a single figure (a hero or heroine) to be prominent throughout a tragedy, and this is one reason that *Andromache* has never been one of the most popular of the canon. By the end of the play the death of Neoptolemus is the key issue, not the fate of Andromache or Hermione: in the last scene scholars can even debate whether Andromache is present (if she is, she utters not a word). It remains true that the play is concerned throughout with the surviving family of Neoptolemus, son of the dead Achilles, greatest of heroes: in the absence of Neoptolemus the aged Peleus represents the male line, and acts as spokesman for heroic nobility in the face of Menelaus' baseness. At issue between the two women is the question of bearing a child to Neoptolemus: Hermione, the legitimate wife, is barren, whereas Andromache has borne him a son whose life is at risk throughout the first half of the play. After the father's death, this child becomes the single hope for the future of Achilles' line: at the end of the play the goddess prophesies that he will father a line of kings in Molossia, in north-western Greece.

Part of the explanation for the changing focus of interest in the play may lie in the limited mythological material concerning Andromache available to Euripides. From earlier sources we can see that at least two points were traditional: that Neoptolemus marries Hermione, and that Andromache was taken back to Greece by him. The potential clash between two women sharing a single man was a natural Euripidean subject. Further details may be drawn from the tradition (for instance, there was a version in which Neoptolemus' visit to Delphi was in order to seek advice on Hermione's childlessness), but the development of domestic drama and personal antagonisms is surely Euripides' own.

Prominent in the play are two further sources of antagonism: hostility between Greek and barbarian, and hostility to Sparta. These are handled in very different ways. Despite the vicious complaints made by Hermione about Andromache's barbarian witchcraft, we see nothing to justify such hostility, and the fate of the princess of Troy, a captive in a foreign country, is handled with much pathos. Peleus when he appears shows her nothing but consideration (though we might ask whether he would have shown as much concern were it not for the presence of the child). Here, as elsewhere in Euripides, it is the Greeks, or the worst among them, who behave in ways we might call barbaric (cf. 244; *Trojan Women* 764). Menelaus shamelessly backs up his daughter's unjustified persecution, deceives Andromache and shows contempt for religious sanctions; but when confronted by the resolution of Peleus, he makes an ignominious departure, pleading a prior engagement. This negative portrayal of the king of Sparta is a late fifth-century BC development: in epic, Menelaus is a worthy and respected hero, and little is made of his 'cuckold' status. Even in Aeschylus' *Agamemnon*, his loss of Helen is treated with fully tragic dignity. That Menelaus is such a hateful and unimpressive figure in several Euripidean tragedies (later, most conspicuously in *Orestes*) can hardly be unconnected with the war Athens was currently fighting against Sparta and her allies; and this suggestion is supported by several passages of generalizing denunciation of Spartan morality elsewhere in the text (esp. 445ff., 595ff., 724–6).

The treatment of Apollo and Delphi in the play has also been linked with contemporary political attitudes. Delphi had promised support for Sparta at the beginning of the war (Thucydides i, 118), and the disastrous plague which swept Athens in 430 and subsequent years could be seen as fulfilment of that promise (Thuc. ii, 54, 4). However, the murder of Neoptolemus at Delphi was already a fairly fixed point in the legend, though variously explained; and although his family and supporters are naturally dismayed, and Orestes' part in the deed is further evidence of Dorian treachery, it remains true that Neoptolemus had behaved rashly in denouncing Apollo before. In Greek eyes, the god has a right to exact revenge, and revenge naturally brings sorrow to the victim's family. The speech of the messenger culminates in an angry question about Apollo's wisdom: 'How then can he be wise?' (1165); but this complaint, though easily paralleled in other Euripidean plays, is not developed here. Indeed, part of the point of Thetis' epiphany seems to be to remind characters and audience that the gods bring good news and good fortune as well as bad.

Andromache shows many characteristic Euripidean features besides those already mentioned. It moves into relatively unexplored mythical territory and therefore exploits the possibilities of surprise. We might expect Neoptolemus himself to appear, or Orestes to reappear; we think Hermione is a fiend, but find that she too can make a convincing victim. The forceful rhetoric typical of Euripidean argument is as conspicuous as ever, embracing marital disharmony, Spartan treachery, personal invective. The heroic achievements of the Trojan war are tarnished, especially through the denigration of Menelaus' own military prowess (616–18). But heroic virtue as a whole is not satirized or rejected: the decisive intervention of Peleus saves Andromache and her son, and Neoptolemus' last stand at Delphi is given all the excitement and glamour of a Homeric duel, even though he faces impossible odds. The conclusion of the play with the divine epiphany is perfunctory to modern taste; yet the situation is already resolved, and Thetis is needed to guarantee the future for both Peleus and the unnamed heir of Neoptolemus. *Andromache* is rarely staged nowadays, but perhaps deserves more attention than it has generally received.

CHARACTERS

ANDROMACHE, *widow of Hector, concubine of Neoptolemus*
MAIDSERVANT *of Andromache*
CHORUS *of women of Phthia*
HERMIONE, *daughter of Menelaus, wife of Neoptolemus*
MENELAUS, *king of Sparta*
CHILD, *young son of Andromache and Neoptolemus*
PELEUS, *father of Achilles, grandfather of Neoptolemus*
NURSE *of Hermione*
ORESTES, *son of Agamemnon, cousin of Hermione*
MESSENGER
THETIS, *goddess mother of Achilles by Peleus*

[The scene is the palace of Neoptolemus in Phthia, a district of Thessaly. Near the central door is a shrine of THETIS *with an altar and statue of the goddess.* ANDROMACHE *is seated as a suppliant in front of the shrine.]*

ANDROMACHE: O land of Asia, o Thebe,[1] my city! I left you long ago, a young bride exulting in her dowry of much gold, and came to Priam's royal home when I was given in marriage to Hector to be the mother of his children. Andromache was a woman to be envied in those early days, but now she knows misery such as no other woman on earth. I saw my husband Hector killed by Achilles and the son I bore him, Astyanax,

10 hurled from the towering battlements when Troy was taken by the Greeks. Then I found myself a slave, I, whose family all men regarded as subject to none, and I came to Greece as the pick of the Trojan spoils, awarded to the islander Neoptolemus as his battle-prize. Here I live in Phthia, in the land that borders on Pharsalia, where the sea-goddess Thetis shared the home of Peleus,[2] far from the company of men, shunning their commotion. Thessaly's people call the place Thetideum in memory of the goddess who became a man's

20 bride. Then this house became the property of Achilles' son, but he has allowed Peleus to rule over Pharsalus, not wishing to assume the throne in the old man's lifetime.

In this house I lay with Achilles' son, my master, and have borne him a child,[3] a boy. Now at first, despite the unpleasantness of my situation, I was constantly led on by hope to believe I should find some assistance, some protection against my troubles, as long as my child came under no threat. But ever since my master has turned his back on my slave's bed and taken the Spartan Hermione to wife, she has made me the butt of her wicked accusations. She claims that I have made her barren and hated by her husband through the use of secret drugs, that I want to live here in the palace in her place, once I have ousted her in her husband's affections. Yet this role of mistress was forced upon me from the beginning and I have now relinquished it. Great Zeus be my witness: I had no wish to occupy that bed. But she will have none of this, indeed she wants to kill me, and her father, Menelaus,[4] is aiding and abetting his daughter. He is in the palace at this very moment, having come from Sparta for just this reason. In terror I have come to this shrine of Thetis beside the palace where I now sit, hoping that she may save me from death. For Peleus and the descendants of Peleus hold it in reverence as a memorial to his marriage with the Nereid.

I have sent my only son away in secret to another home, fearing he might be killed. His father is not here to help me and can be of no use to his son, since he is away in the land of Delphi, making atonement to Loxias for his mad behaviour in going once to Pytho and asking Phoebus for satisfaction for his father whom the god had killed.[5] He hopes that by asking forgiveness for his earlier offence he may find the god gracious in the future.

[*A* MAIDSERVANT *enters from the palace.*]

MAIDSERVANT: My lady, I do not shrink from calling you by this title, since I paid you this respect in your own home in the days we lived at Troy and showed myself a loyal servant there, to you and your husband while he lived. Now I've come with news for you; I'm sorry for you and this outweighs any fear of being found out by one of my masters. Menelaus and that daughter of his are hatching a terrible plot against you; you must be on your guard!

ANDROMACHE: My dear friend, companion in slavery (for fellow-slave you are to her who was once your queen and now is wretched), what is it they are doing? What cunning web are they now weaving? Is it my death they want? Have I not suffered everything else?

MAIDSERVANT: It is your son's murder they intend, poor lady, the boy you smuggled out of the palace. Menelaus has now left the house to get him.

ANDROMACHE: No, not that! Does he know my son has been sent away? How can he have found out? Oh my poor boy! This is the end of me!

MAIDSERVANT: I don't know; others in the house told me this.

ANDROMACHE: Then it is all over. My child, they will seize and kill you, these two vultures, while the man who is called your father continues to linger in Delphi.

MAIDSERVANT: Yes, but if he was here you'd never be treated like this, I think; as things stand, you haven't a single friend.

ANDROMACHE: Has there been no news of Peleus, saying that he would come?

MAIDSERVANT: He is an old man to be coming to your help now.

ANDROMACHE: Well, more than once I've sent, asking him to come.

MAIDSERVANT: You don't imagine any messenger pays you attention, do you?

ANDROMACHE: Of course not! Well then, are *you* prepared to take a message for me?

MAIDSERVANT: How will I explain my absence from the house for so long?

ANDROMACHE: You'll think of a hundred schemes; you're a woman.[6]

MAIDSERVANT: It's dangerous; Hermione is a guard to be taken seriously.

ANDROMACHE: You see? You disown your friends in trouble.

MAIDSERVANT: I do not! Never lay that charge at my door! I will go; after all, a slave-woman's life is a small matter if any harm should come to me.

ANDROMACHE: On your way, then! [MAIDSERVANT *leaves*.] I
will make the heavens echo to the dirges and lamentations
and tearful cries to which my life is forever bound. It is natural
in women to take pleasure in the woes that beset them,
recounting them constantly over and over. But I have not one
but many sorrows to lament, the city of my fathers gone,
my Hector killed and the grim fate I am yoked to, falling
undeservedly into a state of slavery. Never should a mortal be
called happy until he has died and you have seen how he   100
has passed through his final day before making the journey
below. [*She now sings an elegiac lament:*][7]

To lofty Ilium Paris brought Helen to share his nuptial bed but
it was for disaster, not in marriage, that she came. Because of her, o
Troy, the warriors of Greece came in their thousand swift ships and
laid you waste with fire and spear, slaying – alas! – my husband
Hector, whom the sea-nymph Thetis' son dragged behind his chariot
round the walls of Troy. And I was led forth from my bridal chamber,
down to the seashore, wearing on my head the loathsome hood of
slavery. Many were the tears that fell from my cheeks when I left   110
my city, my chamber, and my husband in the dust. Oh my sorrow,
my piteous sorrow, why should I still look upon the sunlight when I
am Hermione's slave? Her oppression has driven me to embrace this
statue of the goddess as a suppliant and here I waste away in tears
like a rushing stream flowing down a rock.

[*The* CHORUS *enters. They are women of Phthia.*]

CHORUS [Strophe]: *O woman, who has remained seated all this while*
on the floor of Thetis' shrine, though I am Phthian and you are of
Asian stock I have come to you, hoping that I may be able to find a
remedy for your desperate woes. They have caused Hermione to   120
clash with you, poor woman, in a bitter feud over two beds, since you
share one man, the son of Achilles.

[Antistrophe:] *Realize your circumstances, consider the hopeless-*
ness of the position you are in. Are you competing against the lady
who is your mistress, you, a Trojan girl, against a Spartan princess?
Leave the shrine of the sea-goddess where sheep are sacrificed. How   130
does it befit you in your distress to disfigure your features with weeping

because your masters use constraint against you? You will succumb to might; why pursue the struggle when you have no strength?

[Strophe:] *Come, abandon the splendid dwelling of the Nereid goddess and accept that you are in a foreign land, from a city that is not of our kind, and that here you see none of your friends, most* 140 *wretched, most abused girl.*

[Antistrophe:] *My heart was racked with pity for you, woman of Troy, when you came to my master's house; but fear makes us stay silent (though truly your plight fills me with pity), fear that the daughter of Zeus' child may learn that I wish you well.*

[*Enter* HERMIONE.]

HERMIONE: This gorgeous diadem of gold[8] upon my head, these finely woven robes in which I am dressed are not heirlooms 150 from the household of Achilles or of Peleus. I brought them here from the land of the Spartans, Laconia, together with my rich dowry, as a gift from Menelaus, my father, and this means I may speak with perfect freedom.

Now you, slave-woman, won by the spear, you want to oust me from this palace and make it your own home; thanks to your drugs my husband detests me, thanks to you my womb is barren and withers away. You Asiatic women[9] are terribly 160 clever in such matters. But I'll frustrate you in this; this house of the Nereid will not help you at all, and neither will her altar or shrine; no, you will die. But should someone, mortal or god, wish to preserve your life, then you must give up those proud thoughts of royalty you once had and crouch humbly, falling at my knees; you must sweep my house clean, sprinkling drops of water with your own hands from jars of beaten gold, and you must realize where in the world you now are. There is no Hector here, no Priam with his gold; this is a city of Greece. But you have lost all finer feeling, you 170 wretch: you have brought yourself to sleep with the son of the man who killed your husband and to bear children to his murderer. You foreigners are all the same, of course: fathers sleep with daughters, sons with mothers, sisters with brothers, closest relatives commit murder against each other, and all is sanctioned by custom. We want none of your practices here. It is wrong for two women to be under the control of one man; if a man wants to avoid strife in his home, he is happy to look no further than one woman in one bed.   180

CHORUS-LEADER: A woman's heart is a jealous thing and always bitterly opposed to rivals in a husband's love.

ANDROMACHE: Ah, what a curse is youth to mankind, youth and the injustice that can accompany it! My fear is that my status as a slave may deny me the right of reply to you for all the justice of my case, while, if I win, it will cost me dear. Those with influence in the world resent being worsted in argument by inferiors. None the less I will not accept convic-   190 tion[10] without stating my case.

Tell me, young woman, what incontrovertible point would have made me confident of ousting you from your lawful marriage? Is Troy a greater city than Sparta? Does it enjoy more good fortune? Do you see before you a woman who is free? What has given me the confidence to seek to take your place in this house? Was it my youth, my physical attractiveness, my great city, the friends that I enjoy? Or was it my aim to have children in your place, little slaves who would trail behind their mother in misery? Will children of mine be accepted   200 as rulers of Phthia if motherhood is denied to you? No doubt I am a great favourite with the Greeks because of Hector! No doubt my name is little known and I was no princess of Troy!

No drugs of mine have made your husband turn away from you; it is your own lack of understanding for each other. Here is your 'drug'. It is not our beauty, woman, but our qualities that charm our husbands. If anything causes you irritation, then you boast of Sparta's greatness and belittle Scyros, you   210 are rich while your in-laws are poor, and Menelaus counts for more than Achilles in your eyes. This is the reason why your husband dislikes you. A woman must acquiesce in her husband's wishes, even if she has been given to one she cannot respect, and avoid competing with him in self-esteem. If you were married to some prince in the snow-bound depths of

Thrace, where many wives in turn supply one husband's bed, would you have killed them? Then people would have seen that you ascribed your own lust for sex to all women. None of this brings you credit; it's true we women are more prone to this affliction than men, but we are better at concealing it.

O Hector, my love, to please you I would never try to thwart you in your affairs if any girl took your fancy; many times in the past I nurtured your bastards at my own breast[11] rather than show any bitterness towards you. By acting like this I kept my husband's love through loyalty. But you are so fearful that you don't allow a single drop of rain to wet your husband's face. You shouldn't try to outdo your mother in loving a husband, woman; if they are sensible, children whose parents set a bad example should not try to copy them.

CHORUS-LEADER: My lady, as far as you can without difficulty, try to reach an accommodation with this woman. This is my advice.

HERMIONE [to ANDROMACHE]: Don't lecture me on morals or try to better me in argument, claiming that you can control yourself where men are concerned, whereas I cannot!

ANDROMACHE: Well, to judge from the position you are taking up, I'm right!

HERMIONE: I hope that my idea of sensible behaviour may never coincide with yours, woman!

ANDROMACHE: You are young to be talking about what should make a woman ashamed.

HERMIONE: You don't stop at talking; you act against me with all your power.

ANDROMACHE: More of the same! Won't you stop complaining about the state of your marriage?

HERMIONE: Are you telling me it's not natural for women the world over to put love first?

ANDROMACHE: Yes, provided their love is of the right kind; but if it isn't, they are in the wrong.

HERMIONE: We live in a city that does not recognize the customs of foreigners.

14

ANDROMACHE: Foreigners feel shame at what is shameful no less than Greeks.[12]

HERMIONE: Oh how clever you are! But still you must die.

ANDROMACHE: Do you see that Thetis' statue is looking at you?

HERMIONE: Yes; it is filled with hatred for your homeland because Achilles' blood was spilled.

ANDROMACHE: Helen was the cause of his death, not I, and she is your mother.

HERMIONE: Ah, will you go so far as to reopen my wounds?

ANDROMACHE: Very well, I'll say no more; my lips are sealed. 250

HERMIONE: Tell me now what I came out to learn.

ANDROMACHE: I tell you that you don't have as much sense as you should.

HERMIONE: Will you leave this holy sanctuary of the sea-goddess?

ANDROMACHE: Yes if my safety is guaranteed; if not, I will never leave it.

HERMIONE: My mind is fixed on this, believe me; I will not wait for my husband to come.

ANDROMACHE: And I will not surrender myself to you first, either.

HERMIONE: I will use fire against you; you will get no consideration from me —

ANDROMACHE: Then burn away; the gods will know what you do.

HERMIONE: — as your flesh is seared with fearful wounds.

ANDROMACHE: Cut my throat, make the goddess's altar run with my blood; she will come for you. 260

HERMIONE: You barbarian creature, you stiff-necked hussy, are you so defiant in the face of death? I'll make you quit this place of sanctuary soon enough without lifting a finger; such is the bait I have for you. However, I'll say no more; you'll see soon enough. Keep your seat there; even if molten lead surrounded your feet, I'll make you shift before the one you put your trust in, Achilles' son, arrives. [HERMIONE turns and leaves through the central door of the palace.]

ANDROMACHE: I do trust him. How strange it is that a god has

270   given men antidotes to dangerous reptiles, but when it comes
       to something worse than vipers or fire, a woman, no one has
       yet discovered a remedy.

CHORUS [Strophe]: *Great were the sorrows he set in train, the son of*
Maia and Zeus, that day he entered the dell on Ida, bringing that
lovely team of goddesses three, armed for the hateful contest of beauty,[13]
280   *to the cowherd's steading, to the lonely young herdsman and his*
unfrequented hearth and home.

       [Antistrophe:] *When they came to the wooded dell they bathed*
their radiant bodies in the waters of a mountain spring and approached
the son of Priam. With extravagant promises they vied in their rancour
with one another and the Cyprian won with her crafty words that
290   *brought delight to his ears, but to the wretched city of the Phrygians*
and citadel of Troy a harrowing destruction of life.

       [Strophe:] *If only his mother had cast him out to die as one*
polluted before letting him make a home on Ida's uplands, on the
day that Cassandra from her prophetic laurel tree cried out for his
death as one who would inflict great harm upon Priam's city. Whom
did she not accost, what elder of the people did she not entreat to put
300   *the infant to the sword?*[14]

       [Antistrophe:] *Then the women of Troy would have escaped the*
yoke of slavery and you, lady, would have won yourself a royal home.
Greece would have been spared the bitter, wayward struggle endured
for ten years by her young men as they fought before Troy's walls;
never would wives have found their marriage-beds cold and empty,
nor would aged fathers lament the loss of sons.

       [MENELAUS, *father of* HERMIONE, *enters with attendants.*
       They have ANDROMACHE'S CHILD.]

MENELAUS: I have come with your son, taking him from the
       other house where you had him sent in secret, unknown to
310   my daughter. You were confident that your safety would
       be assured by this statue of the goddess and this boy's by those
       who hid him. But events have proved you to be less clever
       than Menelaus, the man before you, woman. Now, if you fail
       to leave this sacred place as empty as you found it, his throat
       will be slit instead of yours. Think then on this: are you willing

to die or is this boy to pay for your crime, the harm you are
doing to my daughter and to me?

ANDROMACHE: Ah, reputation, reputation, how many thousands of men owe it to you that their lives are inflated to great
heights though they are worthless? Can one so petty as you   320
have once commanded the squadrons of the Greeks and taken
Troy from Priam? A man whose daughter's childish complaints
have made him behave so pompously that he seeks to defeat
a wretched slave-woman! You are not fit, I think, to be Troy's
conqueror,[15] nor does Troy deserve you.   330

Come Menelaus, let us talk this business through. Let us
assume I am dead by your daughter's hand; she has brought
my life to an end. She will no longer escape the taint of guilt
for shedding another's blood. And you will also have to face
up to public opinion by answering to a charge of murder; as
an accomplice you will have no other choice open to you.
However, suppose I manage to escape death myself, will you
take my boy's life? Do you imagine his father will accept his
child's death lightly? Troy would not see him as such a   340
weakling. No, he will follow the path of duty, he will let the
world see him acting as Peleus and Achilles, his father, would
wish: he will show your daughter the door. Then, when you
offer her in marriage to another man, what will you tell him?
That her husband was vile and her virtuous heart prompted
her to shun him? He will be unimpressed. Who will take her
for his wife? Or do you mean to keep her in your house,
husbandless, growing into a grey-haired widow?

Wretched man, do you not see it, the mountain of waves
that threatens to engulf you? How many times would you
rather find your daughter supplanted in her husband's love   350
than undergo what I have described? It is not right to punish
trivial offences too harshly, and, if we women are a dangerous
plague, that is no reason for men to copy our ways. As for
me, if I am using spells against your child and making her womb
infertile, as she claims, then freely and without constraint
abandoning the altar's refuge, I will of my own accord submit

360 myself to the judgement of your son-in-law; I owe him just as much in damages if I am guilty of making him childless.

There, you have my case. But as far as your own thinking goes, one thing about you makes me afraid: strife over a woman also made you destroy the wretched city of the Phrygians.[16]

CHORUS-LEADER: You have spoken too freely for a woman before men; your mind has lost any sense of proportion.

MENELAUS: Woman, this is a trivial dispute and, as you say, unworthy of a king such as me, and of Greece. But let me tell you, capturing Troy is less important to every man than gaining what he desires to have. I stand by my daughter in this (for 370 losing a husband's love I judge to be a serious matter). All other misfortunes that may befall a woman are of secondary importance, but in losing a husband she loses her life. My son-in-law has the right to command my slaves and members of my family and I to command his as well. Between those who are genuinely friends no private ownership exists; their goods are shared. If, while waiting for him to appear, I fail to order my own affairs as well as I can, then I am feeble and have no eye to the future.

Come, leave the goddess's shrine here; for, if you die, this 380 boy escapes death, but if you refuse to die, I will kill him. One or other of you is bound to forfeit life.

ANDROMACHE: Ah, what a cruel chance and choice of life you put before me! If I win my life, contempt is my reward; if I lose it, wretchedness. Menelaus, what you propose is dreadful and all for so little cause – can you not relent? Why kill me? For what? Which city have I betrayed? What child of yours 390 have I killed? Which house have I set fire to? Because I had no choice, I have slept with my master; will you then kill me and not him, the one who made this happen? Will you ignore the cause and rush on to the effect, though that was secondary?

[*Turning away from him in despair:*] Oh, my sorrows, my sorrows! My wretched homeland, what I am undergoing is monstrous! Why did I have to bear a child and crown one burdensome grief with another? I witnessed Hector's bloody

end as the chariot wheels dragged him along, and Troy piteously consumed by fire, I became a slave myself and was   400
dragged by the hair down to the ships of the Greeks. When
I came to Phthia, they gave me as a bride to Hector's murderers.
What pleasure then has life for me? Which way should I look
for relief? To my past or my present fortune? This boy was
all I had left, the one ray of solace in my life. Now they are
going to kill him; they have decided it.

Well, not if my wretched life is all it costs! There is hope
for him if he escapes with his life, but for me only disgrace if
I fail to die for my child. There you are, I now leave the   410
altar and give myself up to you to slaughter, murder, throttle
by hanging. My child, your mother is now going to Hades so
that you may not die. If you cheat death, remember your
mother, what I suffered and how I died, kiss your father and
tell him of my fate, weeping and clasping his hands as you do.
Everyone regards his children as his very life, that's clear
enough. If any man despises children, having none of his own,
he may be spared some grief but his happiness is rooted in
sorrow.   420

CHORUS-LEADER: Your words have touched my heart; it is
only human to feel pity at misfortune, even when it is a
stranger's. [*To* MENELAUS:] You should try to make peace
between your daughter and this woman, to free her from her
anguish.

MENELAUS [*to his servants*]: Seize her, you men,[17] lay hold of her
I say! She will hear words she does not like. I have you now!
To make you leave the goddess's holy altar I made the threat
to kill your son and so induced you to give yourself up to me
and have your throat slit. So much then for the fate that lies
in store for you. As for this boy, my daughter will decide   430
whether she wants to kill him or let him live. Now, into this
house with you, so that you may learn that a slave should
never show insolence to those of free birth.

ANDROMACHE: Oh no! You tricked me! I have been deceived!
MENELAUS: Proclaim it to all; I make no denial.

ANDROMACHE: Is this what passes for shrewdness among those who live by the Eurotas?

MENELAUS: Yes, and Trojans would agree: do harm to those who have harmed you.

ANDROMACHE: Do you think the gods are not the gods and do not judge us all?

MENELAUS: I will bear such judgement, whenever it comes. But you I will kill now.

ANDROMACHE: And this little chick, tearing him from under my wings?

MENELAUS: No, I'll give him to my daughter to kill, if she wants.

ANDROMACHE: Ah, not that! Oh, I ought to be mourning for you already, my child!

MENELAUS: You certainly have no grounds for confidence as far as his future is concerned.

ANDROMACHE [*breaking into rage*]: Inhabitants of Sparta,[18] most hated men on earth, devious plotters, masters of lies, hatchers of wicked schemes, whose thoughts are twisted and rotten, never direct, your successes throughout Greece are built on crimes! Every vice belongs to you; you commit murder without end and know no shame in seeking your own profit; constantly you are discovered saying one thing but thinking another. I curse you! I am not so appalled by the prospect of death as you suppose. The day that ended my life was when the wretched city of the Trojans fell, and my glorious husband who often with his spear drove you trembling off the beach into the sea. And now you show yourself to a woman in all the terror of your armour and threaten me with death. Then do the deed! There will be no words of flattery on my tongue when I take my leave of you and your daughter. You are a great man in Sparta; well, greatness was mine in Troy. Do not derive any pleasure from my present misery; it may come to you also.

[MENELAUS *and servants leave, taking* ANDROMACHE *and her* CHILD *with them*.]

CHORUS [Strophe]: *Never will I approve of mortals having two bed-fellows, or of sons by different mothers, a source of quarrelling and bitter recrimination in the home. I would have my husband be content with one marriage-bed, unshared by another woman.*   470

[Antistrophe:] *In cities also two rulers are harder to bear than one; this adds one burden to another and creates dissension among the people. So, too, when two poets have crafted a poem together, the Muses love to put them at loggerheads.*

[Strophe:] *When sailors are swept along by rushing winds, in the matter of steering, two points of view, or a whole body of experts,*   480 *are no match for one man of average ability exercising his independent judgement. In palaces and in cities, when men want to find the right solution, it is one man who achieves what is needed.*

[Antistrophe:] *The Spartan woman, daughter of commander Menelaus, gives proof of this; like fire she raged against her rival in love and, to satisfy her bitter enmity, she seeks to kill the wretched woman of Troy and her child. To shed such blood is an offence against*   490 *heaven, against custom, against decency. This deed of yours will yet turn your fortunes to ill, lady.*

[MENELAUS *and attendants re-enter with* ANDROMACHE *and her* CHILD, *who now wear fetters.*]

But here I see the pair of them clasping one another before the palace, with sentence of death passed upon them. Poor woman! And you, unfortunate boy, who are to die because of your father's lust, though you have no part in this strife and bear no responsibility in the eyes of the rulers!   500

[ANDROMACHE *and her* CHILD *lament their fate in lyrics and appeal for mercy to* MENELAUS.]

ANDROMACHE [Strophe]: *Now I am sent on my journey below the earth, my wrists bloodied from the cords that bind them fast.*

CHILD:[19] *Mother, mother, your little chick here shares your journey!*

ANDROMACHE: *What a pitiful offering we make, you elders of Phthia's land!*

CHILD: *Father, come to save your family!*

ANDROMACHE: *O my dear child, there will you lie under the earth,*   510 *a corpse with a corpse, close to your mother's breast!*

CHILD: *No, no! What is going to happen to me? Oh mother, we are wretched indeed, you and I!*

MENELAUS: *Away with you beneath the earth! You come from a city that was our enemy and two reasons compel the two of you to die: you are condemned by our decision and your son here by my daughter*

520 *Hermione. It is pure folly to leave an enemy's son to be an enemy when one has the chance to kill him and rid the house of fear.*

ANDROMACHE [Antistrophe]: *O husband, my husband, son of Priam, if only I had your spear and sturdy hand to champion me!*

CHILD: *Oh, pity me! What charm can I find to turn death away?*

ANDROMACHE: *Clasp your master by the knees and ask his mercy, child.*

530 CHILD [*falling at* MENELAUS' *feet*]: *Oh please sir, be kind sir, don't let me die!*

ANDROMACHE: *My eyes brim with tears; they pour down like a stream unwarmed by the sun from a smooth rock. Oh, I am wretched!*

CHILD: *Ah, what am I to do? How can I escape from this terror?*

MENELAUS: *Why do you fall at my feet in entreaty? You might as well address your appeals to a wave or a rock washed by the sea! My own family will receive my help but you have no means to charm my*

540 *love; it cost me much in heart and limb to win Troy and your mother. She is the one you will have to thank for your journey down to Hades.*

CHORUS-LEADER: But here I see Peleus approaching, with all the haste his old legs can muster. [*Enter* PELEUS *with a manservant.*][20]

PELEUS: You there, and you, the one in charge of this blood-letting, I ask you, what is this, what's it all about? What has caused this sickness to fall on my house? What deaths are you plotting without trial? Menelaus, stop right there! Don't be

550 in such a hurry to flout justice! [*To his servant:*] Quicker! Lead me on! This business must be tackled at once it seems, and now, if ever, I need to find the strength of my youth. The first thing is to breathe some spirit into her, like a wind filling a ship's sails. [*To* ANDROMACHE:] Tell me, what is your crime that these men should be leading you and your

son away with your wrists tied with cords? You go to the slaughter like a ewe suckling a lamb, while your master and I are away.

ANDROMACHE: They are taking me away with my child to die, old man, just as you see. What can I say to you? It was not a *single* desperate summons I sent to bring you; I cannot count the messengers I despatched. I take it you know from hearsay of the bad blood that exists in the palace between this man's daughter and myself, and how it is spelling my ruin. And now they are leading me off, after tearing me from the altar of Thetis, the mother of your noble son, the lady you worship and venerate. They have neither passed sentence on me in a proper trial nor waited for my master to return home; no, they have taken advantage of the fact that my boy and I lack any protection. He is completely innocent! But still they are going to make him share his wretched mother's death. Oh, I beg you, old man, falling at your knees – I cannot use my hand to grasp your precious beard – save me, for the love of heaven! Otherwise we shall die, a miserable end for me, old man, but one that also brings no honour to you and yours.

PELEUS [*to* MENELAUS' *men*]: Loosen this woman's cords I say, and untie both her hands before someone regrets it!

MENELAUS: And I say do not! I am not your servant – I have far stronger claims to ownership of this woman than you.

PELEUS: In what sense? Will you come here and try to run my house for me? Are you not content to lord it over those in Sparta?

MENELAUS: It was I who took her from Troy as the prisoner of my spear.

PELEUS: Yes, but it was my grandson who gained her as his prize.

MENELAUS: Is his property not mine and mine his?

PELEUS: Yes, to treat with respect but not to abuse and kill without consent.

MENELAUS: Make no mistake, you'll never take this woman from my hands.

560

570

580

PELEUS: I will, once I've used this staff to give you a bloody head!

MENELAUS: Then lay a finger on her, so I can teach you a lesson. Come towards me![21]

PELEUS: Do you call yourself a man, you coward with cowards for ancestors?[22] How can you enjoy a good reputation, at least in the eyes of real men? Someone who let a Phrygian make away with his bedfellow, leaving the rooms of his house unlocked, with no servants to guard them, on the assumption that he had in his home a virtuous wife, when in fact no woman was more promiscuous!

No Spartan girl[23] could keep her virtue, even if she wanted to; they leave their homes empty and share the running track and wrestling ground with young men, baring their thighs in loose-fitting shifts – it is quite unacceptable! Is it then any wonder that you fail to rear women of any modesty? Helen is the one you should put that question to, the woman who left your home to go rioting off to another country with her young man. And then, to recover a woman like that, you raised so huge a force of Greeks and led them to Troy? Once you had found her to be unfaithful you should have washed your hands of her instead of going to war, letting her stay there and even paying money to avoid ever taking her back into your home. But your thoughts took a different course: you sent many a brave man to his death, you made elderly mothers wait in vain for returning sons and robbed grey-haired fathers of noble offspring. And one of these is my wretched self. I see in you the fiend who murdered Achilles. Back you came from Troy, the only warrior without a scratch to show, and as for the splendid weapons you took there in their fine coverings, you brought them back quite unblemished.

I told him, your son-in-law to be, not to form any tie of kinship with you or to take into his home a filly sprung from so wicked a dam; the mothers' faults come out in their daughters. Let me give you a piece of advice, all you fellows who would be husbands: choose the daughter of a good mother. Another thing, just look at the monstrous way you treated your brother, urging him to let his own daughter's throat be slit[24] like a complete fool! Were you so afraid of not recovering a worthless wife? No, you utter coward, when Troy lay at your feet (I will go back to your great moment), you failed to kill the woman you had won back; one glimpse of her breasts[25] and you cast aside your sword, conquered by the Cyprian, letting her kiss you and fawning on the faithless bitch! And then you come to my grandchild's home and create havoc in his absence, threatening this wretched woman and her son with a dishonourable death. He'll make you sorry for it, you and that daughter of yours in the palace, though the boy may be a bastard three times over! Poor soil often yields a better crop than rich, let me tell you, and many a bastard is a better man than a true-born son.[26] Why don't you take your daughter back to your own home? Better for men to choose marriage-relations and friends from the poor and honest than from the wealthy and unprincipled. You are beneath contempt!

CHORUS-LEADER: The tongue can set men at each other's throats, all from a trivial beginning. People who are wise take good care not to fall out with friends.

MENELAUS: How could wisdom ever be attributed to the old or to those once famed among Greeks for their intelligence? Take your case, Peleus; although you are the man you are, son of a famous father, although you have formed a connection with us by marriage, you make this woman, a foreigner, an excuse for insulting us and bringing shame on your own head! You ought to have banished her beyond the waters of the Nile, beyond Phasis, and continually asked for my assistance, coming as she does from Asia where so many young Greeks fell in death, killed by the spear. She has a share, too, in your son's blood; Paris, who killed your son Achilles, was Hector's brother, and she was Hector's wife. And this is the woman you share the same home with, taking meals with her without qualm and allowing her to bear children under your roof to

630

640

650

become your bitter enemies! Then, when I want to kill her,
660 acting in your interests, old man, as much as my own, I have
her snatched from my grasp!

And yet, consider it; I may raise the question quite properly:
if my child produces no children, and this woman does have
offspring, will you let them rule as kings of Phthia? Will men
of foreign birth govern Greeks? Am I then the foolish one if
I show my distaste for what is unjust, and are you the man of
670 sense? Oh, you are old, old! As to my leadership of men,
you will help me more by speaking of it than by not. The
trouble Helen caused was not of her choosing but the work
680 of the gods,[27] and this more than anything benefited the men
of Greece. They lacked knowledge of weaponry and combat
and so grew into proper warriors. It is experience that teaches
men all things. If I stopped myself from killing my wife when
she appeared before my eyes, it was a case of exercising
self-control. You would have done better in my view not to
have killed Phocus.[28] I have not spared you in this encounter
but goodwill towards you, not anger, is the reason. If you
continue in this irascible vein, your endless talking will get
690 worse while I will simply profit from my forethought.

CHORUS-LEADER: Let us have no more now of these foolish
words – this would be the best thing by far – before the two
of you come to grief together.

PELEUS: Oh, how misguided the custom is in Greece! When an
army sets up a trophy of victory over the enemy, it isn't the
hard-working troops who get the credit for the achievement,
oh no, it's the general who wins the reputation, though he
was only one man wielding his spear among countless others,
and he gains more esteem for contributing no more than a
700 single soldier. Just like you and your brother – you sit back
puffed up with pride at the success of Troy and your role as
generals there, though other men's sweat and toil filled
your sails.

I will make you realize that Paris of Ida was not so dangerous
a foe as Peleus, if you don't get out of my house this instant,

you and your childless daughter, and go to perdition! My son's
son will drag her by the hair from room to room of this house.   710
A barren heifer herself, she will not tolerate others giving
birth, having no children of her own. But if misfortune
has struck her in the matter of children, must we impose
childlessness on ourselves? [*To* MENELAUS' *servants*:] Damn
you, men, leave her alone! I want to find out if anyone will
stop me untying her wrists. [*To* ANDROMACHE:] Stand up.
My hands may not be steady but I will loosen these knotted
thongs that tie you. [*To* MENELAUS:] You cruel swine, did
you have to bruise her wrists like this? Did you imagine it was
an ox or lion you were binding in a noose? Or were you   720
afraid she might grab a sword and revenge herself on you? [*To*
ANDROMACHE'S CHILD:] Over here, child, come under my
arms; help me to loosen your mother's bonds. I will raise you
in Phthia to be an enemy they will fear. [*To* MENELAUS:] If
Sparta's sons were not hardy warriors, famed with the spear,
let me tell you, in everything else you would be no better
than anyone else.

CHORUS-LEADER: Old men do not know how to control
themselves; their quickness of temper makes them hard to
manage.

MENELAUS: You rush into insults with too much eagerness. I
have come to Phthia not of my own choice and so I will   730
neither do anything unbecoming nor let it be done to me.
For the moment, as the time at my disposal is limited, I will
go back home; there is a certain city not far from Sparta[29]
which was formerly our friend but is now behaving like an
enemy. I want to attack it at the head of my troops and bring
it under our control. When I have settled matters there to my
liking, I will be back. Then face to face for all to see, I will
state my case before my kinsman and listen to his. Now, if he
punishes this woman and behaves with moderation towards
me in the future, he will find me moderate in return, but if   740
it is anger that he shows, he will find me angry. These words
of yours do not distress me; your power of speech is that of a

shadow cast by a man; you are quite incapable of doing anything except talking. [MENELAUS *and his attendants leave.*]

PELEUS [*to* ANDROMACHE *and her* CHILD]: Lead on, my child, stand here under my arm, and you also, poor lady; it was a savage storm you met with but now you have reached the harbour's calm.

ANDROMACHE: Old sir, may the gods be generous to you and 750 yours for saving my son and my unhappy self! But have a care! These men may lie in wait for us where the road lacks travellers and take me off by force when they see you are an old man, while I am weak and my son a child. Think well: we don't want to make our escape now only to be captured later on.

PELEUS [*in exasperation*]: I want no cowardly talk such as this! How like a woman! Proceed! Who will lay a hand on you? The man who touches you will be sorry! Thanks to the gods I have at my command throughout Phthia a host of horsemen 760 and numerous men-at-arms. My back is straight; I am no old man, as you suppose, and when it comes to a man of his stamp, I will merely confront him before recording my victory over him, for all my grey hairs. An old man with courage is better than a host of youngsters; what's the point of rippling muscles if you're a coward? [*They all leave the stage.*]

CHORUS [Strophe]: *I would rather not be born at all than lack parents of good stock and a share in the inheritance of a wealthy house. Should* 770 *some disaster befall a man, the well-born have no lack of remedy; honour and glory attend upon men from noble families and their names are proclaimed for all to hear. Time does not rob the nobly-born of what they leave behind; even in death their valour shines forth.*

[Antistrophe:] *It is better not to have a victory that sullies* 780 *reputation than to overthrow justice by force and win hatred. Such gain brings men delight at first but in time it withers in their hands and voices of reproach beset their house. This is the way of life I approve, this the one I wish to make my own, to wield no power in my home or my city that transgresses justice.*

[Epode:]³⁰ *Aged son of Aeacus, I do believe that at the Lapiths'*   790
side you fought it out most gloriously with the Centaurs, that on the
ship Argo you braved the inhospitable waters, passing the Clashing
Rocks which guard that sea on a memorable voyage, that when Zeus'
son flung his bloody net over Troy, that city once so renowned, you
came back to Europe sharing with him the glory.   800

[*Enter Hermione's* NURSE, *a slave-woman still in her service.*]
NURSE: O ladies, dear ladies, what a day this has been – one trouble
after another! There's my mistress in the house, Hermione, left
all alone by her father; now she's having second thoughts³¹
about her actions, the way she planned to kill Andromache
and her son, and she's bent on ending her own life, afraid her
husband will strip her of privilege and banish her from this
house for her behaviour. The slaves on guard only just   810
stopped her as she tried to hang herself, removing from her
grasp the sword she had snatched up. Such is her remorse, her
awareness that what she has done is wrong. Now, dear ladies,
I'm exhausted from trying to keep my mistress from using the
noose. Please go inside the house and rescue her from death;
new friends arriving on the scene are more persuasive than
familiar ones.

CHORUS-LEADER: Indeed we hear the shouting of servants
inside the house; this is what you came to report. It seems   820
the poor woman means to show the depth of her grief at her
terrible action. She is coming from the house now, trying to
escape the servants' hands in her eagerness to die.

[HERMIONE *enters, distraught, with some servants behind.*]
HERMIONE [Strophe]: *Oh, what misery! I shall rend my hair and*
tear my face with nails that wound!
NURSE: What will you do, child? Do injury to your own body?
HERMIONE [Antistrophe]: *Oh, my agony! Away with you, veil of*
fine threads, I fling you off my hair into the air!   830
NURSE: Cover your breast, my child, fasten your dress!
HERMIONE [Strophe]: *Why should I cover my breast with my dress?*
My crimes against my husband cannot be hidden from men's eyes;
they are plain for all to see.

NURSE: This distress you feel, is it because you plotted to murder your rival for your husband's love?

HERMIONE [Antistrophe]: *Distress? It is my arrogant heart that torments me. To think I should have been shameless enough to attempt this deed. Oh, I am cursed, cursed in the eyes of men!*

NURSE: Your husband will forgive you for this error of
840   judgement.

HERMIONE: *Why did you wrest the sword from my grip? Give it back, dear friend, give it back! I want to drive it home into my heart. Why do you not let me hang myself?*

NURSE: And if I let you take your own life when you have lost your senses, what then?

HERMIONE: *Ah, pity me for my fate! Where is the welcome bolt of lightning to end my life? Whereabouts can I leap from a rock, high over the sea or the wooded hills, to end my life and swell the ranks*
850   *of the dead?*

NURSE: Why trouble yourself over this? Disasters are sent from the gods and, sooner or later, afflict all men.

HERMIONE: *You left me, father, left me all alone on the shore without a ship to board. My husband will destroy me, it is certain, he will destroy me! I shall no more have this house of my lord as my home. Which god shall take me as his suppliant, whose statue[32] should I rush to clasp? Should I fall at the knees of a slave-woman, a slave*
860   *now myself? How I wish I might be a dark-winged bird, to fly from Phthia's land where the pine-wood craft passed between the dusky cliffs, first of ships[33] to brave the ocean.*

NURSE: My girl, I didn't like the way you went too far earlier, when you treated the Trojan woman unjustly, and now, too, this fear of yours that goes beyond the limit makes me lose patience. Your husband will not throw over his marriage with you as you imagine; he will not be influenced by the worthless
870   pleas of a woman who isn't Greek! In you he has no captive of the spear won from Troy but the daughter of a noble father, coming from a city of great prosperity, who brought with her hand a rich dowry. Do not fear, your father will not betray you by allowing your banishment from this house. Go inside

and stop showing yourself in front of the palace here before people start to talk!

CHORUS-LEADER: And here is a stranger, not a man from these parts but foreign looking, coming towards us with hurried steps. [*Enter* ORESTES.][34]   880

ORESTES: Ladies, I speak as a stranger: is this palace the royal dwelling of Achilles' son?

CHORUS-LEADER: You are quite right. But, tell me, who are you that asks this question?

ORESTES: The son of Agamemnon and Clytemnestra – Orestes is my name. I am journeying to the oracle of Zeus at Dodona.[35] Now that I have reached Phthia, it seems a good idea to inquire of my kinswoman, Hermione of Sparta, to see if she is alive and enjoying good fortune. Her home is far distant from mine but she is dear to my heart.   890

HERMIONE: Son of Agamemnon, you are as welcome a sight as a harbour to storm-tossed sailors! [*Sinking to the ground in front of him*:] I beg you, by these knees, pity me for the state you see me in, the way I am abused by Fortune! I clasp your knees with my arms – let them serve as my suppliant wreaths!

ORESTES: Ah, what is this? Do my eyes deceive me? Is this not the royal mistress of the house I see before me clearly, the daughter of Menelaus?

HERMIONE: Yes, the only child that Helen his wife, daughter of Tyndareus, bore to my father in his palace. Rest assured.

ORESTES: Phoebus, Healer, release us from our woes! What is   900
wrong? Is it gods who persecute you or men?

HERMIONE: It is partly myself, partly my husband, partly some god. From all sides my doom approaches.

ORESTES: What misfortune could befall a woman, if she has as yet no children, apart from marital problems?

HERMIONE: You have put your finger on my troubles; that was astute of you.

ORESTES: Has your husband rejected you for some other woman?

HERMIONE: His concubine, the prize of his spear, Hector's wife.

ORESTES: Ah, that's no healthy state of affairs, when one man has two women.

HERMIONE: Precisely; and my reaction to this was to protect 910 my own interests.

ORESTES: Did you act as women usually do and hatch some plot against your rival?

HERMIONE: Yes; I planned to kill her and her bastard child.

ORESTES: And did you kill them, or did some accident snatch them from your grasp?

HERMIONE: It was old Peleus who respected the weaker party.

ORESTES: Did you have an accomplice to share in this murder?

HERMIONE: Yes, my father, who came from Sparta for this very reason.

ORESTES: Are you telling me the old man had the better of him in combat?

HERMIONE: No, my father gave way out of respect for his years. And now he has gone, leaving me defenceless.

ORESTES: I see; you fear your husband because of what you have done.

HERMIONE: You understand; he will kill me, and justifiably. It 920 is beyond doubt. Oh, I beg you, in the name of Zeus, protector of our family, give me passage from this land to the furthest place on earth or to my father's royal seat. This palace seems to me to have a voice that urges my banishment; the land of Phthia hates me. If my husband returns home from Phoebus' oracle before then, he will make me die a shameful death, or else I will become the slave of his imported bedfellow, the woman who had me as her mistress before!

How then did I come to commit this crime, as it might be 930 called? I was crushed by the visits of wearisome women,[36] filled with their own self-importance, who kept giving me this advice: 'Are you going to let this vile slave-woman, this piece of war-baggage who occupies your home, take turns with you in your husband's bed? By Argos' queen, if she was under my roof, she wouldn't enjoy such favours and live to tell it!' Now when I heard these Siren words, I became puffed

up with folly. What need had I to keep watch on my husband
when I had at my disposal all that I required? I enjoyed great
wealth, I was mistress of my house, and any children I might   940
have produced would have been true born, while hers would
be bastards and, thanks to her, slaves to my own.

No, never, never (I will not say it once only) should sensible
married men allow women access to their wives in their homes.
They instruct them merely in how to be wicked. One abets
her in destroying the marriage, hoping to profit in some way
from it; another, already false to her own husband, encourages
her to join her in infidelity, while many act out of sheer
promiscuity. This is why men find corruption in their homes.   950
Keep close watch then on the doors of your house, using bolts
and bars. No good comes of women paying visits to a house,
indeed a lot of harm.

CHORUS-LEADER: You deal too harshly with womankind. I
can understand your feelings here, but just the same, women
ought to draw a veil over the failings of their sex.

ORESTES: He was no fool, the fellow who taught men to give a
hearing to accounts coming from the other side. So it was
with me; because I knew of the turmoil in this house, caused
by the quarrel between you and Hector's wife, I bided my   960
time, keeping an eye out to see if you would stay here or take
fright at the slave-woman's murder and seek to flee from the
palace. I came, not because of any information from you, but
to bring you away from the palace here, hoping that you
would give me a hearing, as now you do. You were betrothed
to me once, but now your home is here, with him as your
husband, and this is due to your father's treachery: before he
invaded Troy's borders he had given you to me as my wife.
But later he promised your hand to the man who has you
now, if he should sack the town of Troy.   970

When the son of Achilles returned to his home here, I
forgave your father and begged Neoptolemus to release you
from marriage, reminding him of how difficult a situation I
was facing, as someone undergoing banishment from such a

house, and pointing out that my cruel fate made marriage possible within a related family but very difficult otherwise. He was insolent, however, and taunted me over the killing of my mother, as the man hounded by the goddesses whose faces drip blood.[37] My family's misfortunes reduced me to 980 humiliation at this and I was hurt, sorely hurt; but I endured the cruel blow and went away reluctantly, deprived of your hand in marriage. Now, therefore, since your fortunes have collapsed and you have no way out of this disastrous trap, I will take you to your home and give you into your father's protection. It is a wonderful thing, the tie of blood, and, when trouble comes, nothing is better than the help of one of your own relatives.

HERMIONE: As to my marriage prospects, my father will concern himself with this. It is not a matter for me to decide. But lose no time – get me safely away from this house before my 990 husband gets here first and takes me prisoner, or old Peleus learns of my escape and sets off after me with horsemen.

ORESTES: Don't worry about an old man's strength. As for Achilles' son – such contempt he showed me – have no fear of him! Such is the net of death[38] woven for him that lies securely fastened in his path, woven by this hand of mine! I'll say no more of this; when all is accomplished, the rock of Delphi shall know. Mother-killer, am I? Well, if only my 1000 guest-friends in the Pythian land stand by their oaths, I'll show him what it is to marry a woman meant for me! He will bitterly regret having asked Lord Apollo for satisfaction for the killing of his father. It will be of no help to him that he changed his mind and now seeks to appease the god; Apollo and my accusations will consign him to a foul end. Neoptolemus will discover my capacity for hate. The god brings reversal of fortune on the heads of his enemies; he does not tolerate their pride. [HERMIONE and ORESTES depart.]

CHORUS [Strophe]: *Phoebus, who raised up Ilium's fair crown of* 1010 *walls,[39] and you, lord of ocean, who ride over the surface of the sea behind your team of dark-blue horses, why did you give up the fruit*

of your handiwork to Ares, master of the spear, abandoning wretched,
wretched Troy to dishonour?

[Antistrophe:] Chariots past number did you yoke on Simois'
banks behind their fine horses; past number, too, the bloody contests
of men you established, contests where no garland was the prize. 1020
Dead and gone are the princes of Ilium, no more in Troy does the
altar fire blaze with fragrant fumes to honour the gods.

[Strophe:] Gone is Atreus' son, slain by his wife's violence, while
she, giving death in exchange, met her end at her children's hands. 1030
A god, a god it was whose oracular order fell on her head that day
Agamemnon's son, leaving his shrine and coming to Argos, took her
life, becoming his mother's murderer. Phoebus, divine one, how should
I believe?

[Antistrophe:] And in the assemblies of the Greeks many lamen-
tations rang out for wretched children, while wives left their homes for 1040
the arms of a new lover. Not on you alone, not on your loved ones
alone, have cruel sorrows fallen; Hellas has been plagued indeed.
Even to the fertile lands of the Trojans the storm of war passed,
sending its bloody rain down on the men of Greece.

[PELEUS *returns, accompanied by attendants.* ANDROMACHE
and her CHILD *are with him but do not speak any further.*]

PELEUS: Women of Phthia, tell me what I ask you. A confused
report has reached me that Menelaus' daughter has left this
house and is gone. I am here because I long to know if this is 1050
true. When members of a family are away, those at home
should work hard to protect their interests.

CHORUS-LEADER: Peleus, your news is true enough. It does
me no honour to conceal the misdeeds that surround me. The
queen is gone; she has fled from the palace here.

PELEUS: What was it made her afraid? Tell me.

CHORUS-LEADER: Her husband – she feared he would expel
her from the palace.

PELEUS: For the plots she was hatching against his son's life?

CHORUS-LEADER: Yes, and her plan to kill his concubine.

PELEUS: Did she leave the palace with her father? Who
accompanied her? 1060

CHORUS-LEADER: Agamemnon's son has come and taken her away from Phthia.

PELEUS: What does he hope to achieve? Does he want her for his wife?

CHORUS-LEADER: Yes, and he also means to kill your grandson.

PELEUS: Lying in wait for him or meeting him in open combat?

CHORUS-LEADER: With the help of men of Delphi in Loxias' holy shrine.

PELEUS: Oh no! Horrifying news! [*To his attendants:*] Quick, one of you, go to the Pythian seat and tell our friends there of this plot before Achilles' son is struck down by his enemies!

[*Enter a* MESSENGER, *one of the men serving Neoptolemus.*]

1070 MESSENGER: Ah, what misery I feel! Here I am, an unhappy man, to tell such a tale of sorrow to you, aged sir, and those who love my master!

PELEUS: Oh, no, no! My heart plays the prophet, full of foreboding.

MESSENGER: Your grandson no longer lives, to tell you plain, old Peleus. Such are the sword-thrusts he has received from the men of Delphi and their friend from Mycenae. [PELEUS *totters and falls.*]

CHORUS-LEADER: Ah, what's this, old man? Do not fall! Get to your feet!

PELEUS: I am nothing. I am ruined! My voice is gone, my limbs too: they no longer support me.

MESSENGER: Stand up and listen to what happened, if you really 1080 do want to help your friends.

PELEUS: O fate, what woes you have inflicted on my wretched head, when I had all but run the distance of my old age! How did he meet his end, my only son's only son? Tell me; it is a tale too awful to be heard, but still I wish to hear it.

MESSENGER: When we arrived at Phoebus' famous dwelling, we spent three whole days from dawn to dusk, letting our eyes take in all that was to be seen. This behaviour apparently caused suspicion. The folk who are the god's tenants started coming together in groups, while Agamemnon's son went

through the town speaking words of hate in each man's ear: 1090
'Do you see this fellow walking through the god's precinct
filled with gold, where men have built their treasuries, back
here a second time on the same business that brought him
before, bent on pillaging the temple of the god?'

This set in motion a wave of anger and resentment in the
town. Civic authorities began filling the council chamber and,
unprompted, those responsible for the god's treasure posted
guards in the colonnades around his temple. Now we knew
none of this as yet and, bringing our sheep, reared on Parnassus'
grassy slopes, we came and stood before the altar with the 1100
local officials and Pythian priests. One of them then said,
'Young man, what prayer would you have us offer to the god?
What is the purpose of your visit?' Neoptolemus made this
reply: 'I wish to make amends to Phoebus for my past misdeed
in asking him for satisfaction for the killing of my father.'
Then it was clear to all how strong a hold Orestes' words had
taken, the story that my master was a liar who had come to 1110
work mischief. He made his way into the shrine, ascending
the steps, intent on making his prayer to Apollo in front of
the inner shrine, and began to occupy himself with the burnt
sacrifice. But, lurking in the shadow of a laurel, a band of men
were waiting for him, swords in hand, one of whom was
Clytemnestra's son, whose cunning mind had devised all this.
My master was standing in plain view, making his prayer to
the god when, armed with sharpened swords, they broke
cover and lunged at Achilles' son who wore no armour. He
stepped backwards, not critically wounded, drawing his 1120
sword, and, seizing some armour from the side-wall where it
hung on pegs, he took his stand on the altar steps, a warrior
terrible to see. And calling out to the people of Delphi, he
asked them this: 'Why do you seek my death when the mission
I have come on is a pious one? What is the crime that makes
you want to take my life?'

So many of them there were close by, but not a man uttered
a word. Instead, they began pelting him with stones they had

picked up. He was battered by these as they came at him in
constant flurries from all sides like a blizzard. He tried to
1130   protect himself with his armour as he warded off the shower
of missiles, holding out his shield this way and that to deflect
them. They made no headway though; the storm of weapons,
arrows, javelins, spits drawn from slaughtered oxen came flying
at him together but ended short of his feet. Then you would
have seen a war-dance to freeze the blood as your boy twisted
to avoid these missiles. When they had formed a circle round
him, hemming him in and denying him a breathing space, he
quit his position on the top of the altar and, with that leap
1140   that won him fame at Troy,[40] he flung himself at them. Like
doves at the sight of a hawk they turned tail and fled. Many
lost their lives in the confusion, either from wounds or trampling one another to death in the narrow passageway. The din
of shouting profaned the holy silence of the sanctuary and
echoed from the cliffs.

Then there was a strange silence as my master stood there,
a radiant figure in his shining armour, until from the depths
of the shrine a voice rang out, a weird, heart-stopping cry,
that stirred the host and roused their fighting spirit. Then
Achilles' son fell, his side pierced by the thrust of a sharpened
1150   sword, but he did not fall alone. And when he hit the ground,
there was not one of them who didn't bring up his sword or
a stone to smash and rend him where he lay. His body, all of
that fine young body, has been destroyed by savage wounds.
Now, as his corpse lay too near their altar, they threw him
outside the temple precinct where men offer sacrifice. We
lost no time in picking him up and have brought him here
for you to make your lamentations, sir, crying out and weeping
1160   for him, before you give him decent burial in the earth.

This is how the god who gives oracles to men, who arbitrates
on justice to all the world, dealt with the son of Achilles, when
he came to offer amends. Like an unforgiving man
he remembered a quarrel in the past. How then can he be
wise?[41]

[*Attendants enter carrying the body of* NEOPTOLEMUS *on a bier. After their entrance into the orchestra they set it down before* PELEUS.]

CHORUS: Here he comes now, our prince, carried shoulder high from the Delphian land to his home. I pity the dead man, I pity you too, old man. The welcome home you are giving to Achilles' son is not the one you would have chosen, and you yourself in your misery   1170 have come to share in one and the same fate as he.

[PELEUS *and the* CHORUS *now lament over the corpse.*]

PELEUS [Strophe]: *Oh, what misery! Such a terrible sight I see here, receiving it with these hands into my house! Ah, this pain I feel, it overcomes me! Good people of Thessaly, we are ruined, finished! My family exists no more, no children are left in my house. My sufferings make a wretch of me. What friend have I left to make my heart happy as he appears?* [*Caressing his grandson's body:*] *Dear lips, dear*   1180 *cheek, dear hands! If only you had been slain by fate below Ilium's walls, by the banks of Simois!*[42]

CHORUS-LEADER: In that case, meeting such an end, he would be held in honour, old man, and your lot would then be a happier one.

PELEUS [Antistrophe]: *Oh marriage, marriage that brought ruin, ruin on this house and my city! O my poor, poor boy, I cannot bear it! I wish that my family had never embraced that despicable marriage of yours for the promise of children and home, wedlock with Hermione*   1190 *that was to spell death for you, my child! If only she had been destroyed by a bolt of lightning*[43] *before that day! If only you, a mortal man, had not made Phoebus, a god, responsible for your noble father's death, because of the bow's deadly work!*

CHORUS [Strophe]: *Cry sorrow, sorrow, sorrow! I shall begin the lament for my slain master with the song reserved for the dead.*

PELEUS: *Cry sorrow, sorrow, sorrow! I, a wretched, unhappy old man, shed tears in my turn.*   1200

CHORUS: *Aye, it is the god's will, the god has caused this disaster to happen.*

PELEUS: *My beloved boy, you have left my house desolate, you have abandoned me to a childless old age.*

CHORUS: *You should have died, you should have died, old man, before your children.*[44]

PELEUS: *Let me tear my hair, let me rain harmful blows on my head*
1210 *with my fists! O men of Phthia, Phoebus has robbed me of the two sons I had!*

CHORUS [Antistrophe]: *Old man, you have suffered terribly and seen misery; what life will you have in the years to come?*

PELEUS: *Childless, deserted, with no end to my suffering, I will drink sorrow's bitter cup to the hour of my death.*

CHORUS: *All for nothing did the gods bless you at your wedding.*[45]

PELEUS: *Gone with the wind is all the promise of that happy day; how*
1220 *little it now deserves those lofty words of praise!*

CHORUS: *Your life is turned upside down; alone will you be in the empty halls of your palace.*

PELEUS: *No more do I have a city to live in; away with this staff of royalty!* [*He flings away his sceptre.*] *And you, daughter of Nereus, dwelling in your gloomy cavern, you shall witness me falling in utter ruin!*

CHORUS: *Ah, ah, what is that moving? What godlike presence do I sense? Girls, look, see! This is some god, speeding through the bright*
1230 *air, who is setting foot on our Phthia's soil, rich pasture for horses.*
[*The goddess* THETIS *appears on a raised platform above the stage.*]

THETIS: Peleus, it is I, Thetis;[46] in memory of our former nuptials I have come here, leaving the dwelling of Nereus behind. First I counsel you against grieving excessively at your present misfortune; I, too, though a goddess and child of a divine father, and so one whose children should never have caused her to weep, I lost the child I bore to you, the foremost warrior of Greece, my swift-footed son, Achilles.

My reasons for coming here I will explain, and it is for you to listen. Take this man who has died, Achilles' son, to the
1240 Pythian hearth and there give him burial where he will bring shame on the men of Delphi and his tomb may proclaim the bloody murder wrought by Orestes. As for his wife, the bride of his spear Andromache, she must make a new home in the land of Molossia, old man, where Helenus[47] will take her

as his wedded wife, and with her this boy must also go, this
last remaining scion of Aeacus. And following in his line as
king of Molossia[48] one ruler after another shall pass his days
in the eye of heaven's favour. It must not be that my family
and yours, old man, and the blood of Troy, should fall like
this into ruin. Indeed the gods take thought for Troy as well, 1250
though Pallas' determined hostility has brought it low.

As for you, so that you may know how blessed you are in
marrying me, I will free you from all the ills that beset mankind
and make you divine, untouched by death and decay. And
then from that day forth you will dwell with me in the palace
of Nereus, god and goddess together. Rising up from there
you shall top the ocean with feet unwetted by the waves to see
the son we love so well, our Achilles, who dwells in his island 1260
home on Leuce's shore within the sea that travellers fear.[49]

But you must first go to the men of Delphi's god-built
town, taking with you this dead body. When you have committed it to the earth, make your way to the hollow cavern
in Sepias' rugged and ancient coastline, and there take your
position. Wait for the moment when I emerge from the sea
with my troop of fifty Nereids who will be your escort. You
must fulfil what is appointed by fate; this is the will of Zeus.
Put an end to your grief for the one who has died; it is the 1270
lot of all men to pay the debt of death, the decree that heaven
has passed for them.

PELEUS: My Lady, noble partner of my bed, child of Nereus,
accept my greetings! In this you act worthily of yourself,
worthily of your own children. I here suspend my grief at
your bidding, goddess, and, when I have given this man burial,
I will go to Pelion's glens where once I clasped your lovely
form to mine.   1280

[THETIS *disappears and* PELEUS *exits.*]

CHORUS: *Many are the forms taken by the plans of the gods and many
the things they accomplish beyond men's hopes. What men expect
does not happen; for the unexpected heaven finds a way. And so it
has turned out here today.*[50]

HECABE

PREFACE TO *HECABE*

Although this play probably preceded the *Trojan Women* of 415 BC by a decade, the two are closely comparable in theme and situation. *Hecabe* too is set in the aftermath of the sack of Troy. But its treatment of the miseries of the vanquished is more complex, for in this play the victim strikes back and takes revenge on one at least of her enemies. This powerful and emotionally gripping drama was one of the three most widely read in antiquity (the other two being *Phoenician Women* and *Orestes*), and was equally admired in the Renaissance; after a period of relative neglect, it has now regained much of its former prestige.

The impact of the play on most ancient and some modern audiences can be explained by mentioning a few of the most striking episodes. The prologue is spoken by a ghost; the first half of the play culminates in human sacrifice, with the slaying of the virgin Polyxena, vividly and pathetically narrated by a messenger; there are two scenes of self-humbling supplication, in which the wretched Hecabe appeals to her oppressors, first Odysseus and later Agamemnon; the finale involves conspiracy and violence, as Hecabe and her women blind the treacherous Polymestor and murder his youthful sons; after this deed we see Polymestor bleeding and humiliated, crawling on to the stage like a wounded wild beast. The characterization of the main figures is strong in its simplicity: in Odysseus we have the consummate politician, shamelessly amoral; in Polymestor, the arch-hypocrite. These villains are set in contrast with the innocents slain for base motives: Polydorus, murdered for the gold, and Polyxena, sacrificed to pay ghastly homage to the dead Achilles. Most interesting is the character of Hecabe herself, of which more below.

As often, Euripides interlaces different strands of legend and creates something more elaborate and emotive. In the *Iliad* Polydorus was a warrior fighting at Troy, whereas here he was only a child when Priam sent him away for his own protection. The sacrifice of Polyxena to Achilles was traditionally part of the legend, but in making the justification for this action the need to win a favourable wind, Euripides links the end of the Trojan war with its beginning: just as Agamemnon was compelled to slay his own daughter Iphigenia at Aulis, to ensure that the expedition could set sail, so a second virgin must suffer now. Another major innovation seems to be the location of the action: the play is set in Thrace, a country which the Athenians regarded as exceptionally savage and bloodthirsty (see e.g. Thucydides vii, 29–30). The ruler of the region, Polymestor, seems to be a Euripidean invention, and is as ruthless and indifferent to conventional morality as Seneca's Atreus or Marlowe's Jew of Malta.

The ghost's supernatural foreknowledge enables him to foretell Polyxena's death, and this makes for gloomy irony as the inevitable killing is planned and accomplished. Further irony results from Hecabe's ignorance about Polydorus' own death: it is when the Trojan women go to fetch water to cleanse Polyxena's body that they discover her brother's corpse; and later in the play, Polymestor mistakes the covered body of Polydorus, the damning evidence of his own atrocious betrayal, for that of Polyxena.

The two halves of the play are thus connected and bound together: in the first, Hecabe loses her daughter and is helpless to defend her; in the second she learns of another equally painful loss, that of her son, the one hope for the future rebuilding of Troy. In the first case the death of Polyxena is monstrous, but is at least the action of openly-declared enemies. By contrast, the treachery of Polymestor, who was an ally and had enjoyed the hospitality of Priam while Troy prospered, is far more horrifying, and his continued deceitfulness on stage is repulsive. But there is also a contrast between Hecabe's helplessness in the first half of the play and her power to take revenge in the second: passive suffering becomes determined plotting and decisive action. The contrast is heightened by the parallel scenes already mentioned, in which Hecabe supplicates Odysseus and Agamemnon. In the former she is pleading for Polyxena's life and fails; in the latter, she begs for Polymestor's death and succeeds. In the dark world of Euripidean tragedy, vengeance is more easily obtained than compassion.

Inevitably Hecabe's character has been the subject of many critical analyses, some of them treating her severely. Does the admittedly loathsome behaviour of Polymestor justify the almost sadistic treatment of the villain by the Trojan women? And what of his sons, surely innocent of their father's crimes yet slaughtered to increase his own punishment? Other points have been made, some perhaps unduly moralistic. Hecabe prevails on Agamemnon to let her have her way with Polymestor by reminding him of his infatuation with her daughter Cassandra; this may startle us, but it is hardly fair to label her a pander, when she is naturally bound to use any argument that comes to hand. More disturbing is the prediction made by Polymestor at the end of the play, in which he foretells Hecabe's transformation into a dog. This has often been read as implying that she has sunk to the level of a beast. It seems best not to weigh the pluses and minuses of moral evaluation too precisely. By any standards Polymestor is despicable and odious, and we surely understand, perhaps even sympathize with, Hecabe's hatred. Yet we must also be shocked and dismayed by the killing of his sons, and by the viciousness of the queen in her horrible triumph. Tragedy characteristically presents extreme situations in which the rights and wrongs are not easily discerned; and in Euripides acts of revenge, as in *Medea*, *Electra*, *Orestes* and elsewhere, are deliberately placed in a complex and many-shadowed light. If every reader agreed about the morality of the heroine, *Hecabe* would be a less disturbing and less influential play.

CHARACTERS

GHOST OF POLYDORUS, *murdered son of Priam and Hecabe*
HECABE, *queen of Troy and widow of Priam*
CHORUS *of captive Trojan women*
POLYXENA, *daughter of Hecabe*
ODYSSEUS, *a Greek commander*
TALTHYBIUS, *a herald from the Greek army*
OLD SERVANT *of Hecabe, now a slave*
AGAMEMNON, *commander-in-chief of the Greeks*
POLYMESTOR, *Thracian ally of Priam*

[The scene is the shore of the Thracian Chersonese where the Greek fleet has landed, delayed by bad weather, after the fall of Troy. On one side stands the tent of AGAMEMNON *and behind are the huts that house the Trojan prisoners-of-war. In the air above the huts the* GHOST OF POLYDORUS *appears.]*

GHOST OF POLYDORUS:[1] I have come here, leaving behind the hiding-place of the dead, the gates of darkness where Hades has established his dwelling, apart from the other gods. Polydorus is my name, the son born to Hecabe, daughter of Cisseus, and to Priam. When the city of Troy was in danger of falling to the spears of the Greeks, my father was afraid and sent me in secret from the land of Troy to the home of a guest-friend,[2] Polymestor of Thrace, warrior-king of a horse-loving people, who farms the fertile plains of this peninsula. Unknown to any, he sent away with me a large quantity of gold to save   10
his surviving sons from penury, should the walls of Troy crumble. I was the youngest of Priam's sons and this was why he sent me away in secret; my young arms were not capable of bearing weapons or wielding a spear.[3]

Now, while the boundaries of that land were fixed and in their place, while no harm had yet come to Troy's protecting walls and Hector, my brother, enjoyed success in battle, this long I was a welcome guest at the house of my father's Thracian friend and, nurtured like some tender plant, I grew in stature, little knowing what my end would be. But when Troy fell   20
in ruin and Hector met his end, when our ancestral hearth was levelled and my noble father fell at the altar built by the

49

gods, slaughtered by Achilles' murderous son, then my father's guest-friend murdered me in my misery to gain my gold. He wanted to possess it for himself in his own home, and so he killed me and threw my body into the rolling sea. There I lie, one moment on the shore, another in the sea's swell, carried along by the constant ebb and flow of the waves, with no one
30 to weep for me or give me burial. Now I have left my body to come here where I hover over my dear mother. For three days now, all the time that the poor woman has been here in the Chersonese since leaving Troy, I have floated over her.

All the warriors of Greece sit idle here on the shore of the Thracian land, despite having ships to sail. The son of Peleus, Achilles, manifesting himself above his tomb,[4] brought the whole Greek host to a standstill, as they were poised to make their homeward voyage, oars ready to sweep the sea. He asked
40 that he be given my sister, Polyxena, as a welcome sacrifice[5] to honour his grave. This privilege will not be denied him; men who loved him will not withold such a gift. It is fated that my sister be led to her death this coming day. Two corpses of two children shall my mother see – my own and this wretched girl's. So that my poor remains may be buried, I will appear in the surf at the feet of one of her slave-women. The powers below have granted my prayer: I shall pass into
50 the hands of my mother and receive the grave's due rites. When this is performed, I will have all that I wish.[6]

But here comes old Hecabe, making her way out of Agamemnon's tent, troubled at seeing me in her dreams. I will leave this place. Oh, my poor mother! After a royal palace you have come to see the day of slavery and all your happiness of former days now finds an equal measure of sorrow. You are being destroyed by some god, who has given you this fate to balance your one-time prosperity.

[*Exit* GHOST OF POLYDORUS. HECABE *comes slowly out of* AGAMEMNON's *tent, supported by fellow slaves.*]

HECABE: Lead her forward, daughters, lead the old woman before
60 this tent, clasp this aged wrist and hold her up, the woman

who was once your queen, women of Troy, but now shares
your slavery. And, resting my weight on your arm, that serves
as my curved staff, I shall hurry my stiff-limbed steps along,
setting one weary foot before the other.

O fiery radiance of Zeus, o night, why am I so troubled
in the darkness by fearful visions? O holy Earth, mother of   70
dark-winged dreams, I wish to avert the vision the night
has sent!

You gods of earth below, keep safe my son, the only anchor
now of my home, who dwells in snowy Thrace under the   80
watchful eyes of his father's guest-friend!

Something unwelcome shall happen; a song of sorrow shall
come to hearts that already have their fill. Never has my heart
known such a relentless trembling or quaking as now it does!

Where should I find the inspired soul of Helenus, women
of Troy, where Cassandra, to tell me what my dreams portend?   90

[*Enter* CHORUS, *with whom* HECABE *now sings a lament.*]

CHORUS: *Hecabe, I have hurried out here to your side, leaving our*
master's tent where I was assigned by lot and designated a slave,   100
when the Greeks drove me away from Troy's city, the booty won at
the point of their spears. No relief can I offer from your sufferings,
lady, but, shouldering a heavy burden of news for you, I come as a
herald of sorrow. In full assembly the Greeks have voted to sacrifice
your daughter to Achilles. That is the news I hear.

You remember the time he scaled the mound and showed himself
in his golden armour, when he checked the ships that were launched,   110
though their sails were billowing against the forestays, with this cry:
'Where are you bound, you Greeks, that you leave my tomb without
its gift of honour?' Then, throughout the host of Greek spearsmen
opinion was divided, and marked dissension surged through the ranks,
some maintaining it was right to give this sacrifice to his tomb, others
that it was wrong. It was Agamemnon who promoted your interest,   120
remaining true to his love for the prophet-maid, Bacchus' follower.[7]
But the sons of Theseus, Athenians born, spoke up, one after the
other, and their two speeches merged in one opinion, that Achilles'
tomb should receive the tribute of fresh blood. They declared they

would never give Cassandra's bed more honour than the spear of
Achilles.

130

On either side there were heated words and passions were even in
the balance until that crafty talker, Laertes' son, that glib flatterer
of the mob,[8] began to use persuasion on the army: 'Do not reject the
noblest Greek of all to spare a slave-girl's throat! Let it not be said
by one of the dead as he stands before Persephone that Greeks failed
to honour Greeks, that when we left Troy's plains we gave no thought

140

to those who died for Greece!'

In no time he will be here, Odysseus will come to wrest the filly
from your bosom, to tear her away from your old arms. Go to the
temple, go to the altar, call upon the gods, those in heaven and those
below the earth! It may be your entreaties will save you from being
robbed of your wretched child; or else you must live to see the maid,

150

crimsoned with blood, prostrate at the tomb, while the darkly-
gleaming spring gushes from her neck, bedecked with gold.

HECABE [Strophe]: Oh what misery I know! What can I say? What
speech, what lamentation, I who have been turned into a wretch by
a wretched old age, by slavery that cannot be endured, cannot be
borne! Oh pity me, pity me! Who is my defender? What family,

160

what city? Gone is my aged husband, gone my sons. Which road
shall I take, this one or that? Where does my safety lie? Where is
he, some god or lesser power to champion my cause? O women of
Troy, you have destroyed me, destroyed me with the terrible news,
the terrible suffering you have brought! No more do I desire to live in
the sun's light.

170

O wretched feet, lead me, lead my aged limbs to the tent here.
O my child, daughter of a mother most wretched, come out, come out
of the tent, hear your mother's cry!

[POLYXENA comes out of the tent of AGAMEMNON.]

POLYXENA: Mother, mother, why are you shouting? What fresh
calamity did you announce, drawing me out of the tent in such
astonishment, like a frightened bird?

180

HECABE: O my child, my unfortunate child!

POLYXENA: This greeting does not bode well; that word spells a grim
fate for me.

HECABE: *How much I want you to live!*

POLYXENA: *Speak out! Don't keep me in the dark any longer! I am afraid, mother, afraid — what is it that fills you with sorrow?*

HECABE: *O child, child of an unhappy mother, —*

POLYXENA: *What is the news you have?*

HECABE: *— the judgement of all the Greeks is that you must be sacrificed at the tomb of Peleus' son.*   190

POLYXENA: *Ah! Mother, what are you saying? Tell me the unenviable evils, tell me, mother!*

HECABE: *I am telling you, child, the news I have received, hard as it is to utter: the Greeks have voted to end your life.*

POLYXENA [Antistrophe]: *O mother, how terribly you have suffered! What have you not endured in your wretched life! And now what further outrage, loathsome, unspeakable, has some god thrust upon*   200
you? No longer now, no longer do you have me, your child, to share in misery the slavery of your miserable old age. You will see me — what woe for you, what woe for me! — snatched from your hands like some calf reared in the mountains torn from its dam, sent on my way with severed throat to Hades, to the darkness of the earth, where in sorrow I shall lie among the dead.   210

[ODYSSEUS *enters from the direction of the Greek camp, accompanied by soldiers.*]

CHORUS-LEADER: But here comes Odysseus, Hecabe, hurrying on his way here to bring you word of something new.

ODYSSEUS: Lady, you know, I think, the decision of the army, the resolution that was passed; just the same, I will tell you this. The Greeks have decided that your daughter Polyxena   220
is to be sacrificed at the high mound of Achilles' tomb. I am appointed by them to escort the girl and bring her there. The man who will oversee this sacrifice and wield the knife is the son of Achilles.[9] You know what you must do: spare us the need to take her from you by force; do not try to match my strength, but realize the limits of your own and the hopelessness of your position; in times of trouble, wisdom lies in thinking what you ought to think.

HECABE: Ah, it seems I am on the verge of a great contest,[10] one

230   full of groans and not without its share of tears. I did not
die, as it now appears, where I should have died; Zeus did not
destroy me but keeps me alive so I may see – oh, the misery
of it! – evils yet more dire than these. If slaves may put to the
free-born questions that cause no pain and do not vex the
heart, it is right that you should answer my questions and I
should hear what you have to say.

ODYSSEUS: Indeed you may – ask away. It's not time I grudge
you.

HECABE: Do you remember the time you came to spy on Troy,[11]
240   a gruesome sight in your tattered clothes, with drops of blood
from your bruised face trickling down your chin?

ODYSSEUS: I do; that is not an experience I will easily forget.

HECABE: And how Helen recognized you and told no one but
me the secret?

ODYSSEUS: I remember the great danger I faced then.

HECABE: How you humbled yourself and clung to my knees?

ODYSSEUS: Yes, so much that my hand grew numb from holding
on to your dress.

HECABE: Why, then, did you say you were my slave at that
time?

250 ODYSSEUS: I thought up no end of excuses to save my life.

HECABE: And did I not actually save you and send you safe from
Troy?

ODYSSEUS: Because of you I look upon this light of the sun.

HECABE: Then are you not shown to be a villain by these
schemes, receiving from me the treatment you admit you did,
but instead of returning my kindness, doing me as much harm
as you can? It is a thankless generation you belong to, all you
who long to enjoy the prerogatives of public-speaking! I pray
I may have nothing to do with you, men who harm your
friends without a second thought if it helps you make a point
that flatters the mob! But what piece of cunning did they
imagine they had hit upon when they voted to execute this
260   child of mine? Did necessity compel them to human sacrifice
at a tomb where oxen's blood more properly flows? Or in

seeking death for those who caused *his* death, does Achilles justly aim death's arrow at her heart?

But no harm has come to him through her fault. He should have demanded Helen's sacrifice at his tomb; she was the one who brought him to Troy and caused his death. If some prisoner-of-war must be singled out for death, some woman of outstanding beauty, then this is not our concern; Tyndareus' daughter has no equal in loveliness and is guilty of wrong-doing far more than we are. This is the argument I bring against   270
the claim that my daughter's death is just.

Now let me tell you the personal claim I have on you. As you admit, you clasped my hand and touched this aged cheek in your supplication.[12] I now in turn touch these same parts of your body; I demand that you show the kindness I showed you then; I beg you not to tear my child from my hands, or put her to death – we have enough dead. She gives me joy, makes me forget my sorrows; she is my consolation for all those I have lost; she is my city, my nurse, the staff that   280
supports me, the one who guides me on my way. Those who have power should not exercise it unjustly or suppose in their prosperity that Fortune will always be their friend. I, too, was prosperous once but am so no longer; a single day robbed me of all my wealth, my happiness. [*She touches his chin in supplication:*] O my friend, show me some respect, I beg you, have pity! Go among the Greek army and counsel them against this, saying it would provoke the gods if you killed women you had refrained from killing in the hour of your victory, tearing them from altars only to show them mercy. In the   290
matter of bloodshed the same law applies to slaves as to you who are freeborn. Your standing will win them over, even if your eloquence fails you; the same plea voiced by men of no repute and men of position does not carry the same force.

CHORUS-LEADER: There is no human heart so hardened as to hold back the tears on hearing your laments, your long and plaintive tale of woe.

ODYSSEUS: Hecabe, take my advice, do not let your anger make

300   you regard as an enemy one who gives good counsel. I am
ready to save you from death as the one who saved me from
disaster, and this is no idle promise. But I will not retract the
motion I put before the assembly: now that Troy has been
taken, they should honour the request of the finest warrior in
the army and execute your daughter as a sacrifice to him. This
is where most cities go wrong, when a man of quality with a
patriot's heart receives no more credit than wastrels. Achilles
merits our esteem, lady, for no man died more nobly for the
310   land of Greece. Would it not be shameful if the man we
treated as a friend while he lived should forfeit that friendship
now that he is dead?

     Very well; what do you suppose shall be said if there is a
further call to arms for our men and the enemy has to be
reckoned with again? Are we likely to take the field or shall
we value our lives more highly, seeing that the dead receive
no honour? For myself, while I live, I should be wholly content
if I had just a little from day to day; but I would wish my
320   tomb to be seen honoured; that is a tribute that lasts generations.

     If you say your treatment is pitiful, then hear my reply to
that: we Greeks have just as many wretched old women and
men as you, and as many young wives bereft of their splendid
husbands, whose bodies lie covered here by Ida's dust. Resign
yourself to this; if our custom of honouring brave men is
misguided, men will call us fools. You foreigners continue to
regard your friends as enemies and to show no respect for men
330   who die nobly; Greece will then reap the benefit and you
may get what your ungrateful hearts deserve.

CHORUS-LEADER: Ah, how debasing a thing slavery always is,
     submitting to what is wrong and giving way to force!

HECABE [*turning to* POLYXENA]: Daughter, my pleas to spare
     your life are gone, flung to the winds and falling on deaf ears.
     See if your own powers are greater than your mother's, and,
     like the warbling nightingale, utter every strain your voice
     commands in pleading for your life. Appeal to Odysseus'
     sympathy, fall here at his knees and try to make him pity

you in your plight (you have a point to argue: he too has
children). 340

POLYXENA: Odysseus, I see you hiding your right hand under
your cloak and turning your face away to stop me touching
your chin. Do not worry; I shall not appeal to Zeus, protector
of suppliants; you are safe. I will go with you;[13] necessity
requires it and I want to die. If I did not have this wish, I
should be thought a woman of no spirit, clinging to life. And
what need have I to go on living? My father was king of all
the Trojans; this was the first thing in my life. Then I was 350
brought up with the fair hope of becoming a king's bride, and
many a suitor competed for the honour of bringing me to his
hearth and home. The Women of Troy acknowledged me as
their mistress; this wretch you see drew all women's eyes as I
moved among them, matrons and unmarried girls, and only
in my mortality did I fall below the gods.

Now I am a slave. Firstly, this name so new to me makes
me long for death. Then again, perhaps I shall fall into the
hands of a cruel-hearted master, someone who will pay money
for me, the sister of Hector and of many another prince, 360
and set me to the forced task of baking bread in his home,
compelling me to live each day in misery as I sweep his house
clean and stand weaving at the loom. Some slave, bought who
knows where, will defile my bed – I, once deemed fit for
kings! It is unthinkable! I will take this sunlight from my eyes
while they are still free, and give myself to Hades as a bride.

Come then, Odysseus, lead me away and end my life. I see
nothing that might encourage me to hope or think that 370
happiness will ever be mine. [*Turning to* HECABE:] Mother,
please do not say or do anything to thwart me in this, but
share my wish that I should die before I suffer the indignity
of a shameful fate. When someone has never tasted sorrow's
bitter cup, he may bear the yoke but its weight galls his neck.
He would be happier dying than remaining alive; life without
honour is a heavy burden to endure.

CHORUS-LEADER: To be born from noble stock fixes a marvel-

380　lous stamp on a person, a mark that is renowned among men, and the title of nobility confers ever more glory on those who are worthy of their birth.

HECABE: These are honourable words you have spoken, daughter, but the cost of such honour is pain. [*Turning to* ODYSSEUS:] If it is necessary that Peleus' son be honoured and that you Greeks avoid censure, then do not kill this girl, Odysseus, but lead me off instead to Achilles' pyre and stab me – I ask no mercy; I am the mother of Paris whose arrow killed the son of Thetis.

ODYSSEUS: Old woman, it was not your death that Achilles'
390　ghost sought from the Greeks but hers.

HECABE: Then at least kill me together with my daughter! That way the earth and the dead man who asks for this shall have twice as much blood to drink.

ODYSSEUS: Your daughter's death suffices; we should not add one death to another. I regret the need for this one.

HECABE: It is absolutely necessary that I share my daughter's death.

ODYSSEUS: How? I am not aware of having a master to answer to.

HECABE: It makes no difference; I will cling to her as ivy embraces an oak.

ODYSSEUS: Not if you listen to those wiser than you.

HECABE: Make sure of this: I will not let go this girl unless you
400　use force.

ODYSSEUS: Well, I won't go away either, leaving her here.

POLYXENA: Mother, do as I say; and you, son of Laertes, be kind to a mother's natural feelings of anger, while you, poor woman, must not oppose him; he has the upper hand. Do you want to fall to the ground, to have your old body dragged, jostled by force, pulled along, to be humiliated by a young man with his strength? That is the fate you can expect. Oh not this, mother, please! You deserve better than this.

O mother dear, give me your precious hand, let me hold

my cheek to yours! Never again will I look upon the sun's 410
orb and rays; this moment is the last. This is the final farewell
you will have from me. O mother, my own mother, I am
leaving, leaving for the world below!

HECABE: My child, how pitiful you are and how wretched
am I!

POLYXENA: I shall lie there, in Hades' realm, far from you.

HECABE: Oh no, no! What shall I do? Where shall I go to end
my life?

POLYXENA: I shall die a slave, though my father was freeborn, – 420

HECABE: But for me, daughter, slavery will continue among the
living.

POLYXENA: – denied the bridegroom and marriage that should
have been my right.

HECABE: And I shall die bereft of fifty children.

POLYXENA: What would you have me say to Hector or your
aged husband?

HECABE: Give them the message that no woman equals me in
misery.

POLYXENA: O loving breast, where you used to hold me close
and give me nurture!

HECABE: O daughter, so wretched in your untimely fate!

POLYXENA: Farewell, mother; Cassandra, my sister, farewell!

HECABE: Others fare well, for your mother this is not possible.

POLYXENA: There is still my brother Polydorus, who lives among
the horse-loving Thracians.

HECABE: Yes, if he is alive; but I have doubts, so completely has
good fortune abandoned me.

POLYXENA: He is alive, and will close your eyes when you die. 430

HECABE: I need not wait for death; my sufferings have already
ended my life.

POLYXENA [*turning to* ODYSSEUS]: Come Odysseus, take me,
cover my head with my cloak; before I feel the executioner's
blade, my heart has melted at my mother's laments and I am
making her melt in mourning. O light of the sun! I can still

address you by your name, but all that belongs to me of you is that little space between Achilles' pyre and the sword. [ODYSSEUS *and his men leave with* POLYXENA.]

HECABE: Help me! I am fainting, my limbs give no support! My daughter, hold on to your mother, stretch out your hand, give it to me! Do not leave me childless! [*To the* CHORUS:] I am
440 ruined, good women! [*She falls to the ground.*]

CHORUS [Strophe]: *O breezes, ocean breezes, that carry swift, seafaring craft over the swollen waters of the deep, where will you bring me in my misery? Whose house will I go to, who will get me as his slave? Shall*
450 *I go to some port of the Dorian land, or of Phthia, where, men say, Apidanus, the father of fairest streams, makes fertile the plains,*

[Antistrophe:] *or, as our oars sweep the sea, shall my sad voyage take me among the islands, where I shall find my pitiful home, where the first palm that ever grew*[14] *and the laurel spread their holy branches*
460 *to ease Leto's pain and honour the birth of Zeus' children? Shall I join the maidens of Delos in singing the praises of divine Artemis, with her bow and diadem of gold?*

[Strophe:] *Or shall I find myself in the city of Pallas, working on the saffron robe of Athena?*[15] *Shall I embroider there the yoking*
470 *of her horses to her lovely chariot, weaving an intricate pattern, worked with flowers? Or shall the subject be the race of Titans that Zeus, son of Cronos, cast into death's sleep with the blaze of his double-forked lightning?*

[Antistrophe:] *Oh, my children, my poor children! My unhappy father! My country, won by the spears of the Greeks and levelled in*
480 *smouldering ruin! I live in a foreign land, bearing the name of slave, I leave Asia, taking Europe's dwellings in exchange for a home in Hades.*[16]

[*The herald,* TALTHYBIUS, *enters from the Greek camp.*]

TALTHYBIUS: Young women of Troy, where might I find Hecabe, who was lately queen of Ilium?

CHORUS-LEADER: Here lies the lady near you, Talthybius, her back on the ground, wrapped tight in her cloak.

TALTHYBIUS: O Zeus, what am I to say? Do you watch over
490 men or are we fools, blind fools to believe this, and is it

chance that oversees all man's endeavours? Is not this woman
queen of Phrygia, rich in gold, is this not the wife of Priam
the all-prosperous? And now all her city has been laid waste
by the spear, while she, an old woman with no children,
reduced to slavery, lies on the ground, fouling her poor head
with dust. Oh, what a pitiful sight! Old man as I am, I pray I
may meet my end before falling victim to a fate so vile!
[*Attempting to help her:*] Rise up, poor woman, lift yourself up
from the ground, raise that white head!   500

HECABE: Ah, who is it will not let me lie here? I am in mourning,
whoever you are; why do you disturb me?

TALTHYBIUS: It is Talthybius; I am here to do the bidding of
the Greeks.

HECABE: You are most welcome, sir! Have you come because
the Greeks have decided to cut my throat at the tomb as well?
That news would warm my heart! Let's not waste any time,
let's be on our way at once! You be my guide, old man!

TALTHYBIUS: Your daughter has died, lady; I have come to
find you so that you may give her burial. I am sent by the two
sons of Atreus and the Greek troops.   510

HECABE: Oh, no! What are you saying? You did not come to
bring my death sentence then; you came to tell me of horror!
My child, you were snatched from your mother and now you
are dead. This means you have made me a mother with no
children. Oh, heaven help me! [*Turning back to* TALTHYBIUS:]
How did you Greeks end her life, how? Did you show pity?
Or were you brutal, old man, killing her as you would an
enemy? Tell me, though your words will cut me to the quick.

TALTHYBIUS: You would have me give solace twice over, lady,
in my tears of pity for your daughter. These eyes will grow
moist again when I tell my sad tale now, just as they did when
she met her end at the grave. There they were in front of   520
the tomb, the soldiers of Greece in full array, ranks high and
low, to witness the sacrifice of your daughter. The son of
Achilles, taking Polyxena by the hand, set her on the top of
the mound and I was standing hard by. Chosen warriors

of the Greeks, a select company, formed her escort, ready to restrain your young heifer,[17] should she try to leap away.

Then Achilles' son took in his hands a cup all of gold, filled to the brim, and, raising this offering to his dead father, he signalled to me to proclaim silence to the whole Greek army. And I, taking up my position before them all, spoke these words: 'Silence, men of Greece, let no man move in all the army, be still, keep silent!' I made them stand, that mass of men, so not a sound was heard. Then he spoke: 'O my father, son of Peleus, receive this soothing offering, I pray, that summons up the dead. Approach, that you may drink the pure, dark blood of this maiden, the gift we make you, the army and I. Show us your favour, grant that we may cast off our ships from their moorings and come, all of us, to our homeland, having won a favourable homecoming from Troy.'

Those were his words, and all the army joined in prayer. Then he seized by the hilt his sword inlaid with gold on both sides, and, starting to draw it from its sheath, he moved his head, signalling to the chosen young Argive warriors to lay hold of the maiden. When she became aware of this, she spoke these words: 'You Greeks, sackers of my city, it is my will that I die. Let no man lay his hands on me; I will bare my throat in good heart. Leave me free, in heaven's name, before you kill me, so that I may die free. I am of royal blood; it would make me ashamed to bear the name of slave among the dead!'

There was a roar of approval from the troops and Agamemnon told the men to let the maiden go. When she heard this verdict from her masters, she took hold of her dress and, tearing it from the top of the shoulder to the waist, exposed her breasts and all her lovely body to the navel, like a statue in its beauty,[18] and, kneeling on the ground, she spoke these bravest of all words: 'Here, young man, is my chest; strike here, if this is your will, or, if you wish to strike in the neck, here is my throat at the ready!' His pity for the girl made him

waver between desire and reluctance, and then with his blade
he severed her windpipe, causing the blood to gush out in
jets. Even in the throes of death she still made every effort to
fall modestly, concealing what should be hidden from the eyes
of men.   570

When the fatal stroke had made her breathe her last, each
Greek stirred himself, no man to the same task: some strewed
leaves over her corpse, others fetched logs of pine to build up
a pyre, while any man not active got short shrift from his busy
neighbour: 'What's this, you idle wretch? Standing there with
no robe, no ornament in your hands to honour this young
woman? Go and fetch some offering for this girl whose courage
is so extraordinary, whose heart is so noble!'   580

As I give such a report of your daughter's death, I see there
is no woman alive so blessed as you in her children, yet so
cursed in fortune.

CHORUS-LEADER: This is some terrible affliction sent by divine
necessity that has engulfed my city and the children of Priam.

HECABE: O my daughter,[19] I am beset by woes on every side; I
do not know which to face first. If I turn my attention to one,
another will not leave me alone, while a third grief, inheriting
sorrow from sorrow, calls me away from there in turn. So
now, too, I would not be able to wipe from my mind the
suffering that you endured and I must mourn. But this news   590
of your noble bearing has curbed the desire to grieve more
than I should. Is it not strange that poor soil, if the gods send
favourable weather, is successful in producing its crop, and
good soil, if it fails to get the right conditions, yields a bad
crop, whereas in the case of men the bad man is never anything
but a villain, and the good man never anything but good, not
changing his nature when disaster strikes but remaining true
to himself always?   600

Such are the arrows my mind has foolishly despatched.
[*Turning directly to* TALTHYBIUS:] Go on your way sir, and
deliver to the Greeks this message: I ask that no one touch
her; let the soldiery be kept away from my daughter. You

know that in a great army the rank and file cannot be governed, while indiscipline in seamen burns stronger than a fire, and the 'bad' man is the one who holds back from bad deeds. [*As* TALTHYBIUS *leaves she motions to an* OLD SERVANT *to come forward:*] Now, my old servant, you must take this urn, dip it in the salt sea and bring it here that I may wash my child in the final bath and lay out the bride who is no bride, maid who is no maid, as she deserves – but how? That would be impossible. Yet, as best I can (for what else can I do?) I will collect finery from my fellow prisoners-of-war, the women who sit by me and have their living-quarters inside these tents, if any of them has in her possession something she has stolen from her own home, unnoticed by our new masters.

O splendid house, you halls so prosperous once, o Priam, so blessed in wealth, so truly blessed in offspring, and myself, this aged mother of children, how total is our ruin, stripped of our former pride! And then do we allow ourselves to swell with pride, one of us in his wealthy home, another in the honourable name he enjoys in his city? But these things amount to nothing; they are idle flights of fancy, the boasts of a foolish tongue. The truly happy man is the one who lives through each day without suffering any harm. [HECABE *goes into the tent. The* OLD SERVANT *leaves.*]

CHORUS [Strophe]: *For me trouble was destined, for me sorrow, that day when Paris first cut down the pine-wood on Ida's slopes,*[20] *bent on voyaging over the salty depths to the bower where Helen lay, fairest of all women, illumined by the sun's golden rays.*

[Antistrophe:] *For suffering and slavery's yoke that galls more than suffering move in a cycle. One man's folly has led to disaster for all, bringing ruin to the land of the Simois and calamity to others; and the dispute that a herdsman on Ida*[21] *decided by judging between*

[Epode:] *three daughters of the gods, found its solution in conflict and bloodshed and the destruction of my home. By the banks of fair-flowing Eurotas, also, many a Spartan maid laments, shedding tears in her home, while mothers, grieving for the sons they have lost,*

*strike their grey heads and tear their cheeks until their nails grow
bloody from the wounds they inflict.*

　[*The* OLD SERVANT *returns from the seashore. Behind her are
other slaves who carry a draped body.*]

OLD SERVANT: Ladies, where is Hecabe, that woman of sorrow,
she who has surpassed all men and women in misery? None
shall seek to take that garland from her.　　　　　　　　660

CHORUS-LEADER: What is this? Your loud words of ill omen
make me pity you. These reports that bring me pain are never
still.

OLD SERVANT: This burden of sorrow I bring is for Hecabe;
when disaster strikes it is not easy for men to curb their tongues.
[*Enter* HECABE.]

CHORUS-LEADER: Here is the lady now, just coming from
inside the tent in time to hear your words.

OLD SERVANT: O my lady, you have suffered so much – no
words of mine can express it. You are ruined, you no longer
live, though alive, destroyed and left without children, without
husband, without city.

HECABE: This is not fresh news; you reproach me with what I
already know. [*Seeing the body for the first time:*] But why have　　670
you come bringing me this dead body of my Polyxena when
I have been told that all the Greeks were zealous in giving her
burial?

OLD SERVANT [*half-aside*]: She is quite unaware and actually
mourns for Polyxena; her latest sufferings have not come home
to her.

HECABE: Oh no! Heaven help me! This is not the inspired
prophetess you bring here, is it? This is not my Cassandra?

OLD SERVANT: That cry you uttered was for one who is alive,
but for this man who is dead you do not grieve. [*She removes
the cloth that covers the corpse:*] Look at this body that I lay bare
and see if the sight surprises you, going against expectation.　　680

HECABE: Oh no, no! So I see my son dead before my eyes,
Polydorus, whom a man of Thrace was keeping safe for me
in his home! This kills me! Oh, what misery! I am alive

no more, no more! [HECABE *now breaks into a song of grief:*]
*O my child, my child, what woe is mine! I lead off a wild, ecstatic
song, newly taught me by the avenging spirit who has sent these
ills.*

CHORUS-LEADER: Then do you understand the terrible end
that overtook your son, poor lady?

HECABE: *Past belief, past belief is this sight, strange, strange. One set*
690 *of woes follows another and not a day shall pass for me without
groans or tears.*

CHORUS-LEADER: Terrible, poor lady, are the sufferings we
endure.

HECABE: *O child, child of a miserable mother, what end brought you
to death, by what fate do you lie here, who on earth caused this?*

OLD SERVANT: I do not know; it was on the seashore I found
him.

HECABE: *Had he fallen to someone's murderous spear, or was he cast*
700 *up on smooth sand?*

OLD SERVANT: A wave of the sea cast him up from the deep.

HECABE: *Oh no, not that, not that! I understand the vision I saw in
my dream (it did not pass me by, that black-winged apparition), the
one I saw concerning you – you, my child, who sees no more
the light of Zeus!*

CHORUS-LEADER: Who then was his killer? Does your dream-
wisdom enable you to say?

710 HECABE: *My very own guest-friend, the Thracian horseman, with
whom his old father placed the boy in secret for his safe-keeping!*

CHORUS-LEADER: Oh no, no! What are you saying? He desired
the gold and so murdered him?

HECABE: *An act that cannot be spoken, cannot be named, past wonder,
more than heaven can countenance or men endure! Where are the
rights of a guest?* [*She stoops to examine the corpse at her feet.*] *O
accursed man, how you rended his flesh, hacking at this boy's limbs*
720 *and showing no pity!*

CHORUS-LEADER: Poor lady, whoever he is, the god who is so
cruel to you, he has brought you more tribulation than any
other woman alive. But here I see your master, Agamemnon,

in person; no more words from us now, friends. [*Enter* AGAMEMNON.]

AGAMEMNON: Hecabe, why have you not come under the terms that Talthybius reported to me, that no Greek should touch your daughter? Why are you so slow to give the girl burial? We have left her untouched but you make no move to come, which puzzles me. So I have come here to send   730 you on your way; we have acted honourably towards her, if there is any honour in this business. [*Noticing the corpse:*] Ha! What man is this I see near the tent? Who is this dead Trojan? Those garments he's wrapped in tell me he's no Greek.

HECABE [*to herself*]: Hecabe you wretch, for wretch is Hecabe's name and mine, what shall I do?[22] Should I fall here at Agamemnon's knees or bear my suffering in silence?

AGAMEMNON: Why do you turn your back on me when I look at you and weep? Why won't you tell me what has happened? Who is this man?   740

HECABE [*to herself*]: It may be he will thrust me away from his knees; I would be adding grief to grief.

AGAMEMNON: I am no prophet, you know; I cannot search out the tenor of your thoughts without hearing them!

HECABE [*to herself*]: Am I reading too much hostility, I wonder, into this man's heart, when it is not hardened against me?

AGAMEMNON: If you do not want me to know anything about this, then, believe me, we are agreed; I, too, have no wish to hear. [*He turns away slowly as if to leave.*]

HECABE [*to herself*]: Without this man's help I would be powerless to avenge my son. Why do I hesitate any longer? I must   750 show courage now, whether luck favours me or not. [*Suddenly turning round and throwing herself before him in supplication:*] Agamemnon, I beg you by these knees, by your chin, by your right hand so blessed by the gods!

AGAMEMNON: What is it you ask of me? Not that you should have your freedom? That is easy for you to gain.

HECABE: It is none of the things you imagine, my royal lord.

AGAMEMNON: Well then, how would you have me assist you?

760 HECABE: Do you see this dead man I am shedding tears over?

AGAMEMNON: I do; but what follows from this I cannot fathom.

HECABE: He is the son I once bore, after carrying him in my womb.

AGAMEMNON: Unhappy lady! Which of your children is he?

HECABE: Not one of Priam's sons who died under Ilium's walls.

AGAMEMNON: Did you have some other child apart from them, lady?

HECABE: Yes, but only to bring me grief it seems: the man you see here.

AGAMEMNON: Where was he when the city came to ruin?

HECABE: His father feared greatly for his life and sent him away.

AGAMEMNON: And where did he send him away to, alone of all his living children at that time?

770 HECABE: To this land where he was discovered dead.

AGAMEMNON: To the man who rules over this country, Polymestor?

HECABE: Here he was sent with gold to guard, the cause of his untimely end.

AGAMEMNON: What was his fate? Who killed him?

HECABE: Who else? His Thracian host took his life.

AGAMEMNON: How could he have done this? Was his heart set on getting the gold, I wonder?

HECABE: Exactly, once he had learned of Troy's misfortune.

AGAMEMNON: Where did you find him? Who brought you his corpse?

HECABE: This woman, when she had come upon it on the seashore.

AGAMEMNON: Was she searching for him or engaged in some other task?

HECABE: She had gone to fetch some water from the sea for
780 cleansing Polyxena's body.

AGAMEMNON: He killed him, it seems, and threw him into the sea – the man he had entertained in his own home!

HECABE: Yes, for the waves to toss, after he had disfigured his body as you see!

AGAMEMNON: You poor woman! There is no limit to your woes!

HECABE: My life has ended, Agamemnon; there is nothing left for me to suffer.

AGAMEMNON: Oh cruel, cruel! Was ever any woman so abused by fortune?

HECABE: None, unless you speak of Fortune herself.[23] But let me tell you my reasons for falling at your knees. If you consider my treatment would not offend heaven, I will submit to it. But if not, be my champion against this man, this guest-friend who pollutes hospitality and has perpetrated so unholy a deed, without fear of the gods, whether below the earth or in heaven.

790

I may be only a slave and powerless, but the gods are strong,[24] and strong is their almighty law. Law it is that dictates our belief in the gods, our life and ability to distinguish wrong from right. If it comes before you for judgement and suffers ill-treatment, if punishment does not follow for those who kill guests or dare to carry off the holy treasures of the gods, then there is nothing secure in this world. So give such behaviour the contempt it deserves, show respect for my status and take pity on me; stand back as a painter would[25] and study me, observe the nature of my woes. I was a queen once, but now I am your slave; I was once the mother of fine children, but now I am an old woman with no children, no city, no friends, the most wretched of all mankind. [AGAMEMNON again moves as if to go.]

800

810

Oh no, what must I suffer next? Where are you going, leaving me here? My appeal will fall on deaf ears, it seems. Oh, what misery I know! Why is it we mortals devote ourselves with all due care to seeking out and mastering all other branches of learning, but, when it comes to the art of persuasion,[26] we show no such zeal? Though this art alone presides over mankind, we spend not a jot more energy on learning it thoroughly; and yet, by paying fees to achieve this end, a man eventually would have the ability to convince others on any

point he wished and to get his way into the bargain! Why
820   then should anyone be confident of his own success? My
children, who once were alive, live no more, and I myself go
on my way, reduced shamefully to a prisoner-of-war, gazing
at the smoke that billows yonder above my city.

There is a further point (it may have no bearing on my
case to introduce the topic of love but still it shall be said): my
daughter, Phoebus' maid, sleeps at your side, the one the
Trojans call Cassandra.[27] What price, my lord, will you put
on these nights of joy you find so pleasurable? What thanks
shall my girl receive for those precious embraces in your bed,
830   what shall my reward be for her services? Listen well to what
I say. You see this dead man here? He is a kinsman of yours
and has a kinsman's rights; honour these!

There is only one thing left for me to say. I wish I possessed
a tongue in all my parts[28] – arms, hands, grey hairs, feet, either
through the skilled work of Daedalus or some god – so that
all of them might combine to clasp your knees and shed tears,
840   urging upon you every kind of plea. O my master, supreme
light to the Greeks, do what I ask, extend the hand of retribution to this old woman! It may be a trifle, this service, but
do it none the less! A good man should champion justice and
punish wrongdoers wherever and whenever they cross his
path.

CHORUS-LEADER: It is strange how everything falls out in life
and the laws of necessity determine things, creating friendship
where hatred once flourished and making enemies of those
who once were allies.

850   AGAMEMNON: Hecabe, I feel pity for you and your son and for
your circumstances. I pity too your hand held out in supplication. For the sake of justice and the gods I want this impious
man to suffer the punishment you require of me, if only you
can find a way to have this satisfaction without my men
thinking I planned this execution of the Thracian king for
love of Cassandra. There is a point, you see, that causes me
embarrassment: this man is an ally in the eyes of my troops,

but the dead man is an enemy. If the man before us has claims
on your love, that is a separate matter that has nothing to do
with the army. In view of this, give due consideration to   860
your situation; you have in me a willing partner in your task
and one not slow to assist but less prompt if it means losing
the Greeks' favour.

HECABE: Ah, no end to my suffering! In all the world there is
no person who is free; either he is the slave of money or
circumstance, or else the majority of his fellow-citizens or a
code of laws prevents him from acting as his better judgement
dictates. Since you are afraid and this makes you pay too much
attention to the mob, I will give you freedom from this fear.
If I devise any means of harming my son's murderer, be my   870
accomplice in thought alone, not in deed! And if the Greeks
riot or attempt his rescue when the Thracian gets the sort of
treatment he has in store, hold your men in check without
letting it appear that I am the cause. As for the rest of the
business, never fear, I will organize everything well.

AGAMEMNON: But how? What will you do? Will you, an old
woman, take a sword in your hand and kill a man of Thrace?
Will you use poison? Do you have allies to help you? What
strength can you count on? Where will you find friends?

HECABE [gesturing behind him]: These tents conceal a fair number
of Trojan women.   880

AGAMEMNON: The prisoners you mean, war-booty of the
Greeks?

HECABE: With their help I will take vengeance on the murderer
of my child.

AGAMEMNON: And how will women get the upper hand over
a man?

HECABE: Numbers can be formidable and, combined with guile,
irresistible.

AGAMEMNON: Formidable indeed; but female strength does not
impress me.

HECABE: No? Was it not women who overpowered Aegyptus'
sons[29] and emptied Lemnos altogether of menfolk?[30] Come,

accept what I say; let us have no more of this talk. Give this woman safe-conduct through the army, I beg you. [*Turning to address the* OLD SERVANT:] Go to the Thracian who is our guest-friend with this message: 'Hecabe, Troy's queen that was, asks you to come on a matter that concerns you no less than her, and to bring your sons; your children also must hear what she has to say.' Agamemnon, delay the burial of my newly dead Polyxena. I want a single pyre to consume them both, brother and sister together, a double loss to their mother, before the earth covers them.

AGAMEMNON: You will have your wish. If the army could sail, I would not be able to oblige you in this, but as it is, the god sends no favourable breeze and we must sit idly waiting, looking out for a chance to leave. I pray for a happy outcome somehow or other. All men are agreed on this, both individuals and communities: bad men should meet a bad end and good men prosper. [*Exeunt* OLD SERVANT, AGAMEMNON *and his men.*]

CHORUS [Strophe]: *Troy, my city, no more shall men speak of you as having escaped the victor's sword; such a storm-cloud of Greeks envelops you, now that their terrible spears have laid you waste. You are shorn of your crown of towers and defiled most piteously by the stain of blackening smoke. Never again will I set foot inside you – what misery!*

[Antistrophe:] *At midnight my end began,*[31] *the hour when the evening meal has passed and sweet sleep drops gently on the eyes. My husband, after leaving the songs and concluding the dancing for the sacrifice, was lying in our bedchamber. His great spear hung on its peg and he had ceased to watch out for the sea-borne host that had left their ships and set foot in Ilian Troy.*

[Strophe:] *I was arranging my hair in the bands of my head-dress and gazing into the glittering depths of the golden mirror before sinking on the cushions of our bed. Then a shout went ringing through the town; this was the battle-order that filled our streets: 'Sons of the Greeks, it has come at last, the time for you to sack Troy's high city and return to your homes!'*

[Antistrophe:] *Wearing only my shift like some girl of Sparta,*[32] *I left my husband's bed and prayed on my knees to holy Artemis, but she had no ears for my wretched appeal. I saw the killing of my husband and was carried off over the salt sea. As I gazed back at the city, for the ship had spread her sails for the homeward voyage and separated me from the land of Ilium, I fainted wretched with grief* 940

[Epode:] *and I cursed the sister of the Dioscuri, Helen, and her cowherd of Ida, Paris the wicked, for the marriage that drove me in ruin from my native land and expelled me from my own home; no marriage indeed, but a form of woe sent by an avenging spirit. May the salt sea never bring her back again! May she never return to her* 950 *ancestral home!*

[POLYMESTOR *enters in answer to* HECABE's *summons. He is accompanied by his two children and some armed men.*]

POLYMESTOR: Priam, dearest of men, and you, Hecabe, dearest of women, I weep to see you and your city, and your daughter, too, so recently killed. What suffering is here! There is nothing in which a man can place his trust, not his good name, not the expectation that success will crown his present good fortune. The gods reduce all this to mayhem, confounding past and future, to make us hold them in awe because we are ignorant of what is to come. But what point is there in lamentations? They do not help us to outdistance disaster. 960 If my absence has caused you annoyance in any way, be angry no more. As it happened, I was in the heart of Thrace when you came here, but on my return your servant met me just as I was setting out from my home and, once I heard the words she had to say, I made my way here.

HECABE [*keeping her face turned away from him*]: Polymestor, such is the wretchedness of my circumstances, it makes me ashamed to look you in the face. When last you saw me, prosperity was mine. Now that I find myself sunk as low as this, I feel shame; I would not be able to look at you without lowering 970 my eyes. Please do not imagine I bear you any ill will.

POLYMESTOR: Why, it is hardly surprising you feel this way.

But what need do you have of me? Whatever made you ask that I leave my home to come here?

HECABE: I have a private matter of my own I want to communicate to you and your children. Please tell your servants to
980   leave us here at the tent.

POLYMESTOR [*to his attendants*]: Leave us; it is safe enough for me to be left alone in this place. You are my friend and the Greek army here has no quarrel with me. [*He waits for his men to withdraw.*] Now, you must make things clear: in what way should a friend who enjoys good fortune assist one who does not? I am ready.

HECABE: First of all tell me of my boy, my Polydorus, whom you have in your house, sent there by his father and me; is he alive? The rest I will ask you next.

POLYMESTOR: Most certainly he is; as far as he's concerned you are fortunate.

HECABE: O my dear friend, how welcome these words are! How
990   worthy of you![33]

POLYMESTOR: And what is the second thing you wish to learn from me?

HECABE: If . . . if he remembers his mother at all.

POLYMESTOR: Oh, yes! He tried to come here to you, slipping past the Greeks.

HECABE: And the gold he had in his keeping when he left Troy, is it safe?

POLYMESTOR: Quite safe, yes, and under guard in my palace.

HECABE: Then keep it safe and do not fall under the spell of your neighbour's wealth.

POLYMESTOR: Certainly not that; I trust I may benefit from what I have!

HECABE: Do you know then what I wish to tell you and your children?

POLYMESTOR: I do not; you are going to explain by what you say next.

HECABE [*lowering her voice*]: My friend, as dear to me now as you
1000   were then, there is –

POLYMESTOR: Is what? What is it that both I and my children should know?

HECABE: — an ancient trove of buried gold belonging to Priam and his heirs.

POLYMESTOR: And this is what you would have me reveal to your son?

HECABE: Yes! Yes! From your own lips; for you are a man who holds the gods in respect.

POLYMESTOR: Why then the need for these children to be here?

HECABE: It would be better for them to have this knowledge in the event of your death.

POLYMESTOR: A good point; here too you speak more shrewdly.

HECABE: Then do you know where the temple of Ilian Athena stands?

POLYMESTOR: Is it there the gold is? What should I look for to help me?

HECABE: A black rock that rises up above the ground.   1010

POLYMESTOR: Is there anything else you want to tell me about what is there?

HECABE: I want you to look after the money I brought with me from Troy.

POLYMESTOR: And where is it? In your clothing or have you hidden it?

HECABE: It lies safe inside the tent here, in a heap of booty.

POLYMESTOR: Where? The Greeks are encamped all around us.

HECABE: The tent set apart for female prisoners-of-war.

POLYMESTOR: Is it safe inside with no men on guard?

HECABE: Not a single Greek is inside, just ourselves. Please come into the tent; the Greeks are longing to spread their sails on the voyage home from Troy. Then, when you have gained   1020 all that you should, you can return with your sons to the place where you gave my son his new home. [HECABE *leads* POLYMESTOR *and his sons into the tent. The* CHORUS *sing a short song, dancing excitedly as they do.*]

CHORUS: *Not yet has punishment come to you; but it shall, I think. Like a man who has tumbled sideways into a stormy sea without a*

harbour, you will cut off your life and forfeit your heart's desire.
1030 Where what is owed to Justice and to the gods coincide, harm ensues
that can only spell ruin! You will be cheated by the hopes you placed
in this journey; they have brought you, poor man, marked for death,
to Hades, and hands untrained for war shall end your life.

POLYMESTOR [from inside the tent]: Oh, agony! My eyes,[34] I am
being robbed of the sight of my eyes!

CHORUS-LEADER: Did you hear the Thracian's cry of pain,
friends?

POLYMESTOR: Children! Again I cry for help – they are butcher-
ing you! No!

CHORUS-LEADER: Friends, unheard-of crimes are being committed inside the tent!

POLYMESTOR: You may be quick on your feet but you will
never escape! I'll use my strength to tear a way into your
1040 hiding place! Look, my sturdy hands are clenched to wreak
destruction!

CHORUS-LEADER: Should we rush inside? The time has come
for friends of Hecabe and the Trojan women to answer the
call for battle!

HECABE [emerging from the tent and addressing POLYMESTOR behind
her]: Go on, smash away, spare no effort, tear open the doors!
Never will you restore the brightness of sight to your eyes,
never see alive your children killed by this hand of mine!

CHORUS-LEADER: Have you really overthrown the Thracian,
my lady? Have you your false friend in your power? Have
you done the deeds you say?

HECABE: You shall see him soon enough in front of this tent, a
1050 blind man making his way with blind, staggering steps, yes,
and shall see the bodies of his two children whom I killed
with the help of Troy's noblest women. He has answered to
me. [POLYMESTOR lurches out of the tent on hands and knees,
blinded. At the same time the corpses of his children are revealed.]
Here is the man now, as you see, coming out of the tent. I'll
get out of his path and make way for the Thracian; his boiling
rage will make him a hard foe to resist.

POLYMESTOR [*chanting a solo lament in his agony, his face streaked with blood from his wounded eyes*]: *Ah, the pain, the pain! Where am I to go, where stay, where find shelter, moving on hand and foot like some four-footed beast of the mountains? Which way shall I turn, this way or that, as I try to get my hands on those murderous women of Troy who have destroyed me? Vile daughters of Phrygia, vile, accursed women, where have you fled? In what crevice do you lie cowering from me? O Sun, if only you would cure, yes, cure these bloodied eyes of mine, restoring light where there is now darkness!* 1060

Aha! Silence! Now I catch the stealthy footsteps of women. Where should I lunge to gorge myself on their flesh and bone, as I feast like a wild beast, dealing out wounds in revenge for my own mutilation, wretch that I am? But where, where am I going? Have I not left my children unprotected for these crazed handmaids of death to tear in pieces after slaughter and cast out in savagery on the mountainside to be a bloody feast for dogs? 1070

Where am I to stay my course, where turn, as I gather up my robe of woven linen, like some ship furling its sails with sea-ropes, making haste to the place where my children lie dead, to give them my protection? 1080

CHORUS-LEADER: Wretched man, you are the victim of suffering that is hard to bear; but when a man's actions bring shame, his punishment is terrible.

POLYMESTOR: *Ah, how I suffer! Men of Thrace, with Ares in your blood, come to me now with your lances, your weaponry, your fine horses! Come you Achaeans, you sons of Atreus! This cry I give is for help, for help, I say! Oh, in the gods' name, come quickly! Come! Does anyone hear me? Is there no one to help? Why are you so slow? I have been destroyed by women, by women taken in war! What has happened to me is monstrous, monstrous! Oh, the pain I feel at my mutilation! Where am I to turn, where direct my steps? Should I soar aloft on wings to the palace in the heavens, where Orion or Sirius discharges the fiery radiance of his eyes, or must I plunge in sadness to the dusky waters that give passage to Hades' realm?* 1090 1100

CHORUS-LEADER: It is forgivable, when a man suffers disaster past endurance, that he rid himself of life's misery.

[AGAMEMNON *enters with men-at-arms.*]

AGAMEMNON: I came when I heard your shouting; it was not with a quiet voice that Echo, daughter of the mountain rock, 1110 raised her cry through the army, spreading confusion. Had we not known that Troy's towers had fallen to the spears of the Greeks, this din would have caused us no little fear.

POLYMESTOR: O Agamemnon, my dear friend – I recognized you from the sound of your voice – do you see how I am treated?

AGAMEMNON: Ah! My poor Polymestor, who has destroyed you? Who has robbed your eyes of sight, making them run with blood, and killed your children here? He harboured heavy resentment against you and your children, it seems, whoever he was.

POLYMESTOR: Hecabe destroyed me, she and the women taken 1120 prisoner – no, not 'destroyed' but something worse.

AGAMEMNON [*maintaining his pretence of sympathy*]: What do you say? [*To* HECABE:] You are the perpetrator of this deed, as he says? You, Hecabe, have dared to do this shocking thing that cannot be undone?

POLYMESTOR: Oh no, no! Do you mean she is somewhere near me? Show me, tell me where she is! I want to grab hold of her, tear her apart, make her flesh run with blood!

AGAMEMNON [*attempting to restrain him*]: Come sir! This is no way to behave!

POLYMESTOR: In the name of the gods I implore you, let me go! Let me use my raging hands on her!

AGAMEMNON: Enough! Dismiss such savage thoughts from your heart and state your case, so that I may hear each of you in 1130 turn and come to a fair judgement[35] on why you have received this treatment.

POLYMESTOR: Well, I will speak. There was a youth, Polydorus, the youngest of Priam's sons and child of Hecabe, whom Priam, his father, sent to me from Troy to raise in my own home, no doubt because he feared the capture of Troy. This boy I killed. Let me tell you my motive for this, how I acted sensibly and with a shrewd eye to the future. I was afraid that if the boy was left to become your enemy he might muster the Trojans and make their city one again; the Greeks then, learning that one of Priam's sons was alive, might send a 1140 second force against the land of Troy and so plunder these Thracian pastures in the course of their cattle-raiding. Then we neighbours of Troy would suffer the consequences, a hardship we have known these past few years, my lord.

Now, when she learned that her son had met his end, Hecabe requested my presence, using some pretence that she would tell me of a treasure trove of gold belonging to Priam and his heirs, hidden away inside Troy. She led me, unattended, together with my children into the tent, so that no one else might witness what was to come. I relaxed and sat down in the middle of a couch. Many women, some on my right 1150 hand, others on my left, were seated beside me, as if they were good daughters of Troy giving welcome to a friend, and expressing admiration for the cloak I wore, woven with Edonian skill, holding it up to the light to stare at it. Others were absorbed in the sight of my Thracian spear-shafts and had removed from me my pair of javelins. All those who were mothers were dandling my children in their arms, filled with admiration, passing them from one pair of hands to another to get them out of their father's reach.

Their talk was so gentle, so amazingly calm, but not for 1160 long; suddenly some of them seized swords they had hidden somewhere in their garments and started stabbing the children, while others, grasping hold of me like octopuses, pinioned my hands and limbs. I was desperate to help my children, but each time I tried to lift my face they held me down by the hair, and whenever I tried to move my hands the sheer number of women made my pathetic efforts ineffectual. But then came the ultimate outrage, worse than all others; they did a monstrous thing. Taking hold of their brooches they stabbed

1170 at the wretched pupils of my eyes, making them run with blood, then took to their heels, escaping through the tent. I leapt to my feet and, like a wild beast, started to chase the murderous hounds, searching out every side of the tent like a huntsman, striking and smashing what was in my path.

Such is the treatment meted out to me, Agamemnon, for attempting to further your interests by killing one who was your enemy. Let me not dwell on this excessively. Whatever criticism women have been subjected to by men in the past, whatever abuse they receive today or are likely to earn 1180 tomorrow, I will summarize the whole tirade by saying this: never has sea or land bred such a creature; whoever encounters them knows this.

CHORUS-LEADER: Spare us your insolence and do not make your own troubles an excuse for such sweeping condemnation of all womankind.

HECABE: Agamemnon, speech should never be allowed to carry more weight among men than actions.[36] Honest deeds should have the support of honest words, but, if a man's actions are 1190 criminal, his arguments in turn should be unsound, and never should he be able to make a good case out of what is wrong. There are, of course, subtle wits who have mastered such skills but their subtlety cannot last for ever and they come to a sorry end; no one yet has escaped the net. My message to *you* is thus expressed in my preamble; as for *him*, I will turn to him now and respond with arguments of my own. [*Looking directly at* POLYMESTOR:] It was to spare the Greeks the effort of a second expedition, you say, and to please Agamemnon that you took my son's life. But when, you hypocrite, would 1200 barbarians ever feel friendship for Greeks? This is unthinkable.[37] So what interest of your own were you furthering by this eagerness to please? Did you want to establish kinship with someone by marriage? Did you have some blood-relative of your own, or what other reason did you have? Was it that the Greeks were likely to ravage your country's crops in the event of another expedition? Whom do you imagine you will convince of this? Gold killed my son, if only you were prepared to admit the truth, that and your hopes of gain.

For explain this: why, when Troy flourished and still had the protection of her circling walls, when Priam was alive and Hector carried all before him in battle, why, if you wanted 1210 to earn this man's gratitude, did you not choose that time to kill the boy you were rearing as a guest in your home, or else go to the Greeks with him as a live hostage? No, when death had descended upon us and the city showed by its smoke it was in enemy hands, then you murdered the one who had come in guest-friendship to your hearth.

But there is more; let me now tell you what exposes your wickedness: if your goodwill towards the Greeks was genuine, you should have taken the gold, which you say you kept not for yourself but for Polydorus, and given it to men who were experiencing hardship and had not set eyes on their homeland 1220 for many a year. Why, not even now can you bring yourself to let it out of your grasp; you still stubbornly keep it in your home. Again, if you had kept my son in safety and were raising him as your duty prescribed, you would enjoy a splendid reputation. It is in times of trouble that good men are the surest friends; prosperity by its nature has friends in every case. If you were in need of money and Polydorus enjoyed good fortune, you would have in that son of mine a treasure to reckon with; but, as it is, you have forfeited that man's goodwill, the 1230 gain you would have had from his gold is vanished, and this is the reward you and your children have reaped.

Now, Agamemnon, I address myself to you. If you offer your help to this man, you will show yourself a man of no principle; you will be extending friendship to one who has no respect for the gods, no feelings of loyalty to those who have a right to it, to a man without piety, who tramples on the obligations of guest-friendship. We shall say that you yourself take pleasure in the company of wicked men because you are like them yourself. But you are my master and I must keep a civil tongue.

CHORUS-LEADER: Well well, how true it is that an admirable cause always gives scope for an admirable speech!

1240 AGAMEMNON: It gives me little pleasure to arbitrate over the misfortunes of others, but none the less I have no choice in this case; it would bring disgrace on me if I took responsibility for this business only to disown it. [*Turning to* POLYMESTOR:] You may as well know that in my opinion you killed your guest not to oblige me, no, nor the Greeks, but in order to possess the gold in your own home. Finding yourself in serious difficulty you say what suits your case. Perhaps, as you say, it is no great matter among Thracians to murder a guest under their roof; to us Greeks this is disgraceful conduct.[38] How then am I to avoid censure if I find you not guilty? Impossible!

1250 Since you could bring yourself to commit a wicked act, you must bring yourself to endure its unwelcome consequences.

POLYMESTOR: What humiliation! It seems I shall be defeated by a woman, a slave, and lose my case to one who is my inferior!

HECABE: And is this not just, given the crime you have perpetrated?

POLYMESTOR: Oh, how I suffer – my poor children here, my poor eyes!

HECABE: You feel pain at this? Ha! Do you think I feel no pain over my son?

POLYMESTOR: You shameless creature, you take pleasure in mocking me!

HECABE: I do! Should I not take pleasure in having my revenge on you?

POLYMESTOR: You will take little pleasure, I think, when the sea spray . . .[39]

1260 HECABE: . . . takes me to the shores of Greece, do you mean?

POLYMESTOR: No; . . . covers you after you fall from the masthead.

HECABE: And who will force me to make this leap?

POLYMESTOR: You will climb up the ship's mast by your own efforts.

HECABE: Oh, and how shall I manage that? With wings on my back, perhaps?

POLYMESTOR: You will turn into a bitch with fiery eyes.

HECABE: How do you come to know of this transformation of mine?

POLYMESTOR: These were the words of Dionysus,[40] who prophesies to the Thracians.

HECABE: Did this prophet give you no warning of the sufferings you now endure?

POLYMESTOR: He did not; otherwise you would never have trapped me by such a piece of trickery.

HECABE: Will it be at my death or while I still live here that I fulfil the prophecy?   1270

POLYMESTOR: At your death; and the name by which your tomb shall be called –

HECABE: Will you say a name that celebrates my change of shape?

POLYMESTOR: – is 'tomb of the wretched bitch', a landmark for sailors.

HECABE: I care nothing for that! Your punishment is what I wanted!

POLYMESTOR: Yes, and Cassandra, your daughter, must lose her life.

HECABE: Damn you! That is what I want *you* to suffer!

POLYMESTOR: She will be killed by this man's wife,[41] a savage guardian of his home.

HECABE: Oh, I pray the years may be many before such madness afflicts Tyndareus' child!

POLYMESTOR [*gesturing again to* AGAMEMNON]: This man, too, she will kill, raising her axe on high.

AGAMEMNON: You, sir, have you lost your wits? Are you in love with punishment?   1280

POLYMESTOR: Kill me, for a bloody bath is waiting to receive you in Argos.

AGAMEMNON [*to his servants*]: Seize him, men, haul him away out of my sight!

POLYMESTOR: My words cause you pain?

AGAMEMNON: Gag him!

POLYMESTOR: Go ahead, cover my mouth; I have said enough.

AGAMEMNON [*to his servants*]: Away with him this instant, cast him out on some deserted island since he continues to abuse my ears with such insolence! And you, Hecabe, poor woman, go and bury these two corpses. Women of Troy, now you must make your way to the tents of your masters. Now I see
1290 the winds arising that will give us passage home. May our voyage to our homeland be a happy one![42] May we say goodbye to the troubles we have known here and see our homes in good order!

CHORUS: *Onward friends, to the port, to the tents, to experience the miseries of slavery; fate cannot be resisted.*

SUPPLIANT WOMEN[1]

PREFACE TO
SUPPLIANT WOMEN

The *Suppliant Women* was first produced in the late 420s BC. In the manuscripts which preserve the text of the play, a short summary composed by some anonymous scholar in ancient times describes it as 'an encomium of Athens'. Most interpretation of the play has been concerned to decide how far, and in what ways, this description requires modification. Some critics have maintained that this play shows Euripides' admiration for Athens in the heyday of its imperial power, and that he is showing in dramatic form what Athens stands for. Others take a much bleaker view, reading the play as a protest against unnecessary war; sometimes these critics go so far as to read major scenes and speeches 'ironically', so as to reverse their apparent meaning. The difficulties which many find with the *Suppliant Women* arise in part from the drama's Athenocentricity, and this play more than most needs to be read with a clear understanding of the background in fifth-century Athenian values and attitudes.

In the famous 'Funeral speech' which he put in the mouth of the great Athenian statesman Pericles, Thucydides includes the following claim: 'we acquire our friends by conferring rather than receiving favours . . . It is only the Athenians who, fearless of consequences, confer their benefits not from calculations of expediency, but in the confidence of liberality' (ii, 40, 4, adapted from Crawley). Thucydides' Pericles does not allude to mythical examples of this practice, but other orators freely appealed to the great and generous deeds of Athens in more ancient times, including the episode dramatized in this play. The dissension between the rival sons of Oedipus, each resolved on gaining sole power in Thebes, culminated in one of the brothers, Polynices, enlisting foreign aid. With his father-in-law,

Adrastus of Argos, he led a disastrous expedition against his native city, the so-called 'Seven against Thebes', which ended in the deaths of both brothers and of all the Argive champions. In revenge, the new Theban ruler Creon decreed that these attackers should be denied burial.

It is at this point, in the aftermath of disaster, that the play begins. Athens has played no part in earlier events at Argos and Thebes, but now finds itself the object of moral pressure from Adrastus and from the mothers of the unburied Argives. After initial resistance, the Athenian king Theseus is persuaded that he must intervene to ensure the proper treatment of the dead warriors. In Aeschylus' play dealing with the same legend he succeeded in achieving this end by diplomacy; but in Euripides, as the confrontation with the arrogant Theban herald makes clear, Theseus can prevail only by embarking on a war he does not seek. War itself cannot be represented on the restricted Attic stage; Theseus' victory is recounted in the traditional messenger-speech, with considerable gusto (650–730).

Thus far the achievement of Athens has been shown as unselfish and beneficial; nor is her glorious mythological self-image tarnished in the remainder of the play. But the scenes which follow do show the human cost of the earlier war of the Seven against Thebes, whom Adrastus commemorates in an unexpectedly positive eulogy; moreover, in a startling and melodramatic sequence, the grief-stricken widow of one hero, Capaneus, kills herself on his pyre, leaving her father desolate. Furthermore, although the burial of the dead satisfies Greek religious custom and fulfils the wishes of the surviving kin, the mothers of the dead inevitably continue to mourn their loss. In the closing scene, in which the sons of the dead Argive champions become the focus of attention, there is a conflict between their youthful determination to avenge their fathers when they grow up, and the distressed exclamations of their mothers who feel that there has been enough suffering. In the final epiphany the goddess Athena declares that the future will indeed see a second expedition of warriors against Thebes, when the sons of the Seven, the so-called 'Epigoni' or 'Successors', will triumph where their fathers failed. The outcome of the war will be different, and it may be shadowed by less guilt and folly than the expedition which has just ended in disaster. Nevertheless, Euripides has shown us in this play how destructive war is, and the goddess's words cannot completely calm these gloomy reflections.

The play seems, then, to contrast the foolish and disastrous war of the Seven against Thebes, led by the misguided Adrastus and the doomed Eteocles, with the just war fought reluctantly and for a sacred purpose by the virtuous Athenian Theseus. It thus resembles the *Children of Heracles*, another play in which Athens takes up the cause of helpless suppliant refugees, and in which the opposing side is again represented by an outspoken and arrogant herald. The *Suppliant Women* has an even sharper ideological edge, since it includes a debate between Theseus and the Theban herald on the contrasting virtues of democratic and monarchic government, with Theseus, as a constitutional monarch, putting the case for democracy in opposition to Theban tyranny. Hence it has been effectively argued that the Attic tragedians saw Thebes as an 'anti-Athens', representative of all that Athens is not, and that the *Suppliant Women* and other tragedies (e.g. Sophocles' *Oedipus at Colonus*) show how other states go wrong, whereas Athens succeeds by her piety and devotion to law and justice.

It can hardly be doubted that the Athenian audience would come away from the theatre with much pride and confidence in Athenian ideals and the Athenian way of life. But it would be strange if the scenes of suffering and mourning as a result of the Argive–Theban conflict found *no* resonances in the hearts of a people at war. It is surely artificial to separate all the latter scenes of the play as the consequences of an unjust war fought by non-Athenians. Questions can also be raised about the debate between Theseus and the herald: is the Athenian's case for democracy really so watertight? Some of the arguments put by the herald receive no answer, and many of the criticisms he makes of rabble-rousing and government by demagogues, while not appropriate to Theseus' Athens, might seem disturbingly applicable to the Athens of the 420s. In other words, Theseus' picture of virtuous kingship and open government represents an ideal, and the wrongful war undertaken without divine authority by the foolish Adrastus offers a warning: Athens may not be like that, but she must struggle to retain her superior integrity. This interpretation allows the more disturbing notes in the play to be given some weight, without going to the implausible extreme of a wholly 'ironic' reading which turns the apparently ideal Athens into a self-deceiving or war-loving society.

Other, more specific, connections with contemporary history have been suggested besides the obvious analogy between Athens' past wars and her present. In particular, the Thebans had refused to relinquish the Athenian dead for burial after the battle of Delium in November 424 BC (Thucydides iv, 97). Although denial of burial to an enemy is a recurring atrocity in Greek myth and history, this incident may have given additional bite to the Theban action within the mythical context of this play. In addition, Athena at the end of the play advises her people to establish a defensive alliance with Argos: one such alliance was indeed contracted in 420 and renewed in 416. Whether this allusion anticipates a hoped-for alliance or provides a 'charter-myth' for one already established cannot be answered without firmer external evidence for the date of the play.

At various times political allusion to contemporary concerns has seemed to critics unworthy of a great tragedian, and hence these possible links with history have been denied or played down. But the existence of allusions of this kind in one of the masterpieces of Greek drama, Aeschylus' *Oresteia*, is indisputable, and there is no good reason to doubt that Euripides sometimes followed the same practice. These hints and allusive references may give added significance to the play, but they do not overwhelm the mythical action which is the dramatist's main concern. (Similar issues arise with the *Trojan Women*, where many interpreters have supposed the dramatist to have had in mind the massacre of the Melian population by an Athenian force in the previous year; but even if that speculation is correct, the play remains a play about Troy rather than Melos.) The *Suppliant Women* is a play about Athens at war, produced in a period when Athens was at war; it treats of democratic leadership and high-minded civic ideals, as well as of folly and suffering. In such a play it was inevitable that the different members of Euripides' audience would see different things that related to their own hopes, aspirations and fears. Nor should the modern reader dismiss the drama as a historical oddity: although the mythical setting may seem remote and alien, the issues at stake in the play – respect for the conquered and observance of basic human decencies – will never lose their relevance.

CHARACTERS

AETHRA, *mother of Theseus*
CHORUS *of Argive mothers and their handmaidens*
THESEUS, *king of Athens*
ADRASTUS, *king of Argos*
HERALD *of Creon, king of Thebes*
MESSENGER
EVADNE, *widow of Capaneus*
IPHIS, *father of Evadne*
SONS *of the dead Argive captains, a secondary chorus*
ATHENA

[*The scene is set before the temple of Demeter and Persephone at Eleusis after the disastrous Argive expedition against Thebes. AETHRA, mother of THESEUS, is seated at an altar surrounded by the CHORUS,[2] the mothers of the seven dead champions of Argos who have been refused burial by the victors. At the doors of the temple in an attitude of despair are ADRASTUS, who had led the expedition as Argos' king, and the SONS of the dead warriors. These boys form a secondary CHORUS to that of their mothers. The women of the CHORUS are attended by handmaidens.*]

AETHRA: Demeter, guardian of this Eleusinian land, and you servants who have the goddess's temple in your keeping, a prosperous life is my prayer, for myself, Aethra, and Theseus, my son. This I ask also for the city of Athens and the land of Pittheus, my father, where he raised me in his wealthy home and gave me in marriage to Pandion's son, Aegeus, in obedience to the oracle of Loxias.

I make this prayer as I gaze upon these old women who have left behind their Argive homeland and sit in supplication at my knees, holding leafy branches that show their status. What they have endured is terrible: childlessness afflicts them, now that their seven noble sons have met their deaths around the gates of Cadmus. Adrastus, ruler of Argos, had led them there in his desire to gain for his exiled kinsman, Polynices, his share in the kingdom of Oedipus.[3] Now that they are dead, slain by the spear, it is their mothers' wish to give them funeral in the earth. But this is prevented by the victors, who withhold

10

93

permission to recover the bodies, so flouting the laws of the
gods.[4] This need these women have of me is a burden that
Adrastus shares with them; there he lies, his face dampened
by tears, lamenting the war and the ill-starred expedition he
led from his home.

He has been urging me to appeal to my son, so he might
be persuaded, whether by means of debate or armed force,[5]
to recover the dead and share responsibility for the burial,
imposing this task equally on my son and the city of Athens.
As it happened, I had come from my house to this sacred place
and was making sacrifice for the successful tilling of this land,
where the fruitful ears of corn were first seen[6] to bristle above
our soil. But finding myself surrounded by these suppliant
branches, imprisoned but no prisoner, I wait here by the holy
altar of the two goddesses, the Maid and Demeter;[7] I pity
these grey-headed mothers, bereft of children, and I respect
their sacred wreaths. I have sent a herald to Athens, calling
upon Theseus to come here, either to relieve his country of
these people and the distress they bring, or to discharge our duty
towards suppliants by performing some act of piety to the gods.
Women who have sense should always act through men.

CHORUS [Strophe]: *I entreat you, old woman,[8] from an old
woman's lips, falling at your knees, recover our children and curb the
lawlessness of those who leave the limbs of the dead in sprawling death
as food for the beasts of the mountains;*

[Antistrophe:] *look upon the piteous tears that well up in my
eyes and the gashes where my hands have scarred this wrinkled old
flesh.[9] What other choice have I? I have not laid my dead sons out
before my house, nor do I see any mounds of earth to serve as burial
for them.*

[Strophe:] *You too are a mother, my lady, you once brought joy
to your husband's heart by bearing him a son; show me now the
concern you have for him, show it; such is the pain and sorrow I feel,
now that my children are no more. Prevail on your son, oh I beg you,
to come to the Ismenus and to deliver into our hands the bodies of
our strong young sons that linger without burial.*

[Antistrophe:] *Less than reverently*[10] *but constrained by necessity I have come with suppliant appeals to this sanctuary of the gods with its blazing altars. There is justice in our claim, and you have power enough to end the misery I feel at the fate of my fine sons. In my pitiable suffering, I beg your son to place my dead child in my wretched hands so that I may embrace the disfigured body of my son.*   70

[Strophe:] *Here is a new contest beginning, as lamentation finds answer in lamentation and our servants' hands are heard.*[11] *Come, you singers in tune with our sorrow, come, you partners in our grief, join the dance that Hades celebrates; draw nails across your white cheeks, making your skin a bloody red; it brings honour to the living when they pay tribute to the dead.*

[Antistrophe:] *The pleasure of all my sorrow, my pain, leads me on, never satisfied, like some incessant waterfall that flows from a sun-beaten rock. Never do I cease in my laments. The death of*   80 *children weighs heavy on the heart and prompts lamentation among women; ah, the pain of it! I long for death and a mind oblivious to these woes!*

[THESEUS *enters, searching for* AETHRA, *his mother.*]

THESEUS: Whose cries of grief did I hear, whose breast-beating and wailing for the dead that resounded from the temple here? How fear has lent me wings, lest something has happened to my mother – she has not returned home for some time now   90 and I have come to find her. [*Seeing the group of suppliants:*] Ah, what's this? Here's a strange sight to talk about – my old mother sitting at the altar, surrounded by women of another city who show their grief in more ways than one! Their aged eyes drop piteous tears upon the ground, but they have also shorn their hair, and the clothes they wear do not suggest visitors to the shrine. What does this mean, mother? Now you must give me the facts and I must listen; I expect it is bad news.

AETHRA: My son, these women are the mothers of the seven captains who met their deaths at each of Cadmus' gates.   100 With their suppliant branches they have encircled me, as you see, child, and are holding me captive.

THESEUS [*gesturing towards* ADRASTUS]: And who is the man over there at the doors who groans so pitifully?

AETHRA: Adrastus, they tell me, king of Argos' people.

THESEUS: And the boys around him? Are they the children of these women?

AETHRA: No; they are the sons of the dead[12] who fell in war.

THESEUS: But why have they come as suppliants to us?

AETHRA: I know their plight, but *they* must now take up the tale, my child.

THESEUS [*turning to address* ADRASTUS]: You sir, with your head
110   covered by your cloak,[13] answer my questions. Bare your head, stop your laments and speak; nothing is ever achieved without using your tongue.

ADRASTUS [*obeying*]: Theseus, glorious king of Athens and her people, I have come here to beg a favour of you and of your city.

THESEUS: What are you seeking? What is it you need?

ADRASTUS: You have heard of the expedition I led to disaster?

THESEUS: Of course; your march through Greece was hardly veiled in silence.

ADRASTUS: The flower of Argos' soldiers perished under my leadership.

THESEUS: Such is the work of war's cruelty.[14]

ADRASTUS: I went to ask the Thebans to let me have those who
120   died.

THESEUS: Putting your trust in Hermes' heralds, to gain burial for the dead?

ADRASTUS: Yes, but after that they refused permission – the ones who had done the killing!

THESEUS: And what did they have to say, when your request is what piety dictates?

ADRASTUS: You may well ask; good fortune is theirs but they don't know how to respond to success.

THESEUS: Have you then come to me for advice? Or is there another reason?

ADRASTUS: My request, Theseus, is that *you* recover the sons of
the Argives.

THESEUS: And where is your great Argos now, then? Were they
empty mouthings, those boasts you made?

ADRASTUS: We lost the battle and are ruined; we have come to
you.

THESEUS: Was this your own decision or that of all Argos?

ADRASTUS: Every one of Danaus' sons begs you to bury their
dead.   130

THESEUS: Why did you lead those seven companies of men to
Thebes?

ADRASTUS: It was to oblige my two sons-in-law.

THESEUS: To which of the Argives did you give your daughters
in marriage?

ADRASTUS: It was not with my fellow-citizens that I formed
this tie.

THESEUS: What? You gave Argive girls to foreigners?

ADRASTUS: Yes, to Tydeus,[15] and to Polynices, a Theban born.

THESEUS: What prompted your desire to have them as kinsmen?

ADRASTUS: Phoebus; a riddling oracle of his, hard to fathom,
influenced me.

THESEUS: What did Apollo say when he ordained marriage for
the maidens?

ADRASTUS: That I should give my girls to a boar and a lion.   140

THESEUS: How did you unravel this pronouncement of the god?

ADRASTUS: Two exiles arrived by night at my gates.

THESEUS: Who were they both? Tell me! You spoke of two
men together.

ADRASTUS: Tydeus and Polynices, and they fought each other.

THESEUS: And you gave your daughters to them, thinking they
resembled wild animals?

ADRASTUS: Yes; the way they fought made me think of a pair
of beasts.

THESEUS: What caused them to leave the borders of their homeland and come to Argos?

ADRASTUS: In Tydeus' case he had been banished for shedding a kinsman's blood.

THESEUS: And the son of Oedipus? How did he come to leave Thebes?

150 ADRASTUS: His father's curse[16] was the cause; he was afraid of becoming his brother's killer.

THESEUS: That was prudent of him, to leave his city voluntarily.

ADRASTUS: Yes, but the one who stayed behind wronged the one who left.[17]

THESEUS: Surely his brother didn't rob him of his inheritance?

ADRASTUS: It was as adjudicator in this matter that I came; I then met with disaster.

THESEUS: Did you consult seers and inspect the flames of burnt offerings?

ADRASTUS: Oh, this pains me! You press me where my fault is most blatant.

THESEUS: Your expedition, it seems, lacked the gods' blessing.[18]

ADRASTUS: Not only that; it was undertaken despite the warnings of Amphiaraus.[19]

THESEUS: You found it so easy to ignore the gods' wishes?

ADRASTUS: My troops were young;[20] their clamouring for action
160 made me hasty, too.

THESEUS: You pursued the course of bravery rather than judgement.

ADRASTUS: O sir, your prowess in war is supreme throughout Greece. Royal lord of Athens, it makes me ashamed to fall to the ground and clasp your knees, an old man now, a king once favoured by the gods. And yet I have no choice but to yield to my misfortunes. Bring safely back, I beg you, the dead bodies of these men; show pity for my suffering and for these mothers whose sons have perished, who face the prospect of
170 a grey-haired old age without children. They have found the courage to come here, stirring tired old limbs to make the journey from Argos, not to witness Demeter's mysteries but to bury their dead, though they themselves should have had funeral rites and received this office from the hands of their sons.

Wisdom will prompt a prosperous man to look at a poor one and a poor man to keep an envious eye on the wealthy, to fuel his own desire for success; so those unscathed by bad fortune will be wise to have regard for the sufferings of others. A poet should compose any songs he creates out of joy; if he does not have this feeling, but is crushed by some personal disaster, he cannot bring joy to others either, having no claim to do so.

Perhaps you may say: 'How is it that you ignore the land of Pelops and lay this burden at Athens's door?' This is an objection I have a duty to answer. Sparta is ruthless and given to duplicity,[21] while the other cities are small and lack strength. Your city alone would be able to shoulder this task; it has regard for the misery of others, and in you it has a fine young leader; a lack of this, the need for a commander, has brought many a city to ruin.

CHORUS-LEADER: Theseus, I add my voice to the same appeal he has made; please take pity on my state!

THESEUS: This is a question[22] I have often debated fiercely with other men. It has been said that the good in life is outweighed by the bad. The view I hold is contrary to this: I say that mankind's blessings outnumber its woes. If this were not the case, our life on earth would have ceased. I praise the god who gave order and balance to our existence, formerly chaotic and brutish, firstly by implanting in us intelligence, then adding the gift of speech that conveys meaning, so that we may comprehend what we say; next, he conferred on us the growing of crops and the rain that falls from heaven to increase the produce of the earth and satisfy our thirst; to this he added protection against storms and the ability to defend ourselves against Apollo's heat, and, further, the means to cross the sea in ships, that those of us whose lands were poor might engage in trade with one another. As to matters that are obscure and unclear to our understanding, there are prophets who reveal the future to us by examining flames, the layers of entrails and the flight of birds.

Now, when the god makes such provision for our lives as this, is it not arrogance on our part to be dissatisfied with his gifts? No, in our presumptuousness we seek to rise higher than him, we imagine in the vanity of our hearts that we are wiser than the gods. To this company you too belong, a born fool who, yoked to the response of Phoebus, gave your daughters to strangers,[23] as if the gods were blessing their marriages, and did violence to your own family, fouling the bright water of its name in this fashion. No man of sense should permit his family's blood to be contaminated, mixing healthy with unhealthy, but should seek to have as sons-in-law men whose prosperity will benefit his house. Heaven makes no distinctions in men's circumstances: the sufferings of the guilty are used to bring down the innocent, though they have done no wrong.

Again, you led out to war every man of Argos, flouting the advice given in the prophets' responses; you treated the gods with contempt and so brought destruction on your city. You allowed yourself to be led astray by younger men who love to make their mark in the city, fomenting wars without just cause and causing the deaths of fellow-citizens, the one to win an army-command, another to seize power and play the tyrant, a third to secure his own profit without caring whether the people will suffer any harm as a result of such treatment. There are three divisions in society:[24] first there are the wealthy, who are harmful and endlessly grasping; then come the poor and needy, who are dangerous as they are ruled by envy and cajoled by the words of corrupt leaders into malicious attacks upon the rich; it is the third group, the moderates, who are a city's lifeline; they are the ones who maintain whatever government the citizen-body establishes.

In view of this, do you expect me to take your side in this conflict? What good ground could I give my fellow-citizens for such a course? This meeting is at an end; if you yourself have been guilty of foolish planning, why should we suffer for your misfortune?

CHORUS-LEADER: He acted wrongly; as for the young men, they behaved as young men will. He deserves your pardon.   250

ADRASTUS: I did not require you to sit in judgement on my faults, my lord. I did not come here for correction or censure of any errors. No, I came in hope of assistance. If you are not prepared to give me this, then I must accept your decision; I have no alternative. [*Turning to the* CHORUS:] Come old women, you must go now. Leave here your green branches with their leaves wreathed with wool, and call to witness heaven and earth, Demeter, torch-bearing goddess and the   260 light of the sun, that we have gained nothing by making these appeals to the gods.

CHORUS-LEADER: Theseus, as Aethra is your mother, you are the grandson of Pittheus, who was a son of Pelops, and we, who are of Pelops' land, share with you this same ancestral blood.[25] What are you doing? Will you betray this tie and expel old women from this land, denying them the rights that are their due? Do not do it! A beast has a cave where it can find refuge, a slave the altars of the gods, and one city in distress gains the protection of another, as a bird will fly in fear from the storm; for in human life there is no such thing as perpetual happiness.   270

[*The* CHORUS *now divides into two groups to strengthen their appeal in the face of* THESEUS' *silence.*]

FIRST SEMICHORUS: *Go down, unhappy ones, leave Persephone's holy floor, go down, throw your arms around his knees and beg him to bring back the bodies of our dead sons – oh, my sorrow! – whom we have lost in the bloom of their youth beneath the battlements of Cadmus.*

SECOND SEMICHORUS [*appealing to* THESEUS]: *Dear friend, revered by all Greece, we fall in misery at your knees and hands and beg you by your chin: take pity on our suppliant state, on our wanderings, as we utter a piteous, piteous dirge for our sons!*   280

FIRST: *Do not look on, my child, I beg you, while our sons, as young and vigorous as you, lie without burial in the land of Cadmus for beasts to devour with relish.*

SECOND: *See the tears in our eyes as we fall at your knees in this way,*
begging you to give our sons burial.

THESEUS: Mother, why do you weep, holding your fine mantle
like a veil over your eyes? Are you moved at hearing their
wretched lamentation? I, too, felt a pang of sorrow. Lift up
your white-haired head and put a stop to these tears;[26] it is by
290   Demeter's holy altar that you sit.

AETHRA: Oh, what pain I feel!

THESEUS: Their sufferings should not cause you grief.

AETHRA: O you women, what you have endured!

THESEUS: But you are not related to them by birth![27]

AETHRA: Am I to tell you, my boy, what will bring honour to
you and Athens?

THESEUS: Of course; women too have much wisdom to offer.

AETHRA: Oh, but I'm still reluctant to declare what is in my
heart!

THESEUS: That's a shameful thing to say, keeping good words
hidden from those you love.

AETHRA: Then I will not stay silent;[28] I will not have cause to
blame myself later for holding my tongue like a coward now.
Men say it does no good for women to make fine speeches
but I won't let this deter me; I won't be cowed into abandoning
300   what I know to be the right course.

My advice to you, my son, is, firstly, to consider the
wishes of the gods and so avoid ruin through slighting them.
Moreover, if there were no obligation to help the wronged at
whatever risk to oneself, you would hear not a word from me.
But this is not so and you must realize how much honour this
action will bring you. Men of violence are refusing the dead the
burial and funeral rites that are their due. I do not shrink from
urging you to make these men recognize their duty by means
310   of Athenian steel. You must check those who are confounding the established laws of all Greece.[29] For it is this, due
observance of the laws, that keeps cities free from civil strife.

It will be said – yes, it will! – that courage failed you, that,
when you might have gained for Athens a glorious crown,

fear made you stand back, that you embraced the task of tackling a wild boar[30] – no great challenge – but when it came to facing helmets and spearpoints, to seeing a battle through to the end, you were shown up as a coward. As you are mine, do not act like this, my son. Do you see how, when men   320 mock your country for lack of judgement, it turns a fierce eye upon them? It is in risking danger that it shows its greatness.[31] Cities that hold back from action and practise secrecy are so cautious that they won't even divulge the direction they're looking in.

Go to help the dead, my son, and these pitiful women in their desperate straits. I do not fear for you as you are setting out with a just cause, and, though I see Cadmus' folk enjoying their success, I trust they will get a different throw of the dice next time. The gods reverse all men's fortunes.   330

CHORUS-LEADER: My dearest friend, your words to this man and to me are nobly spoken; this proves to be a double joy.

THESEUS: What I have said, mother, deals accurately with this man; I have demonstrated what kind of counsels marred his judgement. But I also recognize the force of your advice to me: it goes against my nature to turn my back on danger. By performing many noble acts I have given Greeks proof that it is my habit to be a constant thorn in the side of the wicked.   340 I cannot then disown this task. What will my enemies say of me when you, my own mother, who have most cause to fear for me, are the first to urge me to undertake it?

I will do it. I will go and reclaim their dead, by persuasion, if I can. If this fails, the issue will be settled, whenever the point is reached, by force of arms and with heaven's blessing. I also wish to have every Athenian's approval for this and so I shall, if it is my wish; but the whole citizen-body will more   350 readily support me if I give them power of decision.[32] For I conferred on them sole rule when I gave this city liberty with equality of franchise.[33] I will take Adrastus with me as proof of what I say to them, and go before the assembly of my townsmen. When they give their agreement to this, I will muster a select force of Athens's fighting men and return here. Then I will remain in armed readiness while I send word to Creon to give up the bodies of the dead.

[*Turning to the* CHORUS:] Old women, remove the holy wreaths that bind my mother so that I may escort her to the house of Aegeus, taking her precious hand in mine. Wretched is the child who does not repay his parents' attentive care, a service that is most noble; for in this way he gets back from his own offspring whatever he bestows on his parents.

[THESEUS *and* AETHRA *depart, followed by* ADRASTUS.]

CHORUS [Strophe]: *Argos, where the horses graze, Argos, home of my forefathers, did you hear, did you hear these pious words of a god-fearing king, words of great importance to Pelasgia and in Argos?*

[Antistrophe:] *If only he would bring our suffering to an end once and for all, stilling mothers' hands that tear cheeks crimson, and by his kindly aid gaining the love of Inachus' land!*

[Strophe:] *An enterprise that is pious and brings peril is a noble source of joy in a city's memory and wins undying gratitude. What, we wonder, will be Athens's decision? Will it conclude terms of friendship with us? Will we win the right to see our sons buried?*

[Antistrophe:] *Give your protection, city of Pallas, give your protection to mothers and save the laws of men from violation! You have reverence for justice and contempt for injustice; to all in misfortune you always give an arm that shields them from wrong.*

[THESEUS *and* ADRASTUS *return from Athens. An Athenian herald accompanies* THESEUS.]

THESEUS [*to his herald*]: Whenever you bear this office you serve your city and myself as you spread your proclamations. Go now across the Asopus and Ismenus' stream and deliver this message to the haughty ruler of Cadmus' people: 'Theseus requests you graciously to grant burial to the dead, presuming on your assent as he dwells in the land that is neighbour to your own, and to enter into friendly relations with all the people of Erechtheus' line.' If they consent, accept their response and come back without delay. If they do not obey, this is what you must say next: 'Prepare to receive a Bacchic

storm of Athenian warriors. Our army here is in position; it   390
is marshalled hard by in readiness for battle by holy Callichorus'
banks.' [*Turning to the* CHORUS:] Athens willingly and gladly
accepted this task when her people realized it was what I
wanted. [*Reacting to the sudden appearance of a* HERALD *from
Thebes:*] But wait – who is this man arriving who breaks into
my speech? I don't know for sure, but it seems he is a Theban
and a herald. [*To his own herald:*] Wait – it may be that he
comes with the same intent as mine and will save you labour.

HERALD: Who governs this land as monarch?[34] To whom should
I convey the words of Creon, ruler of Cadmus' land, now   400
that Eteocles is dead, killed by the hand of Polynices his
brother, at the city's seventh gate?

THESEUS: First of all, stranger, you were wrong at the outset of
your speech in seeking a monarch here; Athens is not ruled
by a single man; it is a free city. Sovereignty belongs to the
people, who take turns to govern in annual succession. Wealth
receives no special recognition from us; the poor man has an
equal voice in the state.

HERALD: You've made a bad move there and given me the
chance to win the game. The city I represent is ruled by a   410
single man, not by a mob. There is no one who makes the
citizens swell with vanity by speech-making, twisting them
now this way, now that, purely to line his own pockets,
charming at first, the favourite of all, but in time a source of
harm, who invents fresh accusations to conceal his former
errors and gives justice the slip.

Another thing: the people are not capable of plain, honest
speech themselves; how then could they give good guidance to
a city? Measured deliberation provides a better understanding
than hasty judgement. Your common farmer, poor as he is,   420
may be no fool, but his labour in the fields would prevent
him from concentrating on politics. What really poisons life
for the better class of person is when a man of no principles
rises from obscurity to a position of great importance through
using his tongue to control the people.

THESEUS: A smart fellow, eh, this herald, embroidering on the
message he's supposed to deliver! Well, since you're the one
who started this argument, it's your turn to listen; you chose
to hold this contest. No enemy is more dangerous to a city
than a monarch, for then, firstly, laws for all citizens do not
430   exist and one man enjoys power, appropriating the law as
his own possession. This means an end to equality. But when
laws are written down, the weak and the rich man alike have
their equal right; the weaker man, when slandered by his
prosperous neighbour, can respond in like terms, and, if his
cause is just, the man of humbler means defeats the great.
Liberty speaks in these words: 'Who with good counsel for
his city wishes to address this gathering?'[35] Anyone who wishes
440   to do this gains distinction; whoever does not, keeps silent.
Where could a city enjoy greater equality than this?

There is this point also: where the people direct a country's
path, they take pleasure in the young citizens they have. But
a monarch thinks of them as his enemies and puts to death all
nobles he considers clever, fearful for his throne. How, then,
would a city have strength any more, when its young men
are cut away and lopped off like stalks[36] in a spring meadow?
Why should a man acquire wealth and property for his children
450   if all his effort goes only to increase the resources of a
monarch? Why should he raise daughters chastely at home,
as propriety requires, to serve as dainty dishes for a monarch's
lust whenever he desires, but bring tears to those whose care
provided this? May I die the day daughters of *mine* are brought
forcibly to a man's bed!

There you have my response to your attacks. But why are
you here? What do you need from this land? Were you not
your city's envoy you would regret this visit and letting your
tongue so far exceed its brief. A messenger's duty is to deliver
460   his master's instruction and then to lose no time in returning.
In future, let Creon send a less garrulous messenger than you
to my city.

CHORUS-LEADER: Oh, how true it is – when success attends

the wicked, their arrogance shows they think their luck will
never end.

HERALD: Well, I'll deliver my message. As for our debate here,
you hold to what you think but I'll settle for the opposite line.
I and all Cadmus' people warn you not to let Adrastus come
into this land. If he enters, before the waning of the god's
radiance, you are to dispense with the holy mystery of these
suppliant wreaths and drive him out; you are also forbidden   470
to take up the dead ones for burial through the use of force,
since there is no relationship that binds you to the city of the
Argives. If you do my bidding, you will steer Athens's ship
safe from stormwaves, but, if not, a deluge of war shall crash
upon you and us and those who side with each of us.

Consider then and do not let anger at what I have said, or
your claim to have a free city, cause you to give some bombastic
reply when your position is so tenuous. No one should put
any trust in hope: it joins many a city in battle, prompting
men to entertain extravagant thoughts. Whenever the people   480
has to vote on war, no man takes his own death into his
calculations any more but imagines this misfortune will befall
someone else. But if death was there during the casting of
votes for every man to see, this madness for war would not
be destroying Greece. And yet every man alive knows the
more powerful of the two arguments; we know what good is
and what bad, how much better for man peace is than war.
Peace it is that, firstly, is the greatest friend to the Muses and
enemy to the powers of vengeance, peace that is gladdened
by the birth of fine children, that rejoices in a city's wealth.   490
These blessings we wickedly reject and take up wars instead,
man against man and city against city, imposing slavery upon
the weaker.

And are you now seeking to help our dead enemies,
attempting to recover and bury men destroyed by their own
arrogance?[37] Then it is not right that Capaneus' body still
smokes from the lightning stroke, the man who attacked our
gates, setting ladders up against the walls, and swore to sack

the city whether this was heaven's will or not; it is not right
that the prophet was seized and swallowed up in a chasm –
chariot, team of four and driver all as one – or that the other
captains lie before the gates, their skulls smashed by stones.
You must now lay claim to a wisdom superior to Zeus' own,
or else admit that wicked men are justly destroyed by the
gods.

No, wise men should love, firstly, their children, then,
their parents and their country, which it is their duty to make
strong, not weak. Rashness in a general or seaman leads to
error; wisdom lies in recognizing the moment *not* to act.
Forethought is also bravery, you must acknowledge.

CHORUS-LEADER: It was sufficient that Zeus punished them;
there is no need for you and your people to add your own
arrogance in this way.

ADRASTUS: You detestable wretch –

THESEUS: Silence, Adrastus![38] Hold your tongue and don't try
to have your say before I do! It is to me, not you, that this
fellow has come with his message; it is for me, then, to give
him an answer. [*Turning back to the Theban* HERALD:] First of
all I will reply to your opening words. I am not aware that
Creon is my master or that his power so exceeds mine that
he can force Athens to this course of action. Before we let
another give us orders in this fashion, the world would stand
on its head. As for this war, it is not of my making; I did not
even join these men when they marched on Cadmus' land.
But in the case of these dead warriors, I judge it right to give
them burial, thereby bringing no harm to your city nor causing
any lethal conflicts to ensue, but preserving the law of all
Greece. Is this not entirely proper? I grant that the Argives
have done you harm, but it has cost them their lives; you have
repelled your enemies in glorious fashion, but with little
honour for them, and justice has been served.

Now that they are dead, allow their corpses to have a
covering of earth, so that each part can return to the place
from which it first entered the light of day, the breath to the

sky, the body to the ground; we do not own our bodies except for the duration of our lives here, and then they must be gathered up again by the earth that gave us nurture. Do you think you are harming Argos by refusing burial to the dead? Far from it; this is something that hurts the whole Greek race, if dead men are deprived of the rites that are their due and kept unburied. Brave men will turn coward if this custom   540
becomes prevalent.

And do you, who have come here to make these terrible threats against me, quiver with fear at dead men receiving burial in the earth? What may happen that makes you so afraid? Will they rise from their graves to raze your land? Will they father sons in underground chambers to take their revenge? What a fatuous waste of speech this is, to harbour base and vain fears.

O foolish men, learn the truth about human suffering! This life we live is like a wrestling match; some of us succeed   550
today, others tomorrow, others, again, have had their success. Fortune, meanwhile, enjoys herself; the unsuccessful man, hoping for prosperity, reveres her as a goddess, while the one who thrives is afraid of losing her favour and so exalts her name. So you should realize these truths, curbing resentment when the wrong done to you is limited and replying in kind only so far as will not rebound on you.

Well, how should we proceed? Give up to us the bodies of the dead for burial, as we wish to grant them holy rites. Deny us, and the consequences are plain: I will come and bury them by means of force. Never shall Greek say to Greek   560
that an ancient law of the gods came to me and the city of Pandion and withered in rejection.

CHORUS-LEADER: Never fear; while you keep the light of Justice shining, you will escape all the slander of men's tongues.

HERALD: Am I to make a brief reply?

THESEUS: Speak up, if there's anything you wish to say; words come easily to you after all.

HERALD: You will never take these sons of Argos from our land.

THESEUS: Now hear me, too, in turn, if you please.

570 HERALD: I will; I must admit you have the right of reply now.

THESEUS: I will recover the dead from Asopus' land and give them burial.

HERALD: Before that you will have to risk your life amid the shields.

THESEUS: I have faced many other struggles on behalf of others.

HERALD: Did your father sire you to be a match for all opponents?

THESEUS: Yes, for all braggarts; good men need not fear my spear.

HERALD: Your custom, and your city's, is to interfere regularly in the business of others.[39]

THESEUS: Yes; and so by great endeavours she wins great prosperity.

HERALD: Come on then, so that our army of sown[40] men may strike you down in the dust.

THESEUS: How would an earthbound snake contribute to the fury of war?

580 HERALD: Suffering will bring that lesson home to you. For the moment you are still a young man.

THESEUS: You will not stir me to anger with your boasts. Get out of my land, taking the foolish words you brought with you. We are wasting time like this. [*The Theban* HERALD *leaves.*] Now we must be off – every soldier, every charioteer, every horse, its bit dripping at the mouth with foam, rushing to the land of Cadmus! I'll march on Cadmus' seven gates in
590 person, keen sword in hand, and myself serve as my herald. But you Adrastus, I order to stay here and not to taint my fortunes with your own.[41] I will take the field with my own fortune, my spear untouched by guilt, as am I. There is only one thing I need: the support of the gods who revere justice. Their union confers victory. A man's brave heart is useless to him if he lacks the goodwill of heaven. [THESEUS *and his herald leave.* ADRASTUS *remains silent on stage. The* CHORUS *divides once more for song.*]

FIRST SEMICHORUS [Strophe]: *O wretched mothers of wretched captains, how my heart is prey to pallid fear!*

SECOND SEMICHORUS: *What is this thought that troubles you so?*   600

FIRST: *I fear for Pallas' army – what will the issue be?*

SECOND: *Of battle, do you mean, or parley?*

FIRST: *Words would be for the better; but if we see bloody deaths in battle and the city echoes with the beating of breasts, then, ah me! what words will fall on me, what blame for this?*

SECOND [Antistrophe]: *But some stroke of fate may fell in his turn the man who basks in the glory of success; this thought lends comfort and cheer to my heart.*

FIRST: *You speak there of just gods.*   610

SECOND: *What others govern our lives?*

FIRST: *I see that the gods assign many different fates to mortal men.*

SECOND: *This shows your earlier fear has broken your spirit. But justice invites justice, bloodshed bloodshed; the gods, who have in their keeping the end of all things, confer on mortals a reprieve from their woes.*

FIRST [Strophe]: *Oh, if only we might come to that plain where the noble towers rise, leaving Callichorus' stream*[42] *behind, river of the goddess!*

SECOND: *If only some god would furnish you with wings, so that*   620 *you might come to the city of twin streams,*[43] *you would know, yes, know how our friends are faring!*

FIRST: *Whatever fate, what doom is in store for the valiant ruler of this land?*

SECOND [Antistrophe]: *We have called upon the gods, but again we call upon them; it is this before all else that gives us faith to resist our fears.*

FIRST: *O Zeus, begetter of the child by Inachus' daughter, heifer-maid, our ancient mother,*[44] *be our ally I pray, and show yourself a friend to this city!*   630

SECOND: *Bring back for the pyre, I pray, your city's ornament and bulwark, so shamefully abused!*

[*A* MESSENGER *arrives from Thebes.*]

MESSENGER: Ladies, I come with much to tell, and it is good news. First there is my own escape to safety (I had been taken prisoner in the battle by Dirce's stream where the seven commanders fought and died), and then I am to bring you word of Theseus' victory. I will spare you a lot of questioning: I was servant to Capaneus, whom Zeus burnt to cinders with the flame of his thunderbolt.

640

CHORUS-LEADER: Dear friend, we thank you for the news of your safe return and your report about Theseus. If Athens's army is also safe, your whole message would be welcome.

MESSENGER: Safe, indeed; they have met with the success that Adrastus and his Argives should have had when he led them out from the Inachus in his march upon the city of Cadmus' folk.

CHORUS-LEADER: How did Aegeus' son come to set up a thanks-offering to Zeus, he and the men who fought at his side? Tell us; you will give us pleasure, as one who was an eye-witness speaking to those who were not.

MESSENGER: The sun's brilliant rays, illuminating the scene for all to see, were striking the earth when I scaled the tower with its fine view and took up my position as a spectator above the Electran Gate.

650

From there I saw the Athenian army in its three divisions: first, the infantry, extending up towards the hill of Ismenus, as I heard it called, with the king himself, Aegeus' famous son, and the inhabitants of ancient Cecropia drawn up beside him on the right wing, and Paralus himself, armed with spears, hard by the spring of Ares; next, I saw the massed horsemen drawn up for battle at the fringe of the army, a body that matched the infantry in number; then, thirdly, below Amphion's sacred tomb, the war-chariots.

660

The Theban troops occupied the ground in front of the city walls. Behind them, in array, lay the bodies of the dead, the men who had caused the conflict to arise. So horsemen were facing horsemen across the field of battle, and chariots chariots, each side with their teams of four. The herald of

Theseus then addressed all present with these words: 'Silence, men, silence! Hear my words, you men of Thebes marshalled here! We have come to fetch the bodies of the dead, wishing to give them burial. It is not our aim to prolong the shedding of blood; our desire is to show respect for the law all Greeks hold dear.' 670

To this statement Creon offered no reply through a herald of his own, but held his position, armed and silent. The charioteers opened hostilities at this point, driving their chariots through one another's positions and setting down combatants to fight it out with the spear. These started to deal one another blows, while the charioteers wheeled their horses round again to support their men in the fight.

This mêlée of chariots was seen by Phorbas, commander of the Athenian horsemen, and by the leaders of the Theban cavalry in turn, who charged one another with varying success on both sides. This I witnessed with my own eyes (for I was at the place where chariots and combatants were locked in struggle); I don't know where to begin in describing all the horror that met my gaze – the dust that billowed up to the heavens, so much of it there was, the drivers caught up in their reins and dragged along, their bodies rising and falling, the streams of crimson blood from men falling dead or tumbling headlong from shattered chariots and crashing to earth, perishing amid the spokes and wreckage. 680 690

Creon suspected that victory was going to our cavalry and so he advanced, shield in hand, to ensure his allies did not lose heart. But there was no question of Theseus' cause being undermined by hesitation; at once he seized his glittering weapons and rushed to the spot. The two sides clashed, with the entire centre of both armies locked in struggle, and men were killing others or being killed themselves, as orders and shouts of encouragement were noisily passed to and fro: 'Strike home!' and 'Hold the Athenians with your spears!' The army of men sprung from the dragon's teeth were mighty fighters and were beginning to turn our left wing with their right, but 700 our own right wing got the better of theirs and put it to flight. The battle hung in the balance, finely poised.

This was when you would have applauded our general; not satisfied with this victory alone, he headed for where our side was in difficulty and his ringing cry made the earth 710 reverberate: 'Hold these tough spearsmen of Thebes in check, my men, or Pallas' cause is lost!' With this he put fire in the belly of every soldier of Athenian stock. Himself wielding his fearful weapon, the club from Epidaurus,[45] Theseus swung freely through the thick of battle, snapping necks and culling helmets from heads as he harvested with his great cudgel. In the end, the very end, the enemy turned and ran. I gave the victory shout, I danced in delight, I clapped my hands. The 720 Thebans were pressing on to their gates. Throughout the city, young and old alike were shouting and wailing as fear drove the citizens to crowd into the temples. Here was Theseus' opportunity to enter Thebes, but he held back; he had come, he said, not to sack the city but to recover the dead.

This is the kind of general one should choose, a man of courage in the hour of danger. Such a man despises an arrogant city, one that seeks in prosperity to climb to the topmost rung of success, and so forfeits the happiness it might have 730 enjoyed.

CHORUS-LEADER: Now that my eyes have seen this day I thought would never come, I *do* believe in the gods. Those who have paid the penalty here know greater misfortune, I think, than I.

ADRASTUS [*breaking his silence*]:[46] O Zeus, why is it men say that wretched mortals have the power of thought? It is you on whom we depend, you who govern our actions according to your wishes at any time. We had in Argos a city we thought none could resist, given the number of our citizenry and the strength of our fighting men. So when Eteocles offered terms 740 of peace, making a fair proposal, we refused to accept and then paid the price with our lives. Eteocles in turn, whom

Fortune smiled on then, like a poor man newly enriched, grew arrogant, and in a short time Cadmus' foolish people paid for their arrogance with their own ruin.

Oh, the stupidity of man! You shoot your arrows beyond the target and, when, as you deserve, troubles crowd around your heads, it is only events that can teach you a lesson, not friends' advice. And you cities who have it in your power to end your sufferings by debate, you reach a conclusion by bloodshed, not parley.

Enough of this; what I want to know is how you got away safe; then I'll question you further. 750

MESSENGER: When the shock of defeat created turmoil in the city, I made my way out through the gate where the troops were entering.

ADRASTUS: Then are you bringing in the bodies of those who brought about this conflict?

MESSENGER: Yes; all those who commanded the seven famous companies.

ADRASTUS: What do you mean? Where are all the others who met their deaths?

MESSENGER: They have been given burial on the slopes of Cithaeron.

ADRASTUS: On this side of the boundary or that? And who buried them?

MESSENGER: Theseus, where Eleutherae's hill casts its shade.

ADRASTUS: And the dead that he did not bury, where have you left them? 760

MESSENGER: Not far from here; all that you were eager for is nearly accomplished.

ADRASTUS: The servants who bore them from the battlefield must have loathed the task.

MESSENGER: No one of servile birth presided over this task.

ADRASTUS: What? Theseus showed them that much reverence?

MESSENGER: So you would have said had you been there when he tended the dead.

ADRASTUS: He washed the wretches' bloody wounds with his own hands?

MESSENGER: Yes, and made ready their biers, covering them with cloths.

ADRASTUS: How terrible to make such contact, how shameful!

MESSENGER: What shame can men incur from one another's suffering?

ADRASTUS: Ah, how I wish I had shared their deaths!

770   MESSENGER: Your tears are useless; you are causing these women distress.

ADRASTUS: They are the ones, I think, who instruct me. But I will go to meet the dead. I will lift my hand in greeting and utter Hades' mournful songs, addressing the comrades I have lost and lamenting – oh, the pain of it! – my state of loneliness. This is the one thing we mortals can never recover once spent, a man's life; when he loses his wealth, it is not past remedy. [*Exit* ADRASTUS.]

CHORUS [Strophe]: *There is happiness for some but sorrow for others. Both Athens and her commanders have won renown and honour in*
780   *war; for us there is the bitterness of seeing the bodies of our sons; but if we only see them, it is a fine sight, since this is a day we did not look to see, though it brings the greatest of sorrows.*

[Antistrophe:] *If only Time, the ancient father of days, had kept us from marriage all our lives! What need had we of children? What*
790   *awful experience did we imagine would overtake us, if we never were joined in marriage? But now the misery we see is beyond all doubt, robbed as we are of our beloved sons.*

[*A funeral procession enters. Five of the seven dead captains*[47] *are carried by Athenian soldiers with* THESEUS *following behind. At the head of the cortège walks* ADRASTUS, *who enters into a sung lament with the mothers of the* CHORUS.]

But here we see them now, the bodies of our dead sons! Oh what sorrow! If only we might perish with these our children, making the descent to Hades who welcomes all!

ADRASTUS [Strophe]: *You mothers, cry out,*[48] *cry out your lamentation*

for the dead below the earth; let your laments ring out in answer to
my own.   800

CHORUS: *O sons, a painful word for your loving mothers to use in
their lament, I call to you who are dead.*

ADRASTUS: *Oh, I lament my woes!*

CHORUS: *Yes, and I mine.*

ADRASTUS: *We have suffered, oh . . .*

CHORUS: *. . . woes outrageous in their pain.*

ADRASTUS: *Fellow-citizens of Argos, do you not see the doom that is
mine?*

CHORUS: *They see me also in my wretchedness, bereft of my children.*   810

ADRASTUS [Antistrophe]: *Bring them to me, bring their blood-stained
bodies, ill-fated men slain unworthily by unworthy hands in whose
number the struggle was continued to its appointed end.*

CHORUS: *Give me my sons, that I may clasp them in my arms and
fold them to my bosom.*

[ADRASTUS *gives the mothers access to their sons.*]

ADRASTUS: *There you are, there you are; they are yours now.*

CHORUS: *What is mine is a sufficient burden of woes.*

ADRASTUS: *Ah, me!*

CHORUS: *What of us, the mothers, have you nothing to say to us?*

ADRASTUS: *You hear me.*

CHORUS: *The suffering you lament is theirs and ours as well.*   820

ADRASTUS: *If only the Theban ranks had slain me in the dust!*

CHORUS: *If only I had never known the embrace of a husband in the
marital bed!*

ADRASTUS [Epode]: *Look upon an ocean of anguish, you mothers of
sons, wedded to sorrow.*

CHORUS: *Our nails have furrowed our cheeks and with dust we have
covered our heads.*

ADRASTUS: *Oh the pain, the pain I feel! May the earth swallow me
up, may a storm-blast sweep me off, or Zeus' fiery thunderbolt fall*   830
upon my head!

CHORUS: *A sorry end you saw to your daughters' marriages, a sorry
end to the prophecy of Phoebus you heard. The Fury who brings
untold tears has left the house of Oedipus and has come to us.*

THESEUS: Now that you have discharged in full your lamentation for these men, I pass over the questions I meant to put to you
840 earlier; and now Adrastus, I ask you:[49] how was it that these men came to be such exemplars of courage? You have the skill, the knowledge; speak to our young Athenians here. They have witnessed the acts of bravery, beggaring description, by which these men were hoping to capture Thebes. One thing I will not ask you, in case I am thought ridiculous: which of the enemy each of them clashed with in battle, sustaining the deadly thrust of the spear. Such reports are worthless, doing no service to the teller or his listeners; how can a man who is
850 in a battle, with volleys of spears flying before his eyes, give a reliable account of where courage has been shown? I could neither ask a question like this nor put any trust in those who presume to answer it. A man facing the enemy head on could barely see beyond his own immediate danger.

ADRASTUS: Well, listen to me now. These men were my friends and so I accept with pleasure your invitation to speak in their praise; I want to tell the truth about them and to give them their just deserts. Do you see this man whom the furious
860 thunderbolt pierced? He was Capaneus, a man of substance, indeed, but in no way did his wealth make him arrogant. His thoughts were no more proud than a poor man's; he shunned the company of men who scorned moderation and preferred the ostentation of expensive dinners. He said that being content with what was sufficient was the mark of a good man, not stuffing himself with food. He was true to his friends at all times, not just to their faces, and chose them with care. Deceit was foreign to his nature and he was the most approachable of men, never losing control of himself in his dealings with
870 his servants nor with fellow-citizens.

The second subject of my speech is Eteoclus, a man in whom a different virtue was seen. Here was a young man who was by no means wealthy but who enjoyed the greatest honour in the Argolid. Many times friends would present him with gold but he did not allow it in his house; he did not wish to jeopardize his freedom of spirit by becoming a slave to money. When men committed crimes this man reserved his hatred for *them*, not their city, since he knew the unfairness of blaming citizens for the failings of their leader.   880

The third of these men in turn, Hippomedon, was of this stamp: from his boyhood onwards he shunned the pleasures of the Muses and a life of ease, preferring life in the wilds, where it gave him joy to pursue bravery by subjecting himself to a rigorous regime; he would engage in hunting, delighting in horses and bending the bow, in order to make himself of better service to his city.

Next there is the child of the huntress Atalanta, young Parthenopaeus, a man of unique beauty who was Arcadian by birth but who came to Inachus' stream and was raised in   890 Argos. On reaching manhood there, he began by observing the rule for all foreigners living in a new city: he gave the citizens no cause for offence or dislike and he avoided stubbornness in argument – the most common way a man makes himself unpopular, whether he is a natural citizen or from another place. He took his place in the ranks, like a native Argive, and fought for his country, taking pleasure in her successes and regretting any misfortunes that befell her. He was loved by as many men as women, but he guarded against committing any impropriety.   900

In the case of Tydeus, my praise, though brief, will be great. His spirit craved honour and this was its wealth, and his mind matched this in action if not in words. Do not then, Theseus, in the light of what I have said, feel surprise that these men dared to die before the battlements of Thebes. A   910 good upbringing instils a sense of shame and every man who has followed the path of honour is ashamed to become base. Courage can be taught, just as the young child is taught to say and hear the things it does not know. Whatever is learned in youth a man is liable to remember until old age. Give good instruction then to the young.

CHORUS [*addressing their dead sons in grief*]: O my child, for sorrow

920 *I reared you and carried you in my womb, enduring the pains of birth!*
And now, alas, the fruit of my labour is in Hades' power, while I in my
misery have no child to tend me in old age, though children were mine!

THESEUS: Yet Oicles' noble son has honour from the gods for
all men to see; they snatched him up, alive, and laid him to
rest in the depths of the earth with chariot and team. And
Oedipus' son, I mean Polynices, is truly deserving of our
praise; he was a guest in my home after he had left Cadmus'
930 city in self-imposed exile, before he crossed over to Argos.
But do you know what I want you to do regarding these men?

ADRASTUS: I know only this one thing: what you command, I
shall obey.

THESEUS: Then Capaneus who was struck down by the flame
from Zeus –

ADRASTUS: Would you have me bury him separately, as a sacred
corpse?[50]

THESEUS: Yes; but for all the others a single pyre will suffice.

ADRASTUS: Where then will you place his monument, once set
apart?

THESEUS: Here, by this temple, when I have erected a tomb of
stone.

ADRASTUS: My servants will see to this task at once.

THESEUS: I shall see to the dead men; [*to his soldiers:*] let the
940 corpses be carried out.

ADRASTUS [*to the* CHORUS]: Accompany your sons, unhappy
mothers.

THESEUS: Not so, Adrastus; your proposal is quite unsuitable.

ADRASTUS: In what way? Is it wrong for mothers to touch their
own children?

THESEUS: The sight of them so disfigured would destroy them.

ADRASTUS: Yes; corpses and their bloody wounds make painful
viewing.

THESEUS: Then why do you seek to impose such grief on these
women?

ADRASTUS: I was wrong. [*To the* CHORUS:] You must remain
here with steadfast hearts; Theseus is right in what he says.

Once we have cremated them, you shall collect their ashes for yourselves.

[*Turning away from them:*] O wretched mankind, why do you equip yourselves with spears and spill each other's blood? 950 Make an end of this! Cease your struggles and live at peace in your cities as tolerant neighbours. Life is such a brief moment; we should pass through it as easily as we can, avoiding pain.

[*The dead are carried to the funeral pyre.* THESEUS *and* ADRASTUS *leave, accompanied by the secondary chorus of* SONS *of the dead.*]

CHORUS [Strophe]: *No more am I blessed in children, no more blessed in sons, no share in happiness have I now with the women of Argos who have brought forth sons! No words of favour can the childless now expect from Artemis who assists in childbirth. My life is now no life, and, like a roving cloud, I am driven to and fro by heartless* 960 *winds.*

[Antistrophe:] *Seven mothers,*[51] *we bore seven sons to our sorrow, the most glorious of Argos' manhood. And now without son, without child, I am old and utterly wretched, to be numbered neither as dead nor as living, my fate hovering somewhere between the two.* 970

[Epode:] *Tears alone are left to me; in my home lie piteous tokens to remind me of my son, locks cut from my head and hair ungarlanded, and libations for the dead departed, and songs that golden-haired Apollo refuses to hear.*[52] *As I greet each dawn with laments, the tears I shed will never fail to soak the folds of the dress upon my breast.*

[*Enter* EVADNE,[53] *widow of Capaneus, dressed as a bride, on a cliff overhanging the temple precinct. She sings in ecstasy at the prospect of being reunited in death with her husband.*]

CHORUS: *But look! There outside the temple I see now the resting* 980 *place of Capaneus, the sacred tomb where Theseus has begun his rites in honour of the dead, and nearby I see also the famous wife of the warrior slain by the thunderbolt, Evadne, the child fathered by lord Iphis. Where have her steps taken her, why does she stand on yonder soaring cliff that towers above the temple here?*

EVADNE [Strophe]: *What radiant light was it that sun and moon* 990 *drove across the heavens that day, where fleet nymphs rode the*

brightness through the dark, that day when with its songs at my
marriage the city of Argos built a tower of happiness for me and my
bronze-mailed bridegroom, Capaneus? Here have I come now, running
1000 *from my home with a Bacchante's wild haste,*[54] *for I seek to share*
the same bright pyre, his tomb, to end in death this life of pain and
weariness. It makes death a thing of happiness when a loved one's
passing away is shared by one's own, should heaven so ordain it.

CHORUS-LEADER: Look, there you see it before you, the pyre,
just below where you stand, a treasure-store of Zeus, on
1010 which your husband lies, destroyed by the fiery lightning
stroke.

EVADNE [*Antistrophe*]: *I see it, yes, I see my end where I stand.*
May fortune attend my leap, as for fair fame's sake I plunge from
this rock into the pyre, and, clasping my husband in loving embrace
1020 *in the fire's radiant glow, my body pressed close to his, I shall pass*
to the halls of Persephone. [*Gesturing towards the pyre below:*] *Never*
shall I betray you as you lie beneath the earth by continuing to live.
Kindle the wedding torch,[55] *begin my nuptials! May posterity in*
Argos look upon this marriage as worthy and blessed, when ashes of
wedded husband unite in the breeze with those of noble wife, a
1030 *guileless spirit.*

[*Enter* IPHIS, *father of* EVADNE, *in agitation.*]

CHORUS-LEADER: But look, here comes your father in person,
old Iphis, to hear your strange, untimely words; he was a
stranger to them before but they will wound his ears now.

IPHIS: You women, like old Iphis no strangers to misery, I come
sorrowful and anxious for two of my kinfolk; I want to take
across the sea to his homeland the dead body of Eteoclus, my
son, whom the spearsmen of Thebes killed, and I am searching
for my daughter, Capaneus' wife, who has rushed in a frenzy
away from home, longing to share her husband's death. Until
1040 now, it's true, she was kept under watch in the house, but
when my recent troubles made me relax my guard, I found
she'd gone. I supposed it most likely that she'd be here. Tell
me if you have seen her.

EVADNE [*from above*]: Why do you question them? Here I am

upon this rock, father, here like a bird I hover over Capaneus'
pyre, poised in misery!

IPHIS: My child, what wind blows you on such a venture? What
made you steal away from home and come to this land?

EVADNE: It would cause you anger to hear what I intend; I do   1050
not want you to hear, father.

IPHIS: What's that? Isn't it right for your own father to know?

EVADNE: You would be a poor judge of my intention.

IPHIS: Why do you wear this dress? Why the need for such
adornment?

EVADNE: This garb has a glorious purpose, father.

IPHIS: It's certainly clear you're not a woman in mourning for
her husband.

EVADNE: Yes, there is a novel reason for my wearing these
garments.

IPHIS: Is this the sight you should present when standing next
to a funeral pyre?

EVADNE: It is; for that is where I go to win a glorious victory.

IPHIS: What victory will you win? You *must* tell me.   1060

EVADNE: Victory over all women that are seen by the sun.

IPHIS: In works that Athena inspires or in prudence?

EVADNE: In virtue; I will lie in death together with my husband.

IPHIS: What are you saying? What does this loathsome riddle
mean?

EVADNE: I am going to leap on to the pyre of my dead Capaneus.

IPHIS: Daughter, don't say such a thing in public!

EVADNE: This is just what I want, and every Argive must know.

IPHIS: But I will not give you permission to do this!

EVADNE: It does not matter; there is no way you can stop me.
See, I let myself go, no welcome act for you but welcome for   1070
myself and for my husband who will burn alongside me! [*She
leaps on to the pyre.*]

CHORUS: *Oh no! Lady, what a terrible thing you have done!*

IPHIS: Daughters of Argos, I am wretched, ruined!

CHORUS: *Your suffering has been terrible, poor man, and will you
bring yourself to look upon this rash deed?*

IPHIS: No one would you find, no man more pitiful than me.

CHORUS: *O you poor man, we pity you! In old age you have inherited the misfortune of Oedipus, you and my long-suffering city alike.*

1080 IPHIS: Oh, what sorrow! Why is it not possible for men to have a second youth and then be old again? In our homes if any errors are made we can have second thoughts and rectify them, but not so in our lives. If we could be young again and subsequently old again, we would put matters right in our second lives. When I saw other men becoming fathers, I began to desire offspring of my own, and this longing was wasting me away. But if I had reached this state and learned from 1090 experience what it is like for a father to lose his child, never would I have plumbed such depths of misery as this!

So be it; what am I to do now, wretch that I am? Should I enter my house? And then witness the building's utter emptiness, and, with it, the lack of any support for my life? Or should I go to the home of Capaneus here? Once, I admit, it gave me joy to make such a visit, when my dear child was alive. But she lives no more, the girl who used to hold me close each time, drawing my head down to kiss me on the 1100 cheek. When old age comes, a father's greatest joy is his daughter. Sons have bolder spirits, less loving when it comes to showing affection. Oh, take me away at once, take me to my home and there consign me to darkness, where I may waste away and starve to death this old body of mine! What good will it do to wait until I have collected my child's bones?

Old age, you are a wrestler hard to throw! How I hate your grip and how I hate all those who seek to prolong life 1110 by using magic foods and potions to channel its course away from death! What they should do, once they become a burden on earth, is die and be done with it, leaving room for younger men.

[*Exit* IPHIS. *The secondary chorus of* SONS *of the dead*[56] *now enters carrying the ashes of their cremated fathers and behind them walk* THESEUS *and* ADRASTUS. *The* SONS *engage in sung lamentation with the* CHORUS *of mothers.*]

CHORUS: *Ah! Here are the bones of our slain sons being carried in procession. Give me your hands, servants, support a frail old woman (mourning for my son has robbed me of all strength); I have lived through many a year and have melted away in grief at my many afflictions. What greater suffering would you devise for the human* 1120 *heart than to look upon one's children dead?*

SONS [Strophe]: *Poor mother, I bear, I bear my father's bones from the pyre, a burden made heavy by anguish, all that I have gathered together in this little space.*

CHORUS: *Oh, the pain! O son of my son, you bring to his loving mother tears for the dead, a tiny handful of ash to replace the man* 1130 *who once stood great in renown in Mycenae.*

SONS [Antistrophe]: *Childless, childless you are; and I, bereft, alas! of my poor father, shall inherit a desolate house and live an orphan's life, deprived of a father's protecting hand.*

CHORUS: *Oh, oh! All for nothing the effort invested in my children, all for no return the pain of giving birth, the nurture of a mother, the care of sleepless eyes, my loving kisses!*

SONS [Strophe]: *They have gone, their lives are at an end. O father, father! They have gone.*

CHORUS: *In the heavens they have their dwelling now, reduced to ashes* 1140 *in the fire; on wings they have made the journey to Hades.*

SONS: *Father, do you hear your son's lament for you? Shall the day yet come when, shield in arm, I shall take revenge for your death? How your son prays for this!*

[Antistrophe:] *Justice for my father may come yet, if it is heaven's will.*

CHORUS: *Does this evil not yet sleep? I cry in sorrow for my fate; I have had enough of lamenting, enough of sorrow.*

SONS: *One day I will appear in armour of bronze and Asopus will welcome me with his glittering stream as I lead an army of Danaus'* 1150 *people to avenge the killing of my father.*

[Strophe:] *I think I see you still, father, before my eyes . . .*

CHORUS: *. . . kissing you on your beloved cheek, . . .*

SONS: *. . . but the encouragement of your words is gone, vanished in air.*

CHORUS: *To us both he has left anguish – to me his mother, and to you a sorrow at your father's loss that will never leave you.*

SONS [Antistrophe]: *I am crushed by the burden of this weight.*

CHORUS: *Bring them to me, let me clasp my child's ashes to my breast!*

1160 SONS: *These words are unbearable, I weep to hear them; they touch my very heart.*

CHORUS: *My child, you have gone; no more shall I see you, loving treasure of your loving mother.*

THESEUS: Adrastus and you women of Argive race, you see these boys carrying in their hands their noble fathers' remains, recovered by me. These ashes my city and I present to them. It is your duty to keep this act in grateful memory, in recog-
1170 nition of my service to you, and to instil the same message in these boys, that they should honour Athens and for ever hand down the memory of this kindness from one generation to the next.[57] I call upon Zeus and the heavenly gods to witness how reverently we treated you.

ADRASTUS: Theseus, we know all the noble service you have rendered the land of Argos, meeting its pleas with benefaction, and our gratitude will never grow old. We have been nobly served and so must do you noble service.

1180 THESEUS: Is there any further way in which I may assist you?

ADRASTUS: Fare well; this is what both you and your city deserve.

THESEUS: And so we shall; I wish you too the same happiness.

[*Enter above the temple the goddess* ATHENA.]

ATHENA: Listen, Theseus, to these words spoken by Athena, telling you what you should do and how to benefit your city by your actions. Do not give these bones to these boys to take away to the land of Argos, yielding them up so lightly, but rather in recompense for your sweat and toil, and your city's, extract firstly an oath. [*Pointing to* ADRASTUS:] And Adrastus here must swear: as Argos' king he has the authority to swear
1190 on behalf of all the land of Danaus' folk. The oath shall be that never will Argives march in open war against this land, and, should others do so, that they will block their path with

spears; but if they do so march, breaking their oath, then they should pray for shame and ruin to befall the land of Argos.

Now listen while I tell you where you must perform the sacrifices to ratify this oath. You have in your home a bronze-footed tripod that Heracles once, while hastening upon another urgent task after his sack of Ilium, told you to set up at the Pythian altar. Make a sacrifice of three sheep, slitting 1200 their three throats above this tripod, and then inscribe the words of the oath inside the round bowl. After this you must give it into the keeping of the god who presides over Delphi, as a record of the oath and an emblem for all Greeks to witness. And when you slit their throats in sacrifice, causing the blood to flow from the wounds, conceal the sharp-edged knife deep in the earth right beside the seven pyres. If ever Argives march against Athens, they will be shown this relic and it will send them home again in fear and shame. Only when this is done should you let the dead leave this land. As for the precinct 1210 where their bodies were purified by fire, hard by the turning to the Isthmus, leave it sacred to the god.

So much I have to say to you. For the sons of the Argives my words are these: when you come of age, you will sack Ismenus' city in vengeance for the killing of your dead fathers. You, Aegialeus, shall be appointed the young commander, taking your father's place, and at your side, arriving from Aetolia, shall be Tydeus' son, the one named Diomedes by his father. As soon as beards have darkened your cheeks, your army of Argives, rich in bronze, must launch itself against 1220 the battlements and seven gates of Thebes. When you are lions full grown and cubs no more, men fit to lay a city waste, the Thebans will truly regret your coming. This nothing can alter. You shall be called throughout Greece 'The Successors', and men of later generations shall sing songs in your memory, such an army will it be that you lead to victory by the gods' favour.

THESEUS: Lady Athena, I will do your bidding; you have always kept me on the true course, free from error. I will bind this

1230 man by an oath. Only keep me on the right track; if Athens enjoys your gracious favour, we shall live henceforth secure.

CHORUS: *Let us go, Adrastus, let us give this man and his city our oath; such labours as they have performed for us deserve our reverent gratitude.*

ELECTRA

PREFACE TO *ELECTRA*

Over all dramas which deal with the legend of Orestes' matricide falls the great shadow of Aeschylus' *Oresteia*, one of the towering achievements of the Greek stage. We can see that it already enjoyed something of a 'classic' status in the late fifth century BC: in Aristophanes' *Frogs* it is the prologue of the *Libation-Bearers*, the second play of the Oresteian trilogy, that is taken as the sample for criticism of Aeschylus; and there are many passages in extant Sophocles and Euripides where we can discern the strong influence of the older tragedian's masterpiece. The story of Orestes' return in disguise, his meeting with his sister Electra, and his killing of the adulterous Clytemnestra and her lover Aegisthus, was told by both Sophocles and Euripides in plays entitled *Electra*; which is earlier cannot readily be established, but both look back to the Aeschylean treatment of the theme, and comparison is inevitable. The imitation and transformation of the *Libation-Bearers* by Euripides seems particularly clear and pointed: it has been suggested that the younger poet may have been reacting to a recent re-performance of the Aeschylean play or plays.

Some of the differences between the two plays arise from the fact that Aeschylus was composing a trilogy, Euripides a single work. The *Libation-Bearers* deals with the revenge of Orestes, whereas his consequent pursuit by the Furies and eventual acquittal at Athens are the subject of the final play of the *Oresteia*. Moreover, in Aeschylus we have already witnessed the crimes of Clytemnestra and the baseness of Aegisthus: although the matricide remains a horrifying deed, we are in no doubt that what they did was wrong and that Orestes has a solemn duty to avenge his father's death. Indeed, Aeschylus makes little of Aegisthus' death: as Orestes says himself, he got what he deserved. In

Euripides the position is different: the play focuses on the deaths of Aegisthus and especially Clytemnestra, and, despite the strength of Electra's hatred, neither is wholly unsympathetic.

Other changes reflect Euripides' regular interests and dramatic preferences. In Aeschylus' *Libation-Bearers* the setting was at first the royal tomb of Agamemnon, later the palace where Clytemnestra and Aegisthus hold sway. Euripides transfers the scene to a rustic hut, in order to incorporate a new character, Electra's rustic husband, an impoverished but virtuous farmer. The greater prominence of Electra, reflected in the title of the play, is also typical, for Euripides' principal figures are often female. In Aeschylus Electra vanished from the play after her brother had returned and embarked on his task, and was never mentioned again in the trilogy; the vengeance is solely the concern of Orestes, the son and heir. In Euripides the emphasis is reversed: Electra is much more fully characterized, and far more determined on revenge, whereas Orestes cuts a rather unprepossessing figure. It is she who undertakes to arrange a trap for her mother, she who presses Orestes on when his nerve fails him. In Aeschylus she had been absent from the stage and the audience's mind when Clytemnestra was slain; in Sophocles she stands outside the palace and utters a dreadful cry of encouragement ('strike twice as hard, if you have the strength', Sophocles *Electra* 1415); in Euripides she herself participates in her mother's murder (1165, 1168, 1225).

The two halves of the Euripidean play, covering first the reunion of Orestes and Electra and second the accomplishment of the revenge-plot, are very different in tone. The first half moves at a leisured pace, with hundreds of lines passing before Orestes is actually recognized (protracted recognition-scenes are something of a speciality of Euripides', with *Iphigenia among the Taurians* offering the prize example). The country setting, the placid dignity of Electra's rustic husband, her own bitterness at her degraded life-style, make for unusual variety of tone, even some near-comedy (71ff., 184ff., 404ff.). We recognize the tendency to diminish the grandeur of tragedy, for which Euripides was criticized, with much exaggeration, in Aristophanes' *Frogs*. Humour is also close to the surface in the remarkable passage in which the old servant brings Electra 'proofs' that Orestes has returned – proofs of a kind that the Aeschylean Electra had accepted, but which the more sceptical Euripidean heroine rejects on grounds of implausibility (cf. General Introduction, p. xxii). Here Euripides is perhaps gently mocking the archaic manner of the great Aeschylus; yet the servant is correct, and this is not simply parody.

The second half of the play, in which first Aegisthus is assassinated while performing sacrifice, then Clytemnestra lured to Electra's cottage and slaughtered, differs radically in tone and emotional intensity. Euripides seems to have gone out of his way to make the killings particularly repulsive. Not only is Electra filled with almost psychotic hatred, but Aegisthus is killed in a shocking, even sacrilegious manner; moreover, Clytemnestra arrives at the cottage because of a false tale that Electra has given birth, and she speaks mildly and reasonably to her ferociously resentful daughter. The Aeschylean characterization is turned upsidedown. Most dramatic of all is the breakdown of the murderers in the final scenes: both brother and sister are shattered by the horrifying deed they have performed. Even Electra's hate is dispelled: she sorrowfully lays a mantle over her mother's corpse, 'we who felt hatred for you as well as love' (1230). There is no sense of triumph, no words of congratulation from the chorus.

Even the divine intervention which concludes the drama seems to do so in a way that is less satisfying than we might expect, and which clearly brings little consolation to the humans involved. We might have expected the appearance of Apollo whose oracle issued the command to Orestes to avenge his father; instead the play ends with the Dioscuri, Castor and Pollux, brothers of Clytemnestra but now divine. Far from putting all to rights, they ordain separation of brother and sister and exile for Orestes. Whereas in Aeschylus he was finally restored to his father's kingdom, in this play he is to wander and settle eventually elsewhere. Electra too must face a future distant from her homeland. Although the Dioscuri do indeed prophesy Orestes' flight to Athens and his acquittal by the Areopagus court (the main subject of Aeschylus' third play, *Eumenides*), the rapid résumé of future events (1250–75) seems to do little to palliate present and continuing suffering. Nor is all resolved even on the divine plane: Castor himself ventures to criticize Apollo for his murderous command: 'Phoebus, Phoebus – I say no more, as he is my royal lord; wisdom is his but wisdom was absent from the command he gave you' (1245–6). The killing of Clytemnestra is still divinely commanded, as it was in Aeschylus; but whereas there it was a grim and terrible necessity, here the deed revolts not only the doers but even the spokesmen of divinity. This complex reworking of Aeschylus embraces but goes beyond both aesthetic and moral criticism: the target and victim is not so much the dead Aeschylus, but the audience themselves, who are made to look again, aghast, at what the myth really means in terms of the human emotional and psychological cost; and if they expect all tragedies to sew things up with a satisfying formal close, or any god to be able to answer all the questions the tragedy poses, the audience are made to think again.

CHARACTERS

FARMER, *husband of Electra*
ELECTRA, *daughter of Agamemnon and Clytemnestra*
ORESTES, *brother of Electra*
PYLADES, *friend of Orestes*
CHORUS *of Argive women*
OLD MAN, *former tutor to Agamemnon*
MESSENGER, *servant of Orestes*
CLYTEMNESTRA, *widowed queen of Agamemnon, married to Aegisthus*
CASTOR AND POLLUX, *divine sons of Zeus, brothers of Clytemnestra*

[*The scene is a peasant's cottage, the homestead of a poor* FARMER [1] *who lives in the mountains overlooking the plain of Argos. It is just before dawn as the owner emerges from his dwelling, near to which is an altar of Apollo with a rough statue of the god.*]

FARMER: O Argos, ancient land, and you, waters of Inachus! From your shores in days gone by King Agamemnon set sail for the land of Troy, when he had raised a fighting force of a thousand ships. To Argos here he returned, having killed Priam who ruled in the land of Troy, and captured Dardanus' famous city, and on the high temple walls he hung many a trophy of foreign conquest. Up to this point he enjoyed success; but in his home he met his end, victim of the treachery of his wife, Clytemnestra, and the violence of Thyestes' son, Aegisthus.

Now he is no more; he has forsaken the ancient sceptre of Tantalus, and Aegisthus is king in Argos, and at his side sits the daughter of Tyndareus, wife of Agamemnon. As for those he left behind in his palace when he sailed for Troy, the lad Orestes and his daughter Electra: his father's old tutor [2] smuggled the boy out when he was in danger of being murdered by Aegisthus and gave him to Strophius to rear in the land of Phocis; but Electra remained in her father's house and when she grew to the full bloom of womanhood, the foremost men of Greece came to ask her hand in marriage. But Aegisthus kept her in the palace and would not let any bridegroom come into contact with her; he was afraid she might bear a child to some prince who would exact revenge

136

for Agamemnon. But even this measure left him a prey to fear: she might bear a child secretly to some man of noble birth. He therefore determined to kill her, but her mother, for all her cruelty, rescued her from his violent hands. As far as her husband's death was concerned, she had an excuse; but she feared the murder of her children might give rise to ill feeling.

This prompted Aegisthus to devise the following scheme. He issued word that gold would be the reward of any man who should kill the exile who had fled the land, Agamemnon's son, and to me he gave Electra to have as my wife, to me, a man with Mycenaeans as forefathers (here at least I am beyond criticism; but for all the distinction of my line, I am not a man of means, and nobility is undermined by poverty³). His aim was to weaken his own fear by giving her to one so weak himself. If a man of standing had won her, he would have roused Agamemnon's spilled blood from its slumber and Aegisthus would then have got his just deserts. Now, as the Cyprian is my witness, I have never brought shame to her bed; virgin she was and remains to this day. I think it a disgrace to take the daughter of a royal house and force her, when my status is not worthy of her. But I groan for the sake of poor Orestes, my supposed brother-in-law, if ever he returns to Argos and witnesses his sister's less than happy marriage. If any man calls me a fool for taking a young maid into my home and not laying a finger on her, I'd have him know he is measuring self-control by his own flawed standards, and is himself the fool he calls me.

[ELECTRA *enters from the cottage, carrying on her head a pot for drawing water.*]

ELECTRA: O black night that nurtures the golden stars! In your shade I go to draw water from the river, carrying this pot that rests on my head, and I cry to my father, uttering my groans to the wide heavens. It is not a question of being reduced by need to this action, but rather that I want the gods to see how brutally Aegisthus treats me. It is to please him, her husband,

60 that my mother, Tyndareus' shameless child, has thrown me out of the palace; she has borne other children to Aegisthus and so turned Orestes and myself into second-class offspring in our own home.[4]

FARMER: Poor woman, why do you give yourself this trouble, toiling away on my behalf and refusing to stop when I tell you to stop, and you raised in a palace?

ELECTRA: In my eyes you are a friend to match the gods; you have behaved impeccably towards me in my sorry condition. It is no small comfort in life, when troubles come, to find

70 someone to cure them as I have found you. You do not ask it of me, but to the best of my strength I must help you carry out your work, trying to ease your toil and so make your burden lighter. You have enough work outside to keep you busy; it is my job to make everything ready in the house. When a man comes home from working his land, it warms his heart to find all in good order under his roof.

FARMER: Well, if that is how you feel, carry on; the spring is no great distance from where we live. Now the sun's rising, I'll drive my oxen to the fields and sow the soil. No shirker could

80 scrape a living by praying to the gods all day; it's effort that's needed. [*Both leave to perform their separate tasks. Two young men with servants enter in travellers' clothes. They are* ORESTES, *the exiled prince, and his friend* PYLADES.[5]]

ORESTES: Pylades, there is no man in this world I trust more than you, no one whose friendship I value more, whose hearth I would more gladly share. Alone of my friends you have honoured Orestes in the sorry state I find myself, victim of Aegisthus' brutality, the man who helped my witch-mother kill my father. Here I stand on Argive soil, newly come from the god's oracle, without any man's knowledge,[6] to punish my father's murderers, their blood for his. In this night just

90 past I visited my father's tomb. There I offered the tribute of my tears, together with a lock cut from my head, and sacrificed a sheep, spilling its blood on the altar, unknown to the rulers whose word is law in this land. As for the city, I

have not set foot inside its walls but have stopped here at the
frontier, as I want to achieve two things: to escape to another
land, should some observer on patrol recognize me, and to
try to find my sister (they say she is a maid no more but lives
a married woman); if we can make contact I want to enlist
her help in the murder and to get reliable information on   100
what is happening in Argos.

But Dawn comes upon us, lifting up her pale features; let
us try a new path. We will come across someone, a ploughman
may be, or some slave-woman, whom we will ask if my sister
lives in these parts. [ELECTRA *re-enters:*] But wait; here I see
a woman, a servant,[7] who carries on her close-cropped head
a heavy pot of water from the spring. Let's crouch down here,
Pylades, and see if we can learn anything from the slave-woman
about the business that has brought us to this land.   110
[*They withdraw behind the cover of the altar as* ELECTRA *comes
forward slowly, carrying on her head the water-pot, now full. She
begins to sing to herself a song of mourning.*][8]

ELECTRA [Strophe]: *Quicken your step (it is time); onward, onward,
weeping as you go. Oh, what misery I know! I was born the daughter
of Agamemnon, my mother was Clytemnestra, hateful child of Tyndareus, and 'Electra the wretched' is the name my countrymen call me.
Ah, what miserable suffering I endure, how loathsome is my life!*   120
*O father, Agamemnon, in Hades you lie, butchered by your own
wife and Aegisthus!*

[Mesode:] *On you go, rouse the same lamentation, give vent to
your tears – there is some pleasure in that.*

[Antistrophe:] *Quicken your step (it is time); onward, onward,
weeping as you go. Oh, what misery I know! O my poor brother,
what city, what household do you wander in, now that you have left*   130
*your pitiful sister behind in our ancestral home, in the depths of woe?
Return, I pray, and rescue your poor Electra from her suffering –
Zeus, ah, Zeus! – step ashore at Argos, a wanderer no more, and
avenge your father for his blood so shamefully spilled!*

[*A servant comes in and is addressed by* ELECTRA.]

[Strophe:] *Take this pot from my head and put it down. I wish*   140 to cry aloud the lament I send my father in the hours of night. A song of sorrow, a song of death have I for you, father; to you below the earth I utter the lamentation that is my constant offering, day by day, tearing my cheeks with these nails and pummelling this shorn head at your death.

150   [Mesode:] Ah, ah, tear at your scalp! I weep for you, father, poor father, as a clear-voiced swan by a flowing river calls upon its beloved sire that has perished in the treacherous coils of a hunter's snare,

    [Antistrophe:] when you had immersed yourself in that most final of baths and had lain down – ah, the pity of it! – to meet your
160 death! How cruelly the axe cut into you, father, how cruelly they schemed against you on your return from Troy! Not with a victor's headband, not with garlands did your wife welcome you back; she made you the wretched victim of Aegisthus' two-edged sword before taking him as her treacherous lord!

    [The CHORUS enters at this point. They are local women of the Argive countryside.]

CHORUS [Strophe]: Daughter of Agamemnon, Electra, I have come to your dwelling in the wilds. A man has come, a Mycenaean, a
170 drinker of milk who roams the mountains;[9] his news is that in two days' time the folk of Argos are declaring a festival and all maidens are to go to Hera's temple.[10]

ELECTRA: My poor heart beats fast, my friends, but not at the thought of fine clothes or golden necklaces; I will not order the dance for the
180 maids of Argos or tread the ground among them with whirling feet. Tears are my companions by night, tears fill my wretched thoughts by day. Look at my dirty hair and these ragged clothes: are they fitting, would you say, for Agamemnon's royal daughter or for Troy that remembers once yielding the victory to my sire?

190 CHORUS [Antistrophe]: Mighty is the goddess; come, borrow from me a closely-woven dress to put on, and gold jewellery to add to the splendour of fine clothing. Do you imagine you will prevail over your enemies by these tears of yours, if you fail to honour the gods? It is prayers, not laments, you must offer the gods in worship if the sun is to shine on you once more, child.

ELECTRA: No god listens to the voice of the unhappy one or heeds my

father's blood, spilled so many years ago. Oh, how I think of them,   200
the murdered one and the wanderer who yet lives! Somewhere he
dwells in another land, poor lad, a vagrant living in servants' quarters,
he, the son of such a famous father! As for me, my spirit pines away
as I live under a common labourer's roof, driven from the palace of
my forefathers to dwell on the crags of a mountain, while my mother   210
has taken another man as her husband and shares with him a bed
whose sheets are stained with the blood of murder.

CHORUS-LEADER: Your mother's sister, Helen, bears responsibility for many troubles that have afflicted the Greeks and
your house.

> [ORESTES *and* PYLADES *come forward, startling* ELECTRA
> *by their sudden appearance.*]

ELECTRA: Oh no! Women, I put a stop to my lament. Strangers,
see, have been hiding at the altar by the cottage and are leaving
their place of ambush! [*To the leader of the* CHORUS:] Let's get
away from these villains – you run along the track, I'll dash
into the cottage!

ORESTES: Stay, poor girl! You have nothing to fear at my
hands!   220

ELECTRA [*throwing herself down before Apollo's statue*]: O Phoebus,
Apollo, I beg you, save me from death!

ORESTES: There are others I should like to kill, less dear to me
than you.

ELECTRA [*as he tries to raise her*]: Go away! You have no right to
touch me – take your hands off me!

ORESTES: There is no one I have a greater right to touch.[11]

ELECTRA: Then how is it you lurk next to my house with a
sword?

ORESTES: Wait. Listen, and soon you will accept what I am
saying.

ELECTRA: I shall wait; whatever I do, I am yours; you are the
stronger.

ORESTES: I come with news of your brother.

ELECTRA: O my dear friend, is he alive or dead?

ORESTES: Alive. I want to give you the good news first.   230

ELECTRA: Then happiness be yours to pay you for such welcome news!

ORESTES: Happiness is a gift I offer for us both to enjoy together.

ELECTRA: Where on earth does the wretch live out his wretched exile?

ORESTES: He goes miserably from city to city, not living under any one set of laws.[12]

ELECTRA: You don't mean he has to beg for his daily food?

ORESTES: No, but an exile cannot rely on his own resources.

ELECTRA: What message have you brought from him?

ORESTES: He asks if you are alive and, if so, what your circumstances are.

ELECTRA: Don't you see straightaway how haggard I look?

240 ORESTES: Worn away by your sorrows – it makes me weep.

ELECTRA: And my head, my hair, shorn by the razor?

ORESTES: It torments you, no doubt, the thought of your brother and murdered father.

ELECTRA: Oh yes, yes! They are dearer to me than anything.

ORESTES: O my poor girl, how do you suppose your brother feels about you?

ELECTRA: He is somewhere else; he shows his love from a distance.

ORESTES: Why do you live here, so far from the town?

ELECTRA: I am a married woman sir, in a marriage that is like death.

ORESTES: Ah, how I pity your brother! To which of the Mycenaeans?

ELECTRA: He is not the man my father once hoped to give me to.

250 ORESTES: Tell me, so I may hear and tell your brother.

ELECTRA [*with a gesture towards the* FARMER*'s cottage*]: I live far from town in his house here.

ORESTES: A common labourer or cowherd is fit for such a home.

ELECTRA: He may lack means but he is a gentleman; in his treatment of me he has been virtuous.

142

ORESTES: Describe this virtue your married lord has shown.

ELECTRA: On no occasion has he ventured to enter my bed.

ORESTES: Was there some pious reason for this, or did he find you unattractive?

ELECTRA: It was my parents – he thought it wrong to bring dishonour on them.

ORESTES: Was he not delighted to find a wife such as you?

ELECTRA: My friend, he thinks the man who gave me away was not entitled to do so.

ORESTES: I understand; he was afraid that Orestes would return some day and punish him. 260

ELECTRA: That was his fear, certainly; but at the same time he knew better than to take advantage of a woman.

ORESTES: Ah! He is a gentleman, the fellow you describe, and deserves a reward.

ELECTRA: Yes, if ever my absent brother does come home.

ORESTES: And your own mother tolerated this?

ELECTRA: Women give their hearts to their lovers, my friend, not to their children.

ORESTES: What was Aegisthus' motive for treating you with such contempt?

ELECTRA: By giving me to a man like this he wanted my children to grow up as nobodies.

ORESTES: Of course – no sons to take revenge at a later date!

ELECTRA: That was his plan; I pray he pays in full for it!

ORESTES: Does your mother's husband know you are a virgin? 270

ELECTRA: No; we keep quiet about this and rob him of the knowledge.

ORESTES [gesturing to the CHORUS]: And are these women who listen to our words well disposed to you?

ELECTRA: They are; they will keep the words between us a close secret.[13]

ORESTES: And how will Orestes deal with this situation, if he comes to Argos?

ELECTRA: What a question! That does you no credit; what time is there like the present?

ORESTES: Suppose he comes, then: how would he kill his father's murderers?

ELECTRA: By daring to do what my father's enemies dared to do to him.

ORESTES: Would you dare to join him in killing your mother?

ELECTRA: I would, and in my hands I'd have the selfsame axe that killed my father!

280 ORESTES: Is this what I should tell him? You have no qualms?

ELECTRA: I would be prepared to die if only I could slit my mother's throat![14]

ORESTES: Ah, would that Orestes could hear this!

ELECTRA: Well sir, I would not know him if I saw him.

ORESTES: And it's no wonder, either, since the pair of you were youngsters when you were separated.

ELECTRA: There is only one person among my friends who would recognize him.

ORESTES: The man they say snatched him away from death?

ELECTRA: Yes, an old man, my father's tutor in time gone by.

ORESTES: And did he receive burial, your father, after his death?

ELECTRA: Burial after a fashion: they flung his body out of the house.

290 ORESTES: Ah no! Not that, surely? [*Recovering his control:*] A man feels the pain even of a stranger's sufferings when he hears them. But tell me, so that with knowledge I may bring your brother this story of yours, one that he must hear, however much grief it causes him. No man without finer feeling can know what it is to pity; intellect is needed for this. And men of intelligence have cause to regret their capacity for such awareness.[15]

CHORUS-LEADER: My heart is filled with the same desire as this man's. Living as I do far from the town, I do not know of the crimes done in Argos and I too want to be told now.[16]

300 ELECTRA: Well, I will speak, if I must (and to a friend I must), of the heavy blows that Fortune has dealt my father and myself. But since you press me to speak, I beg you, sir, take word to Orestes of what my father suffered and what I still suffer. Tell

him firstly of the sort of clothes I wear, fit for a serving woman, of the dirt that weighs me down and the kind of dwelling I live in, I who was raised in a king's palace! Tell him how, to keep clothes on my back and avoid going without, I work long hours at the loom, making clothes for myself, and how I fetch and carry water from the spring with my own hands. I have no part in religious festivals, no share in the dancing, and as a virgin still I shun the company of married women. I am ashamed to think of Castor, my kinsman, who wanted me for his bride before he joined the gods. 310

Then there is my mother: surrounded by the spoils of Troy she sits on the throne, while Asian maidservants have their place at her side, the women my father won when he sacked their city, wearing their Trojan gowns fastened with clasps of gold.[17] Further, though inside the palace my father's blood has turned black and rotten, the man who took his life steps into his very chariot and rides around in it, his murderous 320 hands triumphantly grasping the sceptre with which my father exercised command over the Greek host. Agamemnon's tomb stands without honour; never yet has it received libations or even a spray of myrtle, and the altar is bare of all ornament. And when wine has made my mother's husband drunk, this splendid man, so we are told, jumps upon my father's tomb and pelts the stone memorial with rocks. These are the words he dares to speak against us: 'Where's your baby boy, Orestes, then? Right here is he, defending your tomb like a hero?' 330 These are the insults[18] slung at him in his absence.

Oh please sir, I beg you, pass on this news! There are many who summon him and I merely convey their wishes: these hands of mine, this tongue, this my suffering heart and shaven head, and the man who was his own father. It would bring him disgrace if, after his father has brought Troy to its knees, he should lack the strength to kill *one* man on his own in single combat, though he has youth on his side and is sprung from a better sire. —

[*The* FARMER *enters from the fields.*]

CHORUS-LEADER: And here I see your husband, making his
340   way towards the house, his labours over.

FARMER: What's this? Who are these strangers I see at my door?
What has brought them to my cottage here in the wilds? Am
I the one they want to see? It brings shame on a woman if she
stands talking to young men.

ELECTRA: My good friend, don't be suspicious on my account.
You will know the truth; these strangers have come to me
bringing news of Orestes! [*To* ORESTES *and* PYLADES:]
Gentlemen, please excuse his words.

FARMER: What do they say? Is the man alive? Does he see the
sun's light?

ELECTRA: He is alive, or rather they say he is; I cannot believe
350   what they tell me.

FARMER: And is he mindful at all of your father's suffering and
your own?

ELECTRA: I can only hope so; a man in exile lacks resources.

FARMER: What word from Orestes have they brought?

ELECTRA: They have been sent by him to observe my degradation.

FARMER: Well, this they've seen in part, and no doubt you've
told them the rest.[19]

ELECTRA: They know; there is no detail they have not been
given.

FARMER: Then my door should have been opened to them a
long time ago! [*To* ORESTES *and* PYLADES:] Come inside
my home; instead of fine words you will be given such
360   hospitality as my house keeps in store. No objections now,
please! You have come from a friend and so you are my
friends. A poor man I may be, but I shall not show a low-born
character.

ORESTES [*to* ELECTRA:] In heaven's name, is this the man who
has been helping you to make a fraud of your marriage to
spare Orestes' blushes?

ELECTRA: This is the one they call poor Electra's wedded
husband.

146

ORESTES: Oh, how true it is:[20] there is no sure way of testing a
man's true worth, for human nature has no rhyme or reason
to it. Before now I have seen a man of no merit whose father
was noble, yes, and goodness flourishing in the children of
low-born parents; I have seen hunger in the soul of a wealthy   370
man and greatness of mind in one of slender means. Take this
man: his importance is small in the eyes of Argos' citizens,   380
he has no great family name to make him swell with pride
and yet, for all his humble origins, he has shown himself no
stranger to nobility. O you misguided men, filled with silly
imaginings, put a stop to your folly and judge a man's nobility
by the company he keeps and how he behaves to others!   390

But let us accept this house's hospitality; we both deserve
it, Agamemnon's son, on whose business we have come, who
is not here, and the man who *is* here. [*To the servants:*] You
men, we must go inside this dwelling. When it comes to
receiving hospitality, I'd rather have an impoverished host
whose intentions were kind than a wealthy one. [*To* ELEC-
TRA*:*] Now, I accept with thanks this man's invitation under
his roof, but I could have wished it was your brother, crowned
with success, who led me into his house, crowned with success.
Perhaps he may come; the answers from Loxias' oracle are to
be trusted, but I put little faith in mortal prophecy. [*They*   400
follow their servants into the cottage.]

CHORUS-LEADER: Now more than before, Electra, my heart
feels the glow of happiness; fortune has at last begun to turn
and we may yet have her blessing!

ELECTRA [*to the* FARMER]: Whatever are you doing? Why have
you invited these strangers into your home when you know
it is so poor and you are so beneath them?

FARMER: Eh? If they are gentlemen as they seem, will they not
be as much at home in humble as in grand surroundings?

ELECTRA: Well, there's nothing grand about your surroundings
and you've made a fool of yourself! Anyway, go now to my
father's dear old tutor who was banished from the town; he
keeps watch over his flocks around the River Tanaus, the   410

boundary that separates the lands of Argos and of Sparta. Tell him to come and to provide some food for us to entertain these new arrivals at our home. He will be pleased, I assure you, and will thank the gods in prayer when he hears that the boy whose life he once saved is alive. We would not get anything out of my father's house from my mother; such news would cost us dear if in her hard heart she came to know her Orestes was still alive.

FARMER: Well, if that's what you would like, I'll deliver this
420 message to the old man. Go into the cottage right away and make your preparations inside. A woman can find many things to eke out a meal if she wants to. There's certainly enough in there still to fill their stomachs for one day. When I am minded to play the host at such a time but fail, I consider what great power money has, both for entertaining guests and to pay for a sick person to be nursed back to life. Money for one's daily
430 food comes to little; every man whose belly is filled gets his fair share, whether he's rich or poor. [ELECTRA *goes into the cottage and the* FARMER *leaves on his errand.*]

CHORUS [Strophe]: *You famous ships that voyaged once to Troy with your numberless oars, in company with the Nereids as you escorted their dancing, where the music-loving dolphin leapt and twirled about your dark-blue prows as he guided Achilles, Thetis' son, the fleet of*
440 *foot, with Agamemnon to the banks of Trojan Simois!*[21]

[Antistrophe:] *The Nereids had left Euboea's headlands behind them, carrying the armour of gold, the shield that was wrought on Hephaestus' anvil,*[22] *and through Pelion, through the holy glens of steep Ossa where the Nymphs keep watch, they had gone, searching for the home where a Centaur father*[23] *reared the son of sea-nymph Thetis, to be a light to Greece and serve the sons of Atreus with his*
450 *swiftness of foot.*

[Strophe:] *In Nauplia's harbour I heard of your famous shield, son of Thetis, from one who had come from Troy, and of the blazons it wore fashioned on its circle to strike terror into the Phrygians. On the rim running round the shield was Perseus,*[24] *cutter of the Gorgon's throat, flying over the sea on winged sandals and holding the creature's*

head, with, at his side, Hermes, messenger of Zeus, Maia's son   460
who dwells in the wilds.

[Antistrophe:] *At the shield's centre shone out the sun's brilliant
disc, swept along by winged steeds, and the stars dancing in the
heavens, the Pleiades and Hyades that made Hector blanch and run.*[25]
On the helmet of beaten gold were Sphinxes, carrying in their talons   470
*the prey their songs had won, while on the breastplate the lioness that
breathes fire*[26] *at the sight of Pirene's steed was bounding away in
swift retreat.*

[Epode:] *On the hilt of his murderous sword a team of four horses
was galloping onward and over their backs swirled a cloud of black
dust. Such were the doughty warriors who fought under your royal
lord, daughter of Tyndareus, the husband you killed alongside your*   480
*lover, you villainous woman. And so in future days the gods will
send upon your head the penalty of death. The day will dawn when
I shall see your blood spilled by the sword beneath your crimsoned
neck!*

[ELECTRA *comes out from the cottage. An* OLD MAN *makes
his way slowly on to the stage.*]

OLD MAN: Where is she, where is she, my princess, my mistress,
the child of Agamemnon, my ward of early days? What a steep
approach it is to this house for the feet of a wrinkled old fellow
like me! Still, it's friends I'm going to; I must drag along this   490
poor bent back and shaky knees. [*To* ELECTRA:] Ah, daughter
(I've just set eyes on you now beside the cottage), here I am,
with a new-born lamb from my fold, taken from under its
mother, and garlands too, and cheeses I've taken from the
press, and this well-seasoned treasure-trove of Dionysus,
worth your respect with its fine bouquet; there's not a lot of
it but it's excellent to mix a cup of it with a weaker drink. Let
someone come and take these things into the house for your
guests. As for me, my eyes are wet with tears; let me wipe   500
them dry with this rag from my clothes.

ELECTRA: Old man, why are your eyes brimming like this with
tears? Can it be that after so long my troubles have reminded
you of troubles past? Or is it Orestes' unhappy exile that makes

you grieve, that and my father whom once you had in your
care and watched growing to manhood – little joy it brought
you and yours!

OLD MAN: Little joy; yet let me tell you what caused my tears
to flow: I went to his tomb as part of my journey and, throwing
510   myself down, I wept to find it deserted. I opened the wineskin
I was bringing for your guests and poured a drink-offering, at
the same time strewing the tomb with sprays of myrtle. Then,
on the altar itself I saw a black-fleeced sheep that had been
sacrificed, its blood not long spilled, and some locks of hair,
cut from a golden head. It gave me a turn, my girl! Who on
earth had dared to approach the tomb? No man of Argos, I
fancy. Maybe your brother was the one who came somehow
with no one's knowledge, and, when he did, paid his respects
to his father's wretched tomb. Compare a lock of that hair
520   with your own[27] and see if it is of the same colour; it is usual,
where two children are of one blood, one father, that they
have a physical resemblance in most features.

ELECTRA: Old man, you speak like a fool if you think a man as
brave as my brother would have come in secret into this land
because he feared Aegisthus. Again, how will a lock of his
hair and mine correspond, the one from a young noble-
man's head, raised in the wrestling-ground, the other a girl's,
groomed by combing? It can't happen. Anyway, old man,
you would find plenty of cases where people who are not of
530   the same blood have similar hair.

OLD MAN: Well then, step in his footprint, child, and see if the
tread of his boot fits your own foot.

ELECTRA: And just how could feet leave any imprint on hard,
stony ground? But if such a trace exists, a brother's and a
sister's foot would hardly be the same size; the man's foot
must be larger.

OLD MAN: Well, even if your brother has returned and visited
the tomb, is there not a piece of clothing you once wove for
him that would help you know him, the clothes he wore that
540   day I snatched him away from death?

ELECTRA: Don't you know that I was still young when Orestes went into exile? If I had actually made clothing for him, how would someone who was then a child have the same garment now, unless his clothes grew with his body? No, either some stranger has shown pity and left a lock of his hair on my father's tomb, or spies sent by my brother have done him this honour.

OLD MAN: Where are your guests? I want to see them and ask about your brother.

[ORESTES, PYLADES *and servants come out of the cottage.*]

ELECTRA: Here they are now, striding out of the cottage.

OLD MAN: They're nobly born all right, but this may prove false: nobility is rarely a guarantee of worth.[28] None the less, [*turning to address the young men directly:*] I bid you welcome, gentlemen.   550

ORESTES: Greetings to you, old man. Electra, which of your friends does he belong to, this old relic of manhood?

ELECTRA: He was my father's tutor, sir.

ORESTES: What? This is the man who smuggled your brother to safety?

ELECTRA: Yes; he it was who saved his life, if he still lives.

ORESTES: Ah, why does he stare at me as if he were examining the stamp on some bright new coin? Is he comparing me to someone?

ELECTRA: Perhaps he gets pleasure from looking at you as one who is a friend of Orestes.   560

ORESTES: Yes, one of his close friends. But why does he walk all round me?

ELECTRA: I too am surprised to see this, sir.

OLD MAN: My lady, make your prayers, daughter Electra, your prayers to the gods!

ELECTRA: For what I lack or what I have?

OLD MAN: So that you may grasp the precious treasure heaven puts before your eyes!

ELECTRA [*humouring him*]: There you are: I call upon the gods. Just what is your meaning, old man?

OLD MAN: Now look at this man, child, this man you love dearly.

ELECTRA: I have been looking for some time now – can you be losing your wits, I wonder?

OLD MAN: Have I lost my wits when I see your brother?

570 ELECTRA: What are you saying, old man? I cannot believe it!

OLD MAN: I say I see him here, Orestes, Agamemnon's son!

ELECTRA: What mark have you seen on him to make me believe?

OLD MAN: A scar along his eyebrow[29] that was cut once when he fell chasing a fawn with you in his father's courtyard.

ELECTRA: What? I do see the mark of a fall!

OLD MAN: Then do you hesitate to clasp the one you love best?

ELECTRA: Not now, old man; your evidence has convinced me! [*Opening her arms to embrace him:*] O my long-lost one, I hold you, the one I never thought to see!

ORESTES: And I hold you at last!

ELECTRA: I never imagined this!

580 ORESTES: And never did I expect it!

ELECTRA: You are he?

ORESTES: Yes, your only ally. And if I draw tight the net I have come to cast, [I yet will have justice for my father].[30] I do not doubt it; otherwise we must stop believing in the gods, if injustice is to triumph over justice.

CHORUS [*dancing in excitement as they sing*]: *You have come, you have come, o day, at last you have dawned, showing, for all Argos to see, the torch she has awaited; long has been his exile as he wandered, poor man, far from his ancestral home. But now, my dear,*
590 *some god, some god delivers our triumph in turn! Raise hands, raise voice, send prayers to the gods that your brother may enter Argos with Fortune's blessing!*

ORESTES [*disengaging himself from* ELECTRA*'s embrace*]: Well, I store the pleasure of your loving greeting in my heart; in days to come I will return this warmth in my turn. [*Turning to the* OLD MAN:] Now you, old fellow – you have come at just the right time – tell me, how am I to punish my father's
600 murderer and my mother, his partner in unholy wedlock?

152

Can I count on the support of friends in Argos? Or are we completely bankrupt, as our fortunes are? Whom should I take as my ally? Should I act by night or in the daytime? What path should I take to tackle my enemies?

OLD MAN: My son, when you find yourself in trouble, you have no friends. It's a god-send, believe me, when a man shares good and bad alike. Now (for, as far as your friends are concerned, your ruin is complete and you have left them no hope), listen to me and learn the facts: winning back your ancestral home and city depends entirely on your own effort, and on luck. 610

ORESTES: Then what is it I should do to achieve this?

OLD MAN: Kill Thyestes' son and your mother.

ORESTES: This is the garland I have come to win. But how am I to get it?

OLD MAN: Not by going inside the city walls, even if you had a mind to.

ORESTES: He has look-outs posted, has he, and an armed bodyguard?

OLD MAN: Aye, that he has; he fears you and doesn't sleep sound.

ORESTES: I see; well, come on, old fellow, give me your counsel on the next step!

OLD MAN: Listen then, for your part, to what I have to say; I've just thought of something.

ORESTES: I hope your advice is good and that I understand it! 620

OLD MAN: I saw Aegisthus when I was making my way here.

ORESTES: Auspicious news! Whereabouts?

OLD MAN: He was near those fields where the horse-pastures are.

ORESTES: What was he doing? I see hope dawning from despair!

OLD MAN: As I saw it, he was making ready a feast in honour of the Nymphs.

ORESTES: As an offering for the rearing of children, or does he anticipate the birth of a child?

OLD MAN: I know only one thing: he was getting himself ready to sacrifice an ox.

ORESTES: How many men were in attendance? Or was he with servants only, and unguarded?

OLD MAN: No Argives were there, only servants of his own household.

ORESTES: Then old man, there is no one, I take it, who will
630   recognize me on sight?

OLD MAN: They are slaves who have never set eyes on you.

ORESTES: Might I count on their support, if I were successful?

OLD MAN: Yes, this is the way slaves are; it works in your favour.

ORESTES: Then how would I ever get close to him?

OLD MAN: By going where he will see you as he makes his sacrifice.

ORESTES: He has his fields just by the road, hasn't he?

OLD MAN: Yes; he will see you from there and invite you to share in the feast.

ORESTES: A dinner-guest he would rather not have asked, god willing.

OLD MAN: The next move in the game is for you to make.

640 ORESTES: You are right. But my mother, where is she?

OLD MAN: She's in Argos, but she will join her husband for the feast.

ORESTES: Why did my mother not accompany her husband when he set out?

OLD MAN: Fear of criticism from the townsfolk made her stay behind.

ORESTES: I understand; she knows the people look at her askance.

OLD MAN: That sort of thing; a sinful woman invites hatred.

ORESTES: How should I proceed then? Shall I kill the pair of them at the same spot?

ELECTRA [*suddenly breaking in*]: Mother's death shall be *my* responsibility.[31]

ORESTES: Then Fortune will take care of the rest.

ELECTRA [*with a gesture to the* OLD MAN]: Let our friend here serve the two of us in this business.

650 ORESTES: Yes; but how do you propose to kill mother?

ELECTRA: Old fellow, go to Clytemnestra and tell her this:

OLD MAN: What message am I to deliver?

ELECTRA: Tell her I have given birth to a child, a boy.

OLD MAN: Just recently, or some time ago?

ELECTRA: Ten days ago, the time a mother needs for purification.[32]

OLD MAN: Just how does this lead on to your own mother's
death?

ELECTRA: She will come when she hears I am recovering from
the strain of childbirth.

OLD MAN: What makes you say that? Do you suppose a woman
like that spares a thought for you, child?

ELECTRA: I think so; and she will shed tears at my child's humble
status.

OLD MAN: Perhaps; but please finish what you have to say: the
race is only half run.

ELECTRA: Well, once she has come, she dies; it's obvious.   660

OLD MAN: All right, I grant she comes right up to the door of
your house.

ELECTRA: Is it not then a short detour for her down to Hades'
realm?

OLD MAN: If only I might die once I have had the pleasure of
seeing this!

ELECTRA: Then your first task for the moment, old fellow, is to
point out the way to my brother here.

OLD MAN: To where Aegisthus is now sacrificing to the gods?

ELECTRA: And then you are to intercept my mother and give
her my message.

OLD MAN: I'll make her think my very words are from your
own lips.

ELECTRA [turning to ORESTES]: Now to your task; it is your luck
to draw blood first in this business.

ORESTES: I will go; I only need someone to guide me on the
way.

OLD MAN: Well, here stands your escort; I'm ready and willing!   670
[The three of them now raise their arms together in prayer.][33]

ORESTES: O Zeus, god of my forefathers and router of my foes, –

ELECTRA: Take pity on us; pitiful are our sufferings.

OLD MAN: Pity, oh pity the children who are sprung from you!

ORESTES: – and Hera, you who preside over Mycenae's altars, –

ELECTRA: Grant us victory, if what we ask for is just.

OLD MAN: Yes, grant them just vengeance for their father! [*All now fall prostrate on the ground.*]

ORESTES: – and you, my father, now dwelling in Hades' realm by a death that heaven abhorred, –

ELECTRA: And sovereign Earth, beaten by these hands of mine, –

OLD MAN: Protect, protect these children so precious!

680 ORESTES: – come now, bringing as your ally every corpse, . . .

ELECTRA: . . . those who helped you to destroy the Phrygians with their spears.

OLD MAN: And all those who loathe sin and wickedness! [*All rise.*]

ORESTES: Do you hear us, my father, so monstrously treated by my mother?

OLD MAN: All this, I know, your father hears; however, it is high time we went on our way.

ELECTRA: He hears it all, I know it; [*taking her brother by the shoulders:*] this means it is now for you to prove yourself a

690 man. For if the word we hear tells of your success, the whole house will shout for joy; but if you die, we shall sing no such song. These are my words to you. [*Turning to the* CHORUS:] And to you, ladies, I make this request: raise the cry that tells of this struggle – make your beacon burn bright! I myself shall keep watch with sword ready in hand. Never shall I yield the victory, never give my enemies the satisfaction of trampling me in the dust![34]

[ORESTES *and* PYLADES *leave with the* OLD MAN *and their servants, and* ELECTRA *goes into the cottage.*]

700 CHORUS [Strophe]: *The tale still lives,[35] ancient in the telling, how Pan, custodian of the fields, by breathing a sweet-sounding melody on his harmonious reeds, once brought away a lamb with lovely fleece all golden, taking it from under its suckling dam on the Argive hills. And the herald, taking his stand on steps of stone, made this*

proclamation: 'Come, Mycenaeans, come to the place of assembly to
see a wondrous sight that portends happiness to the ruler who lays
claim to it!' Then with dance and song the people did honour to   710
the house of Atreus' sons.

[Antistrophe:] Censers of beaten gold were set out and fire blazed
on altars throughout the town of Argos. The flute, servant of the Muses,
sounded its lovely voice and higher and higher in its beauty rose the song
of the golden lamb. Then came the trickery of Thyestes: in secret he   720
had slept with Atreus' loving wife and had taken the wondrous creature
to his own house; then, going into the assembly, he announced that he
had in his own home the horned beast with fleece of gold.

[Strophe:] Then it was, yes then, that Zeus changed the course
of the glittering stars and the radiance of the sun and pallid face of   730
the dawn. With the hot flame of divine fire the regions of the West
were assailed; to the North went the water-burdened clouds, and the
home of Ammon, becoming dry, withered for want of moisture, thus
deprived of the lovely rain from Zeus.

[Antistrophe:] The story runs – but little trust do I put in it –
that the golden-faced sun, to chasten mortals, turned round his fiery   740
course and reversed it to bring misfortune on men. These tales, so
feared by mortal men, benefit the worship of the gods.[36] But you did
not remember these tales, sister of the glorious brothers,[37] when you
took your husband's life.

CHORUS-LEADER: Aha! Friends, did you hear a shout or was it
just a foolish imagining on my part, as when Zeus appears to
thunder below the earth? Look, Fortune's wind swells for all
to see. [Turning excitedly towards the cottage:] My lady, leave
your house, Electra!   750

ELECTRA [coming out]: What is it, friends? How do we stand in
the contest?

CHORUS-LEADER: I know only one thing: I hear the desperate
cry of a man being killed.

ELECTRA: I, too, heard it; it was some way off but I caught it
just the same.

CHORUS-LEADER: The sound travels a long way, yet it is clearly
heard.

ELECTRA: Is it an Argive shriek or from my friends?

CHORUS-LEADER: I don't know; the tone of the shouting is all confused.

ELECTRA [*supposing that* ORESTES *has failed*]: This is my own sentence of death you are affirming. Quick! Let me do the deed!

CHORUS-LEADER: Wait! You must learn the truth of your situation.

ELECTRA: It's hopeless! We've lost – his messengers should have come![38]

760   CHORUS-LEADER: They will; it is no easy task to kill a king.

[*A* MESSENGER *runs in.*]

MESSENGER: The day is yours, maids of Mycenae! I bear a message to all who love him that Orestes has triumphed and Agamemnon's murderer, Aegisthus, lies upon the ground. We must give thanks to the gods.

ELECTRA: Who are you? How can you prove to me that what you say is true?

MESSENGER: Don't your eyes tell you that I'm your brother's servant?

ELECTRA [*recognizing him suddenly*]: O my dear friend, my fear made me forget your face; now of course I know you! What is it you say? He's dead, my father's loathed murderer?

MESSENGER: Dead, yes; I tell you the same news twice over,
770   but it's what you want to hear.

ELECTRA: You gods, and all-seeing Justice, you have come at last! But how did he kill Thyestes' son? What was the manner of his death? I must know!

MESSENGER: When we had left this house we joined a road wide enough for two wagons, and so came to the place where Mycenae's new king was. As it turned out, he was standing in a well-watered garden plucking sprigs of soft myrtle to wear on his head. Then, when he saw us, he called out, 'Hello, strangers! Who are you and where have you come from? What
780   country do you call home?' To this Orestes replied, 'Thessaly; and we are bound for the Alpheus to make a sacrifice to Zeus

of Olympia.' On hearing this Aegisthus said, 'For the present you must share my hospitality and take part in our feast. As it happens I am sacrificing an ox to the Nymphs. If you make an early start tomorrow morning, you will travel just as far. Let's go into the house' – as he said this, he took us by the wrist and began to lead us in – 'I won't take no for an answer!' When we were in the house, he gave this instruction: 'Let 790 water be brought at once for our guests, so they may take their positions around the altar near the holy water!' But Orestes said, 'We have recently been cleansed by pure water from a running stream. If it is proper for strangers to join townsfolk in sacrifice, then, Aegisthus, we are ready. We will not reject your offer, royal lord.'

So much they said to one another publicly. Then the servants, putting down the spears with which they had been guarding their master, busied themselves with the task, every man of them. Some brought the bowl for the victim's blood, others raised baskets on their heads, while others again set 800 about kindling the fire and began to set up cauldrons around the hearths. The whole building rang with noise. Then the man who shared your mother's bed took barleymeal and began to sprinkle the altars, uttering these words: 'Nymphs of the rocks, grant that we may often offer up an ox, myself and my wife, Tyndareus' daughter, in our home and that we may continue to prosper, while our enemies come to grief' – he meant by this you and Orestes. My master prayed to the opposite effect, not pronouncing his words audibly, that he might regain his ancestral home.   810

Then Aegisthus took from a basket a straight-bladed knife with which he cut a lock of the bullock's hair and he threw it with his right hand upon the holy fire. The servants then hoisted the bullock on to their shoulders and he proceeded to cut its throat. This done, he addressed your brother again: 'One of the skills of which Thessalians boast is quartering a bull in fine fashion, that and breaking in horses. Take this blade, stranger, and show if this reputation among your countrymen is true.' Orestes grasped in his hand a well-wrought weapon of Dorian make, and, flinging his handsome cloak back from his

820 shoulders, he chose Pylades as his helper in the task, pushing the servants back. Then, taking hold of the bullock's foot, he extended his hand and laid the white flesh bare; and, quicker than a runner could complete both lengths of the horse-track, he flayed the beast and opened up its flanks.

Aegisthus took in his hands the sacred parts and began examining them.[39] The entrails lacked a liver-lobe, and the portal vein and gall-bladder nearby indicated that no good at all was in store for the one examining them. His looks darkened

830 and when my master asked him, 'Why are you upset?', he replied, 'Stranger, I fear some trickery from abroad. The man who is my greatest personal enemy and public enemy to my house and throne is Agamemnon's son.' Orestes then said, 'What? You fear the stratagem of an exile when you are ruler of a city? Someone fetch me a Phthian cleaver instead of this Dorian blade, so I can hack through the chest and we can enjoy dinner!' This was given to him and he proceeded to chop up the beast. Aegisthus took the innards and began examining them, separating the parts as he did so. Now, while he was bending down engaged in this, your brother, standing

840 on tiptoe, dealt him a blow in the top of his spine, breaking through the joints of his back! His whole body twisted up and down in convulsions and in his agony he kept shrieking as he met his bloody end.

When the servants saw this they lost no time in rushing for their spears: it was a lot for two men to take on. But Pylades and Orestes did not lose their nerve; they stood their ground and faced the others, brandishing their weapons. Then Orestes spoke out: 'I do not come as an enemy of this city or of my own servants; I have taken vengeance on the man who murdered my father. I am wretched Orestes. You men served

850 my father through many a long year; do not kill his son now!' Now, when they heard these words, they held back their spears. He was recognized by an old man who had seen many

years of service in the palace. At once they gave way to loud shouts of joy and put a wreath on your brother's head. He is coming to display before your own eyes a head – no Gorgon's head does he carry but that of Aegisthus whom you loathe. Blood has been paid for blood, a loan that has cost him dear, as his death now shows. [*Exit* MESSENGER. *The* CHORUS *now express their delight in a lively dance, inviting* ELECTRA *to join them.*]

CHORUS [Strophe]: *Come, dear friend, join our dancing steps, like a fawn leaping lightly into the air for joy. Your brother has won – he wears the crown and has accomplished a greater victory than any to be gained beside Alpheus' stream. Come, sing a song of triumph to accompany our dance!*   860

ELECTRA: *O light, o radiant sun with team of four, o earth and night that filled my sight before, now can I open my eyes in freedom, since my father's murderer, Aegisthus, has met his end! Come friends, let me fetch such finery as I have and my house holds to adorn the hair*   870 *of my victorious brother; I will crown his head! [She goes into the cottage.]*

CHORUS [Antistrophe]: *You bring ornaments now to dress his head. Our dancing, dear to the Muses, shall proceed. Now shall they rule in justice, those who in earlier days were the beloved kings of our land, now that they have overthrown the enemies of justice. Come, let us shout aloud in harmony with joy!*

[ORESTES *and* PYLADES *return,* ORESTES *holding a sack. At the same time his attendants bring on the body of Aegisthus.* ELECTRA *comes out of the cottage as they arrive. She has two newly-made garlands in her hands.*]

ELECTRA: Orestes, son of the father whose victory was won   880 under Ilium's walls, glorious in your own victory, receive this wreath to bind your flowing locks! No useless race have you run on its homeward course but one that has brought the death of your enemy, Aegisthus, who killed your father and mine. [*Turning to* PYLADES:] And you, Pylades, his comrade-in-arms, reared by a god-fearing man, take from my hand this

garland. You win an equal share with him in this feat. I pray
I may always see you both prospering!

ORESTES: Think first of the gods, Electra, as the ones who have
890   caused this good fortune; then you may praise me too who
served both them and Fortune. For it is quite true, you see
before you the killer of Aegisthus. [*He lifts Aegisthus' head from
the sack.*] But to make the truth of this plain, look, I carry the
dead man himself. Throw this out, if you like, for beasts to
tear, or else impale it on a stake and press it down as prey for
birds, children of the air. Before you called him master, but
now he is your slave. [*He flings the head at* ELECTRA*'s feet.*]

ELECTRA: It makes me ashamed but none the less I want to
900   speak.

ORESTES: What is it? Speak out – no need for fear now!

ELECTRA: I am ashamed to insult the dead in case I become a
target for someone's critical tongue.

ORESTES: There is not a single person who would blame you.

ELECTRA: My fellow-citizens are hard to please and quick to
apportion blame.

ORESTES: Sister, say whatever it is you wish; the enmity we bear
this man goes beyond any terms or truce.

ELECTRA [*slowly focusing attention on Aegisthus' head*]: Very well;
what should I say[40] by way of introduction to my tale of woes,
what ending should I make? What words should I choose to
be the centre of my tale? And yet each morning in the early
hours I never stopped rehearsing the very words I wished to
910   say to your face, if I ever became free of the fears that haunted
me then. Now I am free and so I will pay you out with the
bitter words I wanted to use against you while you lived.

    You destroyed me; you orphaned me, and this man too,
robbing us of the father we loved, though we had done you
no wrong, and then you shamefully married our mother after
you had killed her husband, the man who still commanded
the army of Greece, you who had never set foot in Troy.
Such was the depth of your folly that you expected to secure
our mother's devotion if you made her your wife and she

defiled my father's marriage-bed! But anyone who seduces 920
a man's wife and then is compelled to marry her should know
he is to be pitied if he thinks she will always be true to him
once she has been false to her former husband. Your life was
a wretched one, though you thought it pleasant enough; you
knew quite well you had offended heaven by this marriage,
while my mother knew she had gained as a husband an enemy
of the gods. A wicked pair, you took each other's fortune on
yourselves, she yours and you that woman's woes.

On every Argive tongue this was said of you: 'The man 930
isn't master in that marriage,[41] the woman is.' And yet what
a disgrace it is when a woman rather than her husband rules
over a house! I cannot bear it when a young man is called in
the city by his mother's name and not by his father's, the
man's. When a man has married a woman of noble birth,
above his station, it is not he but she who becomes the centre
of interest. This is what took you in completely though you
did not realize it: you claimed to be important because wealth
made you powerful. But wealth makes a poor long-term
companion. It is not wealth but character on which 940
a man should rely. This is what never deserts him and will
always shoulder misfortune, while wealth knows nothing of
justice and keeps company with fools; wealth is like a flower
whose bloom is quickly shed, and it vanishes from a house
like a bird on the wing.

As for your behaviour towards women,[42] I say nothing (as
a virgin I may not properly speak of it), but I will hint at it
for those who have ears to know. You took liberties with
them, confident in the fact that you lived in the palace of a
king and enjoyed good looks. Oh, I never want a husband
like that, with features like a girl's; give me a man who looks
the part! His children have hearts that are wedded to the war
god but good looks serve only to adorn the dance. Away 950
with you, ignorant fool! Time has laid you bare and you have
met your deserts! Let no criminal, then, think he has

outstripped Justice if he has run the first lap well, until he reaches the finishing line and has ended life's race.

CHORUS-LEADER: Terrible were his acts and terrible the payment he has made to you and this man; mighty is the strength of Justice.

ELECTRA: Well, now you servants must carry his body inside and place it out of sight; when she comes, my mother must not see the corpse before she is killed. [*Aegisthus' remains are taken into the cottage.* ORESTES *suddenly stiffens as he catches sight of figures approaching in the distance.*]

ORESTES: Wait!⁴³ Let's find a different way!

ELECTRA [*following his gaze*]: What! It's not a rescue party you see from Mycenae, is it?

ORESTES: No, it is my mother, the woman who gave me birth.

ELECTRA: What good timing! She walks right into our net. Yes! The carriage and her dress mark her out.

ORESTES: Oh, what are we to do? Are we going to kill our mother?

ELECTRA: You don't feel pity, surely, at the sight of your mother?

ORESTES: Oh sister! How can I kill her, the one who reared me, who gave me birth?

ELECTRA: Just as she killed your father and mine.

ORESTES: O Phoebus, how harsh, how foolish was your command!

ELECTRA: Where does wisdom lie if Apollo be judged foolish?

ORESTES: Your word was that I must kill my mother, the last person I should.

ELECTRA: What harm comes to you, I ask, if you avenge your father?

ORESTES: I shall be sent into exile for killing my mother, though before, my hands were undefiled.

ELECTRA: Yes, but if you fail to protect your father, you will be guilty of impiety.

ORESTES: I know it; but shall I not be punished for shedding my mother's blood?

ELECTRA: And what if you shirk taking revenge for your father?

ORESTES: Did some evil spirit make that pronouncement, taking the god's shape?

ELECTRA: And take his seat on the sacred tripod? I doubt it. 980

ORESTES: I cannot believe this command from the oracle was well made.

ELECTRA: Do not turn coward or lose your manhood! Go on to set the same trap for her [44] as she used with Aegisthus to kill her husband!

ORESTES [*turning to go into the cottage*]: And so I shall; I take my first terrible steps, and terrible is the thing I shall do. If this is heaven's will, so be it; this is an exploit that brings me pain, not pleasure.

[PYLADES *follows* ORESTES *into the cottage.* CLYTEM-NESTRA *arrives in a carriage. She is attended by female captives from Troy.*]

CHORUS: *Hail, my lady, queen of the land of Argos, daughter of Tyndareus and sister to the noble sons of Zeus who dwell among* 990 *the stars in fiery heaven and hold powers to save mortal men on the roaring sea! We offer our greetings and revere you as we do the gods for your wealth and great happiness. The time is ripe, my royal lady, to pay regard to your fortunes.*

CLYTEMNESTRA: Leave the carriage, women of Troy, and take my hand so that I may step down from it. The temples of the gods have been decked with Trojan spoils, while I possess 1000 these women, the flower of the Trojan land, in return for the daughter I lost[45] – a prize of little worth, yet one that brings honour to my house.

ELECTRA: Well then, mother (as a slave myself, banished from my ancestral home and living in a wretched hovel), let me take hold of your royal hand.

CLYTEMNESTRA: Slaves are here for that; do not trouble yourself on my account.

ELECTRA: Why not? You made a slave of me when you forced me to leave my home, and when it became the property of new owners so did I, like these women, orphaned and left without a father. 1010

CLYTEMNESTRA: Well, that was due to the scheme your father
devised against his own family, the very ones he should least
have treated so. I will tell you the way it was; and yet when
a woman gains notoriety, there is bitterness in what is said
about her. This, in my view, is excusable; but if, once the
facts are known, her conduct deserves to be condemned, then
it is right to treat her with contempt; however, if this is not
the case, such an attitude is indefensible.

When Tyndareus gave me in marriage to your father, it
was not a condition that I or any child of mine should be put
to death. But your father came to our home and took away
my daughter to Aulis where the fleet was at anchor, winning
her over with the promise of marriage to Achilles, and there
he stretched her over the altar and slashed my Iphigenia's
white throat. Now, if he had been seeking to avert the capture
of his city or to benefit his home or to save the lives of the
rest of his children by killing one for the sake of many, then
I could have forgiven him.[46] But the truth was this: Helen
was a loose woman and the man who married her did not
know how to punish an unfaithful wife; these were the reasons
why he killed my daughter. Well, even so, wronged though
I was, I would not have lost control or killed my husband.
But home he came with a crazy woman in tow,[47] a visionary,
installing her as his concubine, and tried to keep two brides
together under the same roof!

Oh, we women are too often ruled by our hearts, I don't
deny it; and, prompted by this, when a husband strays, spurning
his wife's bed, the woman wants to imitate her husband and
to find love elsewhere. And then it's we who find ourselves
openly criticized, while no blame attaches to those who are
responsible, our husbands. Now, if Menelaus had been
snatched away in secret from his home, would I have been
obliged to kill Orestes to save the life of my sister's husband?
How would your father have reacted to that, I wonder? Then
was it right that Agamemnon, the murderer of my child,
should escape death, and that I should suffer such treatment

1020

1030

1040

at his hands? I killed him; I turned to the only path that lay open to me, appealing to his enemies. Which of his friends would have shared with me in killing your father?

Say whatever you wish and put your case freely, showing how it was not just for your father to die.   1050

CHORUS-LEADER: There is justice in what you have said but it is a shameful justice. A wife who has sense should agree with her husband in all matters. Any woman who disputes this, I simply take no account of.

ELECTRA: Remember the words you spoke last, mother, giving me the right to speak freely to you.

CLYTEMNESTRA: Yes, my child, and I say it now as well; you have my word.

ELECTRA: And would you punish me, mother, if my words offended you?

CLYTEMNESTRA: Certainly not; let me put your mind at rest.

ELECTRA: Then I will speak and here is how I will begin my preface. O mother, how I wish you had a better heart! You   1060 and Helen possess a beauty that deserves to win praise, true sisters born, but both of you are strangers to chastity and unworthy of Castor.[48] Once Helen was carried off she gladly succumbed to love, while you brought down the finest man in Greece, offering as your excuse that you killed your husband for the sake of your child!

People do not know you as well as I do. Even before your daughter's sacrifice had been ratified, when your husband had only recently set out from home, you were teasing out those   1070 locks of golden hair in the mirror. When a woman whose husband is away from home takes trouble to make herself beautiful, then mark her down as a strumpet. She has no need to show a pretty face out of doors unless she is looking for what she should not be. You were the only woman I know among all the women of Greece who took pleasure in any Trojan successes and frowned at their failures, because you did not want Agamemnon to return from Troy. And yet you had the opportunity to be honoured as a virtuous wife. You   1080 had for your husband a man who was not Aegisthus' inferior, whom Greece had chosen to be her commander-in-chief. When Helen, your sister, had behaved in such a way, you could have won great renown; bad deeds attract people's attention and provide a standard of comparison for judging the good.

If, as you say, my father killed your daughter, in what way did I or my brother do you wrong? Why was it that, after killing your husband, you did not grant us our ancestral home but rather brought an outsider into your marriage-bed, setting 1090 this as the price for wedlock? Your lover did not suffer exile, but your son did; your lover did not suffer death, but I did; I may be alive but he has made me endure twice my sister's death. If bloodshed, sitting in judgement, requires bloodshed, then I and your son Orestes will kill you in vengeance for our 1100 father. If justice was in *that* deed, justice is also in this.

CLYTEMNESTRA: My child, it has always been your nature to love your father. This is a fact of life: some children are devoted to their fathers, others in turn give greater love to their mothers. I will forgive you; I am not as happy as you might think, my child, at what I have done. Oh, pity me! I am sorry for what 1110 I devised! I let my anger against my husband drive me too far!

ELECTRA: These sighs come too late, when you have no remedy. My father is dead; why don't you bring back your son who wanders in exile from this land?

CLYTEMNESTRA: I am afraid; I look to my interests, not to his. His father's death makes him angry, they say.

ELECTRA: What about your husband? Why do you keep him so bitterly opposed to us?

CLYTEMNESTRA: That is the way he is; and you too have shown stubbornness.

ELECTRA: Yes, for I feel pain; still, I will stop being angry.

CLYTEMNESTRA: In that case, he will no longer show you resentment.

1120 ELECTRA: He is proud; he has my home as his residence.

CLYTEMNESTRA: You see? You stir up fresh quarrels again!

ELECTRA: I will say no more; I fear him . . . as I fear him.

CLYTEMNESTRA: Enough of talking like this. Why did you summon me, child?

ELECTRA: You heard, I think, that I had given birth; I want you to make the thanks-offering, for I don't know how – whatever the custom prescribes for the baby's tenth day. I have never had a child before; I have no experience of what to do.

CLYTEMNESTRA: This is the task of someone else, the woman who delivered you.

ELECTRA: I had no midwife; I had my baby without any help.

CLYTEMNESTRA: Is your house so far from neighbours that could lend a helping hand?

ELECTRA: No one wants poor people as friends.

CLYTEMNESTRA: But look at how dirty you are, how shabbily dressed for a woman who has only just given birth to a child! I will go inside to offer sacrifice for the child's tenth day. When I have obliged you in this, I will go on to the plot where my husband is making a sacrifice to the Nymphs. [*Turning to her attendants:*] You servants, take this team of horses to the stalls and let them eat. Whenever you think I have discharged my sacrifice here, attend on me; I must humour my husband as well.

ELECTRA: Then enter my humble home; do please take care that your clothing isn't stained by all the smoke inside the cottage when you offer up the kind of sacrifice you must to the gods.[49] [*She waits for* CLYTEMNESTRA *to disappear.*] The basket has been duly prepared for the rite and the knife whetted that felled the bull; next to it you will receive your own blow, and fall. In Hades' halls, as in life, you shall clasp the man whose bed you shared. So much kindness will I give to you as you answer to me for my father's death! [*She follows her mother into the cottage.*]

CHORUS [Strophe]: *Wickedness reaps its reward; the fortunes of the house veer round and blow a different course. In that hour my own great king was felled in his bath, and roof and coping of the palace resounded with his cry: 'You monstrous woman, why do you mean*

1130

1140

1150

to kill me when I have returned after ten years to my beloved homeland?'

[Antistrophe:] *Retribution for adultery sweeps back and brings her to judgement, the woman who with her own hands took an axe and with its sharpened blade slew her wretched husband when at last he had returned to his home, the sky-high battlements fashioned by* 1160 *Cyclopes. Poor husband, whatever the grievance that possessed the unhappy lady in that hour! Like a mountain-bred lioness that ranges the dense thickets she performed this deed.*

CLYTEMNESTRA [*from inside*]: O children, in heaven's name, do not kill your mother!

CHORUS-LEADER: Do you hear the cry from inside the house?

CLYTEMNESTRA: Oh, no, no!

CHORUS-LEADER: I, too, cry out in grief for her, done to death by her own children.

CHORUS: *God deals out justice, sooner or later. Monstrous is your suffering but what you did to your husband, heartless woman, gave* 1170 *the gods cause for anger.*

[ORESTES *and* ELECTRA *come out from the cottage slowly, their clothes stained with blood. The corpses of Aegisthus and Clytemnestra are revealed* [50] *to the audience.*][51]

CHORUS-LEADER: Ah, here they come, stepping forth from the cottage, dressed in red from their mother's blood, marked by the trophy that proclaims their wretched sacrifice! There is no house, there never was, more to be pitied than that of Tantalus.

ORESTES [Strophe]: *O Earth, o Zeus who sees all that men do, look upon these foul and bloody deeds, two bodies stretched upon the* 1180 *ground, struck down by my hand in recompense for my woes.*

ELECTRA: *A sight indeed to make one weep, my brother, but I am responsible. Oh what have I done, venting my fury on our mother here, the woman who was the mother of her little girl!*

CHORUS: *O mother who bore these children, what a fate is yours! Monstrous, worse than monstrous is your suffering at the hands of your children! But justly have you paid for taking their father's life.*

1190 ORESTES [Antistrophe]: *O Phoebus, what you proclaimed in song*

*was justice veiled in darkness. All too clear, though, is the anguish you
have wrought; a murderer's fate have you assigned to me, far from
the land of Greece. To what other city am I to go? What host, what
host who fears the gods will tolerate the sight of me, the mother-killer?*

ELECTRA: *Oh what is to become of me? Where should I go, where will
I be invited to join the dance or to give my hand in marriage? What
husband will welcome me into the bridal-bed?*　　　　　　1200

CHORUS: *Again, again your thoughts veer round at the wind's
prompting; they are righteous now but were misguided then, my
friend, when you stirred a frightful act in your brother against his will.*

ORESTES [Strophe]: *Did you see how the poor woman thrust a breast
outside her dress, showing it to us as we sought to kill her, oh, the
thought of it! sinking to the ground, the body that bore us? My heart
melted!*

CHORUS: *I know well; you went through agony when you heard the*　1210
cry of mourning from the mother who gave you birth.

ORESTES: *This was the cry she uttered as she laid her hand on my
cheek: 'My child, I beg you!' And she hung on my cheeks, so that
the weapon all but fell from my hand.*

CHORUS: *Poor lady! How did you bring yourself to look at her when
you killed her, your own mother breathing her last?*　　　　1220

ORESTES [Strophe]: *I threw my hood over my eyes as I put my mother
to the sacrifice, plunging my sword into her throat.*

ELECTRA: *Yes, and I urged you on with encouragement, my hand
joining yours on the sword-hilt. I have committed the most terrible of
acts.*

ORESTES [Antistrophe]: *Take hold of her, cover my mother's body
with a robe and seal her wounds! [Addressing the corpse:] It seems
the children you bore were to become your murderers.*

ELECTRA: *See, with this robe we cover you, we who felt hatred for you
as well as love, to mark an end to great sorrows for this house.*　1230

[*The gods* CASTOR *and* POLLUX *appear on high.*]

CHORUS: *See, above the palace roof they come, whether they are spirits
or of the heavenly company of gods! No mortals travel so. What
makes them appear so clearly to the sight of men?*

CASTOR: Son of Agamemnon, hear! It is your mother's brothers,

the Heavenly Twins, who call you, Castor and his brother
1240   Pollux. We have come to Argos having just quelled a
storm at sea that threatened ships, when we saw the killing of
our sister here, your mother. She now has her just deserts but
you have not acted justly. Phoebus, Phoebus[52] – I say no more,
as he is my royal lord; wisdom is his but wisdom was absent
from the command he gave you. We must acquiesce in what
has happened here. From this time on you must pursue the
course that Zeus and Fate have determined for you.

Give Electra to Pylades to have as his wedded wife. You,
1250   Orestes, must leave Argos; you may not set foot in this city
now that you have killed your mother. The terrible Spirits of
Destruction,[53] the dog-faced goddesses, will drive you hither
and thither, a wanderer reduced to madness. But make your
way to Athens and reverently embrace the holy image of
Pallas; she will keep them away from you, terrifying them
with her fearful serpents so that they do not touch you. She
will hold above your head her shield with its Gorgon's face.

There is a hill of Ares,[54] where the gods first sat to give
their vote on the shedding of blood, when cruel-hearted Ares
1260   in anger at the rape of his daughter killed Halirrhothius, son
of the ocean's king. From that time on there has existed a
tribunal that is most holy and secure. There must you also
stand trial for murder. Votes cast in equal number shall save
you from the penalty of death. Loxias will take the blame on
himself, since his oracle prescribed your mother's killing. And
for future generations shall this law be established, that the
defendant shall always be acquitted if the voting is equally
divided.

1270   As for the terrible goddesses, grief-stricken by this decision
they will pass below to a cavern in the earth, close by the hill
itself, where they will give oracles holy in the sight of pious
men. You must make a city of the Arcadians your home, by
the River Alpheus, near to the precinct of Lycaeus. The city
shall be called after your name.

So much have I said to you. As for the corpse of Aegisthus

here, the townsfolk of Argos shall cover it with a tomb. Your mother will be given burial by Helen and Menelaus, who has lately arrived in Nauplia from taking the land of Troy. Helen never went to Troy;[55] she is here, now that she has left the palace of Proteus in Egypt. Zeus despatched a phantom of Helen to Troy for men to fight over, spilling one another's blood.

As for Pylades, let him leave Achaea's land and journey to his home, having as his one who is both maid and married woman;[56] let him take your brother-in-law in name to the land of Phocis and bestow on him much treasure. Now you must direct your steps across the Isthmian country and make your way to the blessed hill of Cecrops' land. Once you have fulfilled the destiny appointed for this bloodshed, you will be rid of these troubles and find happiness.

CHORUS: *Sons of Zeus, is it lawful for us to converse with you?*

CASTOR: *It is; this slaughter does not pollute you.*[57]

CHORUS: *How was it that you, who are gods and brothers to this woman who has perished, did not debar the Spirits of Death from this house?*

CASTOR: *Fate and necessity directed her to her destined end, together with the foolish utterances of Phoebus' tongue.*

ELECTRA: *May I too share this conversation, sons of Tyndareus?*

CASTOR: *You may; I will ascribe this bloody deed to Phoebus.*

ELECTRA: *What Apollo, what manner of oracle ordained that I should become my mother's murderer?*

CASTOR: *Shared were the deeds and shared the fate, but a single curse inherited from your ancestors has destroyed you both.*

ORESTES: *O my sister, so many the years since I set eyes on you, so swiftly now am I denied your loving presence! We will take our leave of each other, I of you and you of me.*

CASTOR: *She has a husband and a home. There is no cause for tears in her fate, except that she will leave behind the city of Argos.*

ELECTRA: *What other grief is greater than forsaking the boundaries of one's native land?*

ORESTES: *But I shall turn my back on the house of my father and face*

173

trial for my mother's murder, submitting to the judgement of a foreign court.

CASTOR: Have no fear; you will come to the holy city of Pallas. Be
1320   strong!

ELECTRA: O dearest brother, let me hold you in my arms, hold you close! A mother's deathly curse severs us from our ancestral home!

ORESTES: Throw your arms about me, hold me fast! Sing a dirge as if at the tomb of one who has died!

CASTOR: This touches my heart indeed. These words you have spoken are moving to hear, even for gods. As with all who dwell in heaven
1330   there is pity in my heart for the many sufferings of mortals.

ORESTES: I will see you no more.

ELECTRA: And I will not come into your sight.

ORESTES: These are the last words I will speak to you.

ELECTRA: Farewell, Argos! [Addressing the CHORUS as she turns to go:] A long farewell to you as well, women of Argos!

ORESTES: O sister, truest heart, are you going already?

ELECTRA: I go, with tears dampening these tender eyelids.

1340 ORESTES: Pylades, go, take Electra as your wife and be happy!

CASTOR: They will turn their thoughts to marriage. But you must run from these hell-hounds [58] and make for Athens! They are tracking you down, with terror they come to do you harm, black of skin and with serpents in their hands, bringing terrible pain as retribution. [ORESTES runs off in panic. ELECTRA and PYLADES leave by a different exit.] We must go in haste to the Sicilian sea [59] to save some ships as they forge their way through the waves. Flying through the upland
1350   pastures of the air we bring no help to the wicked, but to those whose lives know piety and a love of justice we bring release from sore affliction and grant them safety. Let no one then consent to do wrong or to share his voyage with those who commit perjury;[60] I say this, speaking as a god to mortals. [The Dioscuri depart from view.]

CHORUS: Fare you well! The mortal who can fare well and not fall victim to some mischance knows happiness.

TROJAN WOMEN

PREFACE TO
TROJAN WOMEN

Whereas the other four plays in this volume are only approximately dated, in the case of the *Trojan Women* we are given a firm chronological anchor by an ancient author who records that it was put on in 415 BC, and that Euripides' productions gained second prize. The full tetralogy was *Alexandros, Palamedes, Trojan Women*, with *Sisyphus* as the satyr-play. 'Alexandros' is a common alternative for 'Paris', son of Priam and abductor of Helen; Palamedes was most famous as one of the Greek leaders at Troy, and according to most versions he was executed thanks to a 'frame-up' devised by Odysseus who was jealous of his cleverness. Surviving fragments of the other plays have enabled scholars to carry the work of reconstruction a little further. It does look as though this is a rare instance of Euripides composing a connected trilogy, each play of which dealt with a different phase of the Trojan war.

The first play, it seems, dealt with the early life of Paris, who had been exposed at birth because it was foretold that he would bring disaster on his people. As is common in stories of this kind, Paris survived and was brought up as a herdsman; *Alexandros* dramatized the episode in which he returned to Troy and after initial confusion was eventually recognized by his family. Overjoyed at his survival, they welcome him back and neglect the divine warnings. The second play, *Palamedes*, must have focused on the feud between Odysseus and Palamedes. Thus the first play would have been dominantly Trojan, the second would have been set in the Greek camp. The surviving play, set in the days just after the taking of Troy, brings the two sides together and picks up some of the subject matter of the earlier plays, as when Helen and Hecabe refer back to Paris' offence, and when various characters refer to Odysseus' villainy. The satyr-play may well have had some relation to the tragic trilogy too, since Sisyphus, a notoriously sly and devious Corinthian, was sometimes said to be Odysseus' true father.

The surviving play begins with a divine prologue, but of an unusual type. Here two divinities meet and converse, eventually reaching an agreement (contrast *Alcestis*, where Apollo and Death are in conflict). Athena, who has long waged ruthless war on the Trojans, makes common cause with Poseidon, who has been a loyal ally to Troy. Her anger has been aroused by the blasphemy of the Greeks in sacking Troy, and above all by Ajax's rape of Cassandra within her own temple precinct. For this the gods resolve to punish the Greeks, dispersing their fleet and wrecking many of the ships on their journey home.

This agreement between Athena and Poseidon is important for the whole effect of the play: we, the audience, know that the Greeks' hubristic behaviour will be punished, and the point is reinforced by the words of the prophetess Cassandra, who foretells the disasters that Agamemnon and Odysseus will have to endure. But the impact of this is limited: there is a sense of satisfaction that the Greeks' brutality will meet with retribution, but we cannot forget that many of them will indeed get home in the end; more important, this ironic foreshadowing does nothing to diminish the misery of the Trojans in the present. Indeed, the very fact that the gods are intervening only to punish increases our sense of their neglect of the victims. This is emphasized by the frequent references to the gods by Hecabe and the chorus, most of which dwell on their abandonment of Troy. As Hecabe comments: 'So all that concerns the gods, then, is that I and Troy should suffer . . . wasted, then, are the sacrifices of oxen that we made' (1239–41). Or again, 'O you gods! Yet why do I invoke the gods? Even before this, they were deaf to our appeals' (1280–81). In a memorable ode, the chorus go further and recall the many connections between the Trojan royal house and the Olympian powers, bonds which the gods have forgotten or ignored (821–58). Even if the rest of the Trojans were to believe Cassandra's prophecies, it is unlikely that the prospect of revenge would do much to dissipate their grief and anger at all that they have lost.

The *Trojan Women* itself, after the prologue, concentrates on the sufferings of the victims, of whom Hecabe is central. As the former queen, she is spokeswoman for the survivors; she is also mother of Cassandra, mother of the dead Paris and the dead Polyxena, mother-in-law of Andromache, grandmother of Astyanax. All the miseries of Troy are on her shoulders. The play advances with remorseless pathos, as scene after scene brings a further blow to the women on stage, and Hecabe above all: first the division of the spoils, whereby each of them is allotted to one of the Greek leaders; then the herald's order that the mad Cassandra must accompany him to Agamemnon's ship; Andromache's miserable entrance, bringing news of Polyxena's death; the savage decree that the child of Hector, the infant Astyanax, must die; the scene in which the hated figure of Helen reasserts her influence over her former husband Menelaus; then, to make the Greeks' brutality still more cruelly manifest, the little corpse of Astyanax is actually brought on to the stage. After they have lamented this loss, there is only a brief breathing-space before the ancient city of Troy is set on fire and finally the women are driven off to the ships, to travel to slavery or death. Hecabe, we know, is not destined to reach Greek soil (see 428–30, and cf. the close of *Hecabe*); but here this is forgotten, and she is what she has been throughout: the representative of her people and the woman who is doomed to lifelong suffering.

The *Trojan Women* has enjoyed special popularity in the twentieth century, not surprisingly in view of the centrality of female suffering and the play's emphasis on the horrors of war. Often modern admiration has drawn additional strength from the belief that Euripides was indirectly criticizing the barbaric behaviour of his own countrymen in their treatment of the people of Melos, an island in the southern Aegean which had been brutally subjugated in the previous year. Because the Melians refused to submit to Athenian imperial control, their male population was massacred and the women and children sold into slavery. The episode, recorded in some detail by the historian Thucydides (v, 84–116), was long remembered as an atrocious 'war-crime'. Whether or not we are to associate Melos and Troy, the play explores in painful detail the meaning of conquest and defeat – especially defeat. This exploration is achieved through all the varied styles and forms of the tragic genre: set-speech, choral song, actor's solo lyric, lyric exchange.

The pathos of the slaughtered child, the lamentation for dead husbands, need no comment. In several speeches Hecabe outlines the gulf between her former prosperity and her present degradation. Rather differently, the chorus describe in a poignant ode the contrast between their deluded joy at the presumed departure of the Greeks and the fear and slaughter that ensued when the Wooden Horse revealed its sinister secret (511–67): this ode surely influenced the greatest ancient treatment of that terrible night, the second book of Virgil's *Aeneid*.

Two scenes less straightforward in their pathos, yet quintessentially Euripidean, may be less easy for the modern reader to appreciate: the scene featuring Cassandra's madness, and the *agon* or 'debate' between Hecabe and Helen about the latter's responsibility for the war. The former involves repeated use of the imagery of marriage; Cassandra enters bearing wedding-torches and singing in the style of a marriage hymn, as though her status as concubine of Agamemnon were something to celebrate. The scene at first presents Cassandra as inspired and raving, but subsequently she speaks more rationally, though still obscurely, to those on stage; in a series of speeches she undertakes to show that the Greeks will be unhappier in their victories than the Trojans (as already mentioned, this takes up the themes of the prologue). But her pronouncements, although understood by the audience, bring no comfort to the Trojan women and arouse no misgiving in the herald; traditionally Cassandra's prophecies were never believed (which was certainly important in the first play of the trilogy), and this is in any case natural when she is arguing so unpromising a case. Nor does her prophetic insight give her comfort for herself: she anticipates her own death, too.

The debate between the aged and dishevelled Hecabe and the young, beautiful and gaudily dressed Helen is a Euripidean *tour de force*. The issue is whether Helen is truly worthy of death as a punishment. The judge is Menelaus, the man least likely to decide the case objectively. Helen's speech is cool-headed, ingenious but paradoxical; according to her way of thinking, it was everybody's fault but her own. Hecabe's response is far more effective, being founded on moral outrage and hard evidence; yet it is also coloured by deep antagonism and wholly understandable hatred. The debate, however, is one in which the force of competing arguments is not the decisive factor: what turns the balance is not logic or evidence, but Helen's beauty and Menelaus' renewed desire. Once they are face to face again, the future is inevitable; indeed, it was a traditional feature of the legend that Menelaus' resolution to kill Helen was dissipated when he was in her presence. Like the *agon* of *Hippolytus*, the scene dramatizes not so much the power of argument as the failure of persuasion and rationality. In short, both this episode and that involving Cassandra illustrate in different ways the helplessness of the Trojan women: even when their grasp of right and wrong, past responsibility and future consequences, is sounder than that of their Greek captors, the very fact of their situation makes it impossible for them to translate their knowledge into effect. This helplessness and frustration is as much a part of the play's tragic quality as the raw suffering which is enacted.

CHARACTERS

POSEIDON

ATHENA

HECABE, *queen of Troy, widow of Priam*

CHORUS *of Trojan women, prisoners-of-war*

TALTHYBIUS, *herald to the Greek army*

CASSANDRA, *daughter of Hecabe, priestess of Apollo*

ANDROMACHE, *widow of Hector*

ASTYANAX, *young son of Hector and Andromache*

MENELAUS, *husband of Helen*

HELEN, *wife of Menelaus, daughter of Zeus*

POSEIDON: I am Poseidon. From the salty depths of the Aegean sea I come, where the Nereids step gracefully in the circling dance. Since the day when Phoebus and I raised walls of stone, straight and true, around this city of Troy, never has my heart lost its goodwill towards the city of my Phrygians.[1] But now it is a smoking ruin, sacked by the spearsmen of Greece. Epeius of Phocis, that man from Parnassus, prompted by Pallas' clever plans, fashioned a horse teeming with men-at-arms[2] and sent it inside the battlements with its cargo of doom.

Deserted are the sacred groves; the gods' shrines run with human blood. By the steps at the altar base of Zeus, Protector of the Hearth, Priam lies, fallen in death. The gold and spoils of the Phrygians, vast treasure, are on their way to the ships of the Greeks. Now they wait for a following wind: after ten summers and winters they long to see their wives and children, those men of Greece who came in war against this city. I, too, am going to leave Ilium the renowned and my altars, resigning victory to Hera, Argos' goddess, and to Athena, who together have brought ruin on the Phrygians.[3] Whenever a city succumbs to the misery of desolation, the worship due the gods also falls sick and loses its accustomed place.

Scamander echoes to the endless wails of captive women
as they learn the masters assigned to them by lot. Some fall to
30   the Arcadians, others to Thessaly's men, others still to
Theseus' sons, the Athenian princes. [*He gestures behind him:*]
In these tents are the women of Troy who are not to be won
by lot; they have been selected for the leading men of the
army, and in their number is Helen[4] of Sparta, Tyndareus'
child, regarded as a prisoner-of-war and rightly so. [*He points
to the woman stretched on the ground:*] As for this wretch here,
should anyone wish to see a sorrowful sight, this is Hecabe
who lies before the entrance, weeping many tears for her
many sufferings. Her daughter, Polyxena, has met a wretched
40   end at the tomb of Achilles, but of this she is unaware. Gone
are Priam and their children, and as for Cassandra,[5] the Lord
Apollo has left her a virgin but filled her with prophetic
madness. And now Agamemnon, indifferent to piety and the
wish of the god, intends to use force to make her his concubine.

And so, dear city, so prosperous once, farewell! Farewell,
you shining towers! If Pallas, child of Zeus, had not brought
ruin on you, you would be standing on your foundations still.

[*The goddess* ATHENA *enters.*]

ATHENA: May I address the one who is my father's closest
relative, a god mighty and revered in heaven, renouncing our
50   former enmity?

POSEIDON: You may, Queen Athena. When kinsfolk meet, it
is no small comfort to the heart.

ATHENA: I thank you for your graciousness. I propose that we
discuss a matter of common interest to us both,[6] my royal
lord.

POSEIDON: Do you bring some news perhaps, from a god, from
Zeus or one of heaven's lesser company?

ATHENA: No; it is for the sake of Troy, where now we stand,
that I have come, hoping to enlist your power.

POSEIDON: Can it be that you have given up your hatred of old
and feel pity for the city, now it is reduced to flames and
60   ashes?

ATHENA: Go back first to my point; will you share my proposal and agree to whatever I wish to do?

POSEIDON: Certainly; but I wish to know what your interest is in this matter. Is it to help Greeks or Trojans you have come here?

ATHENA: I want to bring joy to the Trojans who were my enemies before, and to give the Greeks a journey home they will bitterly regret.

POSEIDON: Why these sudden leaps from one mood to another, these random impulses of love and hatred, so excessively strong?

ATHENA: Are you unaware of the insult done to me and my temples?

POSEIDON: I do know; it was when Ajax dragged Cassandra off by force.[7]   70

ATHENA: And the Greeks did not punish him severely, or even reprimand him!

POSEIDON: Despite the fact that your strength enabled them to sack Troy.

ATHENA: This is why I want your help in teaching them a serious lesson.

POSEIDON: I am yours to command. What will you do?

ATHENA: I want to make their journey home[8] one of bitterness and pain.

POSEIDON: While they are still on land, or once they have taken to the briny deep?

ATHENA: When they make their homeward voyage from Ilium. Zeus will send down rain and hail in torrents and make the sky dark with hurricanes. He says he will put in my hands his fiery thunderbolts to strike the Greeks and set their ships   80 ablaze. Then it is for you to play your part: make the Aegean sea roar with monstrous waves and churning waters, fill Euboea's sheltered gulf with corpses, so that in future the Greeks may know to treat my shrines reverently and to hold the other gods in awe.

POSEIDON: It shall be done; this favour needs no lengthy

pleading. I shall make havoc with the waters of the Aegean
sea. The shores of Myconos, the rocky coasts of Delos, Scyros,
90   Lemnos, and Caphareium's headlands will house the bodies
of many a dead man. Now make your way to Olympus, take
from your father's hands the lightning bolts and watch for the
moment when the Greek fleet is under full sail. [ATHENA
leaves. POSEIDON *turns to survey what remains of Troy, then
addresses the audience.*]

Mad is the man who sacks cities, violating temples and
graves, the holy places of the dead; the desolation he makes
seals his own doom in time to come.[9] [*He leaves. Slowly,*
HECABE *rises from the ground.*]

HECABE: *Up, unhappy creature; lift your head and neck from the
ground. This is Troy no more; no more are we the royal house of*
100   *Troy. Fortune is changing course and you must endure it. Set your
course by the wind, sail as fate directs. Do not steer your ship of
life head-on against the waves, sailing as you do at the whim of
chance.*

*Oh misery, misery! Am I not in anguish, and should I not lament
when my homeland, my children, my husband are no more? O my
forebears, your proudly swelling sail is shortened now; you amount*
110   *to nothing after all! What should I leave unsaid, what tell to the
world? What should I lament? Oh, pity me for the harshness of this
bed where I lie, my back stretched out on a hard couch – what a state
I am in! Oh my head, my temples, my ribs! How I long to twist
and turn my back and spine now to one side of my body, now to the
other, swaying to the ceaseless flow of my tearful refrain! Even this*
120   *is music to those in misery – to chant the joyless dirge of their
doom.*

[HECABE *has now finally risen completely from the ground.*]
*O prows of ships, with the hated paean of flutes and the sound of
cheerful pipes, you came on speedy oars over the purply deep, passing
by the safe harbours of Greece to sacred Ilium, and in her bay (ah*
130   *me!) you hung your twisted cables, Egypt's crop,[10] as you came in
quest of Menelaus' hateful wife, that disgrace to Castor and stain on
Eurotas' name. She is the murderer of Priam with his crop of fifty*

sons, she is the one who has driven wretched Hecabe on to this shore
of ruin. Ah me! Look at the seat I occupy here, hard by the tents of
Agamemnon! An old woman, they lead me from my home to slavery,   140
my head pitifully ravaged in lamentation. You wretched wives of
Trojan warriors and you virgin brides of the spear, Ilium is consigned
to smoke. Let us lament her. Just as the mother bird starts up her cry
for her fledgelings, so I shall begin the song for you, a song far different
from that one I used to begin in honour of Troy's gods, when Priam
leaned on his sceptre and my foot gave the loud stamp to start the   150
dancing.

[*The* CHORUS *of Trojan women now enters in two halves.*]

LEADER OF FIRST SEMI-CHORUS: *Hecabe, what is the meaning*
of these shouts and cries from you? What are you talking about? I
heard your piteous cries of lamentation ringing through the tents. Fear
sweeps through the hearts of the Trojan women who sit inside these
tents bewailing their slavery.

HECABE: *Children, the Greeks are on the move, their oarsmen already*
going down to their ships.   160

LEADER OF FIRST: *Ah me, what do they intend? It has come, I*
suppose, the hour when they will carry me off in their ships from my
homeland?

HECABE: *I do not know, but ruin is my expectation.*

FIRST SEMI-CHORUS: *Oh no, no! Women of Troy, sisters in sorrow,*
leave your tents to hear the sufferings in store for you! The Greeks
are setting sail for their homes.

HECABE: *Ah, ah! Do not, I beg you, send out here my raving, maddened*   170
Cassandra to suffer outrage from the Greeks; I have sorrows enough
to pain me. Oh, misery! Troy, wretched Troy, you are no more and
wretched are those who leave you, in life as in death.

LEADER OF SECOND SEMI-CHORUS: *Ah me! Trembling with*
fear, my queen, I have left these tents of Agamemnon to hear you.
Can the Greeks have reached the decision to end my wretched life?
Or are the sailors already taking their places in each ship, oars at   180
the ready?

HECABE: *My child, I came here sleepless in the dawn, my heart stricken*
with shuddering fear.

LEADER OF SECOND: *Has some herald come already from the Greeks?*
Who is to have me for his miserable slave?

HECABE: *You are near, I think, to the drawing of lots.*

SECOND SEMI-CHORUS: *Oh no, no! Pity me! What man of Argos*
or of Phthia will take me away from Troy? Who will take me to an
island place?

190 HECABE: *Alas! Who shall have me, a miserable hag, for his slave?*
Where, where on earth shall I go, poor old decrepit Hecabe, resembling
one dead, the shadowy image of a corpse? Oh, the thought of it! Shall
I be set to keep watch at some doorway or given charge over children,
I, who reigned as queen in Troy?

CHORUS [Strophe]: *Oh, such misery! These laments for your shameful*
state, how pitiful they are to my ear! No more shall I send my whirling
200 *shuttle backwards and forwards at Trojan looms. For the last time*
I look upon my parents' home, and then no more. I will have sufferings
harder to bear, forced to share the bed of a Greek – cursed be that
night and such a fate! – or reduced to pitiful slavery as I draw water
from Pirene's holy spring. If only we might go to the land of
210 *Theseus,*[11] *famed and fortunate! But never to the swirling Eurotas,*
loathsome dwelling of Helen, to face slavery under Menelaus, sacker
of Troy.

[Antistrophe:] *I have heard tell of Peneus' proud land, lovely*
pedestal of Olympus, that it teems with prosperity and plentiful
fruitfulness. There I would choose to go after Theseus' sacred land,
220 *so loved by heaven. And there is Etna's land, home of Hephaestus,*
that faces Carthage; Sicily, mother of mountains – I hear her proclaimed
for her crowns of valour. Then there is the country that is its neighbour
as sailors cross the Ionian sea, the one watered by Crathis,[12] *fairest*
of rivers, that tinges men's hair a fiery gold and with its holy waters
nurtures the land, making it rich in prosperity through its noble men.

230 *But here comes a herald from the Greek army, with fresh news*
in his purse, his hurried steps now coming to an end. What does he
bring? What is his message? We are slaves now, after all, and belong
to the Dorian land. [*Enter* TALTHYBIUS.]

TALTHYBIUS: Hecabe, as you know, I have come to Troy many
times as herald from the Greek army and so am well known

to you, lady, from the past. I am Talthybius and I am here to
bring you fresh news.

HECABE: *This is it, dear women, this is it, the words I have dreaded
all this while!*

TALTHYBIUS: The lots have now been drawn for you, if this
was your fear.   240

HECABE: *Ah me, what is to be our new home – some city of Thessaly
or of Phthia or in the land of Cadmus?*

TALTHYBIUS: You have each been assigned to a different man,
not all together.

HECABE: *Who has won each of us? Which woman of Troy can expect
a happy fate?*

TALTHYBIUS: These are matters I know, but you must ask about
each woman in turn, not all at once.

HECABE: *Then who received my child, my poor Cassandra, tell me?*

TALTHYBIUS: She was chosen as a special prize by King
Agamemnon.

HECABE: *To be the slave of his Spartan wife?*[13] *Not that!*   250

TALTHYBIUS: No; to warm his bed in the hours of darkness.

HECABE: *What? The maiden of Phoebus, to whom the golden-haired
god gave the gift of life-long virginity?*

TALTHYBIUS: Desire for the entranced girl left its arrow in his
heart.

HECABE: *Then throw away the sacred sprays, my child, cast off the
holy wreaths you wear as the god's livery!*

TALTHYBIUS: Yes; is it not a great honour, to gain a king's bed?

HECABE: *What of the youngest child you took from me? Where is she?*   260

TALTHYBIUS: Do you mean Polyxena? Who is it you ask about?

HECABE: *She is the one. To which man has she been yoked by the lot?*

TALTHYBIUS: She has been appointed to serve at the tomb of
Achilles.[14]

HECABE: *Oh no! I gave her birth so that she might be an attendant at
a tomb! But what custom friend, what ordinance is this that the
Greeks have?*

TALTHYBIUS: Think of your daughter as fortunate; hers is a
happy state.

HECABE: *What do you mean by that? Tell me, does she see the*
270   *sunlight?*

TALTHYBIUS: Her fate is such that her troubles are at an end.

HECABE: *What of poor Andromache, wife of Hector the warrior, how
does she fare?*

TALTHYBIUS: She too was selected; Achilles' son took her for
himself.

HECABE: *And whose slave am I, the old woman who needs a stick to
serve her as a third foot?*

TALTHYBIUS: Ithaca's king, Odysseus, got you as his slave.

HECABE [*breaking into a ritual lament*]: *Ah, ah! Beat your cropped*
280   *head, Hecabe, tear both cheeks with your nails! Oh, pity me, pity
me! The lot has condemned me to serve a foul, treacherous master,*[15]
*an enemy of justice, a lawless beast, who with his lying tongue twists
everything from one side to the other and then back again, causing
hatred where once there was love. Cry woe for me, you women of*
290   *Troy. I am ruined, finished, mocked by fate, the wretched victim
of the cruellest of lots!*

CHORUS-LEADER: Lady, you know what is to happen to you.
But which Greek of the Peloponnese or the north controls
my fate?

TALTHYBIUS [*to servants in attendance*]: Inside with you, men!
You must bring Cassandra out here at once so I can deliver
her to the commander, and then bring the others those
prisoners they have won.

     Ha! What is that glare from a pine torch burning inside?
Are the Trojan women starting a fire in the depth of the tents
300   now that they are about to be carried off from Troy to Argos,
or what is it they are up to? Are they setting fire to their own
bodies out of some desire to die? There is no doubt in such
cases that freedom chafes at the yoke of adversity. Open up,
open up! I don't want the blame for what would benefit *them*
but enrage the Greeks!

HECABE: No, they are not starting a fire. It is my child Cassandra
who is rushing out here in a state of frenzy.

     [*Enter* CASSANDRA *at a run from the tent, dressed as Apollo's*

priestess and brandishing a torch. She sings excitedly in celebration
of her forthcoming 'marriage' to Agamemnon.]

CASSANDRA: *Raise up the torch!*[16] *Bring it here, bring me light! I pay*
reverence to this temple − look, look! − I light it with the blaze of
these torches! O lord Hymenaeus! Blessed is the bridegroom, blessed 310
am I, promised in marriage to a king in Argos! O Hymen, lord
Hymenaeus![17] *Since you, mother, continue to grieve for my dead*
father and our country with tearful lamentations, I shall honour my
own wedding by holding up this flaming torch − see its dazzling 320
brilliance! − offering to you, Hymenaeus, and to you, Hecate, the
light that custom prescribes when virgins are wed.

   Step high with quivering foot! Bring on, bring on the dance −
evan! evoe!![18] *− as in my father's happiest days! Sacred is the dancing*
band. Lead it, Phoebus! In your temple amid the bay trees I offer
sacrifice. O Hymen, Hymenaeus! Hymen! Dance, mother, join the 330
dance, weave your steps with me, circling in and out, to show you
love me! In honour of the bride loudly sing the wedding hymn, with
songs and shouts wish her happiness! Come, you Phrygian girls in
your lovely robes, honour in song the husband who is fated to share
my marriage-bed! 340

CHORUS-LEADER: My queen, seize hold of your daughter in
her madness before she goes skipping off into the midst of the
Greek army!

HECABE: Hephaestus,[19] you carry the torch at mortal weddings
but this flame you kindle here is one of misery − how my
high hopes are dashed! O, my child, I never thought to see
your marriage celebrated amidst the spears and lances of
Greeks! Let me have your torch. You rush in such distraction
that you are not holding it straight. Your circumstances have
not brought you to your senses, my child, and still you remain
unchanged. Take the torches inside, women of Troy, and 350
let your tears serve as reply to her wedding songs.

CASSANDRA: Mother, the victory is mine! Deck my head with
garlands and rejoice in my royal marriage! Escort me on my
way and if you think me less than eager, give me a hard push!
As Loxias exists, the Greeks' glorious king, Agamemnon, will

find me a wife more hard to bear than Helen ever was. I will kill him;[20] I will sack his home as he has mine, taking revenge for my brothers and father.

360

But I will not speak of this; I will not sing of the axe that will enter my neck and others', of the conflict that will see a mother killed thanks to my wedding, or the overthrow of Atreus' house. Instead I will show that this city is more fortunate than the Greeks.[21] Possessed I may be but to this extent I will escape my frenzy's grip. In their desire to hunt down Helen they made one woman and her passion the excuse for killing countless men. Their general in his wisdom, to

370

further a cause he should have hated, destroyed what he held most dear,[22] foregoing the pleasures of children at home to gratify a brother, all for the sake of a woman, and that one who had not been abducted by force, no, she left of her own free will. When the Greeks came to the banks of Scamander, one by one they died, yet they were not fighting because they feared to lose their territory or to defend the high towers of their native city. Those who fell in battle never saw their children, were never dressed for the grave by loving wives, but lie in foreign soil. A like fate awaited their families at

380

home: their wives died as widows, their parents without sons after raising their offspring in their homes, never to see them again. Not one of them shall have the offering of blood poured into the soil at his tomb.[23]

But the Trojans in the first place – and this is their greatest glory – met death fighting for their homeland. Those who died in the field were carried as corpses into their homes by comrades and received their covering of earth in the land of their fathers, wrapped in their burial cloths by the hands of

390

their own families. As for those Trojans who survived the fray, each day that came they spent with their wives and children, pleasures denied to the Greeks.

As far as Hector's fate is concerned, a matter of pain to you, let me tell you the truth of it. He has died and left us, but not before winning the greatest name for valour, and for this we have to thank the coming of the Greeks. Had they stayed at home, his greatness would have gone unknown. Paris took as his wife the daughter of Zeus; without this marriage he would have had at home a wife of no interest to anyone. Avoidance of war is the duty, it is true, of all intelligent men; but should it come to it, it is a crown of some distinction to a city to perish nobly, as it is inglorious to meet a coward's end.

For all these reasons it would be wrong for you, mother, to pity this land or my becoming Agamemnon's mistress. I will use this union of mine to bring down those whom you and I most hate.

CHORUS-LEADER: It amuses you to laugh at your own misfortunes and chant prophecies, but perhaps you will show they were not as true as when you sang them.

TALTHYBIUS [*showing impatience after his earlier incredulity*]: Had not Apollo afflicted you with madness, you would pay heavily for seeing the commanders off from this land with such offensive language. But it's true, after all, those men of importance and wisdom in the world's eyes are no better than those judged to be nonentities. Take Atreus' well-loved son, most mighty king of all the Greeks, who fell under this demented creature's spell and chose her for his bed. Now I'm just a poor man but never would I have taken a fancy to someone like her. [*To* CASSANDRA:] As for these words of yours, praising the Trojans and criticizing the Greeks, I'll let the winds blow them away, seeing as you're not right in the head. Follow me to the ships; you'll make a fine little bride for the general! [*To* HECABE:] And you be ready to come when Laertes' son wishes to take you! It's a decent woman[24] you'll be going to serve, as men say who came to Ilium.

CASSANDRA [*indignant at his tone*]: He's a smart one, this servant! Why is it heralds have an honourable name, when they are the one thing that every human being detests, these lackeys of kings and states?

You say my mother will be going to the house of Odysseus?

What then of Apollo's pronouncements, revealed to me, that say she will die here? The rest I leave unsaid; I will not insult her.[25] Poor Odysseus, he little knows what sufferings are in store for him! The day will come when he thinks my sufferings and the Trojans' as desirable as gold. After ten long years to follow those spent here he will reach, alone, his native land. He must face terrible Charybdis, who has her dwelling in that narrow, rockbound strait, and the Cyclops, eater of raw flesh, who haunts the mountains. Ligurian Circe will he know, who transforms men into swine, and shipwreck on the salty sea, the rapture of the lotus and the sacred cattle of the Sun, whose bloody flesh will one day find utterance and tell a tale to wound Odysseus' ears. To be brief, he will descend, alive, to the kingdom of Hades and will get safe across the waters of that lake only to find on his return troubles past numbering in his home.[26]

But why do I proclaim the woes awaiting Odysseus? On your way, Cassandra, lose no time! Let me be wedded to my bridegroom in Hades! A wretched, degrading burial shall you have, great captain of the Greeks, for all your seeming majesty, with night, not day, for witness! I too will be flung out, yes, a naked corpse, and some ravine flowing with storm water will offer me up to wild beasts to divide among themselves near my husband's grave, me, the servant of Apollo! [*Tearing off the articles that mark her as Apollo's priestess:*] O sacred ribbons of the god I love as no other, mystic emblems, farewell![27] I take my leave of the festivals I gloried in before. Away with you, I tear you from my skin! I want to give them to the swift breezes to carry to you, Lord of Prophecy, while my body is yet undefiled. Where lies the general's ship? Where am I to step on board? Quick! Not a moment to lose! Watch out for that breeze to swell your sails so you can take away from this land one of the three Furies, myself!

Mother, goodbye! Shed no tears for me, Troy, dear homeland, brothers who lie under the earth, and you, my father, who sired me, you will receive me soon enough; like a conquering hero will I pass to the world below, after 460 bringing ruin on the house of Atreus' sons who destroyed us. [CASSANDRA *leaves the stage.* HECABE, *overcome with emotion, collapses on the ground.*]

CHORUS-LEADER: Guardians of old Hecabe, do you not see how your mistress has fallen speechless and lies prostrate? Lay hold of her! Idle creatures, will you leave an old woman who has fallen? Lift her up!

HECABE: Let me lie where I have fallen (services unwanted are never welcome, my maids); they merit falling, the sufferings I know, have known and yet shall know. O you gods![28] Sorry allies are those I call upon, but to call upon the gods has some point when misfortune strikes one of us mortals. I wish 470 therefore first of all to sing of my blessings; thus I will cause my hearers to pity my sufferings the more. Of royal blood myself, I married one of royal blood; then I gave birth to children who would be fine warriors, no ordinary men to mock my labour but pre-eminent among Trojans. No woman of Troy or Greece or foreign birth could ever boast of sons like these. And then I saw them fall to the spears of the Greeks. I had this hair of mine cut off at the graves of my dead sons. 480 I wept for Priam, their father, not hearing the end from others' lips but with my own eyes seeing him butchered by the household altar. I saw the capture of my city. The daughters I raised in purity to grace the arms of no common husbands, I raised for others – they have been taken from my hands. No hope have I now that they will ever set eyes on me again or I on them.

And last of all, to crown my wretched sorrows, I will go to Greece in my old age to live a life of servitude. All the 490 tasks that are most burdensome to these old shoulders they will inflict on me. I will become a doorkeeper, a servant who watches over the keys – I, the mother of Hector! They will put me to baking bread, with the hard earth for this poor old

back of mine to rest upon – no more the comfort of a royal
bed. For clothing I will wear around this worn-out skin
worn-out rags that bring shame on my one-time prosperity.

Oh, what misery is mine! Because of one marriage, because
of one woman, what sufferings have been and will *yet* be my
500 lot! O my child, my Cassandra, wracked by divine ecstasy,
your purity has been destroyed, and in such cruel circumstances! And you, my poor Polyxena,[29] where, oh where are
you? Of all the children I bore, not one, male or female, is
here to help his wretched mother. Why then do you set me
on my feet? What hopes can you have? Lead me on my way,
the woman who once strode so proudly through Troy but is
now reduced to slavery, lead me to my billet on the ground,
to my stony pillow, and there let me fall and weep away my
life, ravaged by tears. Fortune has her favourites but not one
should be called happy – do not think it – this side of the
510 grave. [HECABE *once more collapses to the ground.*]

CHORUS [Strophe]: *Sing me, Muse, a song of Ilium, a tearful song
unheard before and worthy of a hero's passing. Now shall I sing a
song of Troy, how that four-footed conveyance of the Greeks brought
us to a miserable end, captives of their spears, on the day they left the*
520 *horse in its golden finery at our gates, its cargo of armed men making
a sound that reached the heavens. There we stood, Troy's citizens,
and raised our voices in a shout from Troy's rocky height: 'Come,
our troubles now are ended! Bring it to the citadel, this sacred effigy,
and offer it to our Trojan maid, daughter of Zeus!'[30] All left their
homes, every young woman, every old man. Showing their joy in*
530 *songs they embraced their own ruin so disguised.*

[Antistrophe:] *All the race of Phrygia hurried to the gates to give
to the goddess that creature made of mountain pine, polished ambus-
cade of Greeks that would bring ruin to Dardanus' land, a gift to the
maiden whose horses are immortal. As if they were launching some
black ship, they cast ropes of hemp around it, and brought it to the
stone dwelling of divine Pallas, where they set it on the floor that*
540 *was to run with our country's blood. When night's darkness had
descended on their joyful labour and the Libyan flute rang forth with*

*its Phrygian strains, the maidens of Troy were lifting their feet high
in the rhythmic dance and singing songs of happiness, while inside
the houses a dark glow lay over the sleepers from the brilliant glare of
torches outside.* 550

[Epode:] *At that hour I was one of those who danced before the
temple of the mountain maid,*[31] *virgin child of Zeus, honouring her
in song. A murderous cry suddenly rang through the city and seized
Pergama. Precious young children flung their arms in panic round
their mothers' skirts. Out from his ambush stepped the god of war,* 560
*and maiden Pallas' work had begun. Around the altars Trojans fell in
carnage, and in their beds the young women, new-widowed as their
husbands were butchered at their sides, became a prize that would bear
children for Greece, bringing sorrow to the homeland of the Trojans.*

[ANDROMACHE, *widow of Hector, enters with her little son,*
ASTYANAX, *in a drawn cart containing Trojan spoils of war,
including her husband's armour.*]

CHORUS: *Hecabe, do you see Andromache here, carried in a cart that
belongs to the enemy? She has with her Hector's son, her own dear
Astyanax, next to her heaving breast. Poor lady, where are you* 570
*bound riding in this cart, with Hector's bronze armour at your side
and the plundered spoils of Troy with which Achilles' son will decorate
the temples of Phthia, far from their Trojan home?*

[ANDROMACHE *and* HECABE *now sing a duet in which they
lament their fate.*]

ANDROMACHE: *It is the Greeks, my masters, who are carrying me
off.*

HECABE: *Oh, no!*

ANDROMACHE: *Why do you sing a song of sorrow that is mine?*

HECABE: *Oh, feel pity!* . . .

ANDROMACHE: . . . *for these sufferings of mine,* . . .

HECABE: . . . *o Zeus!,* . . .

ANDROMACHE: . . . *and what has befallen me.* 580

HECABE: *My children!*

ANDROMACHE: *That is what we once were.*

HECABE: *Gone are our days of greatness, gone is Troy –*

ANDROMACHE: *Poor city!*

HECABE: — *and gone my noble sons!*

ANDROMACHE: *Oh the pity, the pity, . . .*

HECABE: *. . . aye, for my . . .*

ANDROMACHE: *. . . sufferings.*

HECABE: *Pitiful is the fate . . .*

ANDROMACHE: *. . . of the city . . .*

HECABE: *. . . reduced to smoke.*

ANDROMACHE: *O come, my husband, I beg you!*

HECABE: *Unhappy girl, you cry out to my son who rests with Hades.*

590 ANDROMACHE: *Come and make your wife safe! You who deal destruction to the Greeks, . . .*

HECABE: *. . . first-born of my offspring to Priam!, . . .*

ANDROMACHE: *. . . lay me to rest in the sleep of death. These yearnings are strong —*

HECABE: *You wretched girl, these are the sorrows that we endure —*

ANDROMACHE: *— for the city that has passed away —*

HECABE: *— and woe is piled on woe!*

ANDROMACHE: *— due to the malice of the gods, from the day that your son cheated death,*[32] *he who brought ruin on Troy's citadel for the love of a wicked woman. Before Pallas' shrine they lie, the bodies of the dead, smeared in blood, stretched out for vultures to carry away;* 600 *a slave's yoke was his gift to Troy.*

HECABE: *O my homeland, my poor homeland, —*

ANDROMACHE: *I weep for you as I leave you, —*

HECABE: *— now you are witnessing your piteous end.*

ANDROMACHE: *— and for the home where I gave birth.*

HECABE: *O children, you are leaving your mother behind in a city without citizens. What weeping and wailing, what grief is here; tears for our home dissolve into tears. Yet the dead man forgets his anguish.*

CHORUS-LEADER: When misfortune strikes people, what pleasure they derive from tears, from lamentations and dirges, and music with sorrow in its strains.

ANDROMACHE: O mother of the man whose spear once felled 610 so many Greeks, mother of Hector, do you see what is happening here?

HECABE: I see the work of the gods, how they exalt to the skies things of no importance and bring to ruin what seems worthy of respect.

ANDROMACHE: I am being led away as booty together with my child. Noble birth descends to slavery; what a monstrous change!

HECABE: A terrible thing is necessity; Cassandra has only now gone from my side, torn away by violent hands.

ANDROMACHE: Oh no, not that, not that! Another Ajax has appeared, it seems, a second one, to plague your daughter. There is another sorrow that afflicts you also.

HECABE: My sorrows are past measure, past numbering. They 620 vie with each other, disaster with disaster.

ANDROMACHE: Your child Polyxena is dead, slaughtered at the tomb of Achilles as an offering to his lifeless corpse.

HECABE: Oh how wretched am I! This is what it meant, the dark riddle Talthybius gave me[33] earlier, I see it now!

ANDROMACHE: My own eyes witnessed her end. I left this cart and covered her with clothing and beat my breast in lamentation for the dead.

HECABE: O my child, I pity you! What an unholy sacrifice they made of you! Oh yes, I pity you! How shamefully you died!

ANDROMACHE: Her death was as it was. But what of me, still 630 living on? Her death was a kinder fate.

HECABE: My child, death and life are not at all the same; the one is nothingness, the other offers hope.

ANDROMACHE: To be dead, I say, is tantamount to never having been born. Death is to be preferred to a life of pain, for one who feels no danger can feel no pain. But when a man falls from Fortune's height to misery, his mind dwells constantly on the loss of his former happiness. Your daughter[34] is as 640 dead as if she had never seen the light of day; she knows nothing of the misery that was hers. But I aimed at a glorious name and, though I won this in generous measure, good fortune eluded my arrow. All the accomplishments that bring credit to a woman I strove to put into practice in the house of Hector. In the first instance, in the matter where a woman gets a bad reputation (whether she attracts criticism or not), namely, not remaining indoors, I suppressed my longing and stayed in the house. And inside the home I would not tolerate the idle gossip of women but was content to have in my own mind a teacher I could trust. I kept a quiet tongue in my husband's presence and let no clouds pass over my face. I knew in which matters I should be superior to my husband and when it was right for me to let him prevail. And it was because my reputation for this reached the ears of the Greek army that my doom was sealed. For once I was a captive, Achilles' son wished to take me as his wife. I shall be a slave in a murderer's house.

Now if I dismiss any thought of my beloved Hector and open my heart to my new husband, it will seem that I have betrayed the dead. But if, alternatively, I turn away from him in loathing, I will earn the hatred of my own master. And yet they say a single night thaws a woman's distaste for a man's bed. But I feel only contempt for the woman who casts off her former husband for a new affair and gives her love to another man. Why, not even the farm-horse, separated from his yoke-fellow and stablemate, pulls without remorse. But animals are devoid of speech and, lacking the use of reason, are by nature our inferiors. But in you, Hector my love, I had a husband who pleased me well, remarkable in intelligence, in birth, in wealth and in courage. You took me, a virgin, from my father's house and were the first to enter my maiden bed. And now you are no more, while I shall be shipped, a prisoner-of-war, to Greece, where the yoke of slavery awaits me. You have tears for Polyxena, but is her end as horrible as the sufferings in store for me? Not even hope have I, something that is left to all mortals, nor do I delude myself that Fortune will show me any kindness, though even fancies like this bring comfort.

CHORUS-LEADER: We are in the same desperate situation, you and I; in lamenting your sad fate you teach me the extent of my own woes.

HECABE: I have not yet set foot on a ship myself, but I know of them from pictures and from what I have heard. If sailors find themselves in a storm not too severe to endure, they work with a will to get clear of the danger, one man standing at the tiller, a second by the sails, another baling out the bilge-water. 690 But if the sea runs high and the storm proves too strong, they submit to circumstance and resign themselves to the rushing waves. So it is with me: the number of my woes makes me dumb; I resign the power of speech, overwhelmed by the waves of misery the gods have caused.

My dear child, you must not dwell on what happened to Hector; your tears will not bring him back. Honour your new lord and, to please your husband, offer him the enticement of your winning ways. If you do this, you will gratify all your 700 loved ones and may raise to manhood this boy, my son's child, to be a tower of strength to Troy, so that sons of your line may one day resettle Troy and our city may live on.

[*The herald* TALTHYBIUS *now enters, returning from the Greek camp, with an armed escort.*] But enough; a new subject displaces the old: who is this servant of the Greeks I see coming for a second time with new decisions to report?

TALTHYBIUS: Wife of Hector, once Troy's finest warrior, do not hate me; the message I will deliver against my will is one 710 determined by Atreus' sons and the Greeks together.

ANDROMACHE: What is it? These words you speak are a grim prelude indeed.

TALTHYBIUS: They have decided that the boy here – Oh, how am I to say it?

ANDROMACHE: . . . is not to have the same master as me? Can this be true?

TALTHYBIUS: None of the Greeks will ever be his master.

ANDROMACHE: Will they leave him here then, a poor remnant of the Trojans?

TALTHYBIUS: If there is a painless way to tell you this terrible news, I do not know it.

ANDROMACHE: Your concern is appreciated but not if it means holding back bad news from me.

TALTHYBIUS: They intend to kill your son; now you have the truth in all its horror.

ANDROMACHE: No, no, no! This wickedness you tell me is
720   worse than the marriage that will be mine!

TALTHYBIUS: Odysseus made a speech in the assembly of the Greeks and won their assent, –

ANDROMACHE: This is monstrous, monstrous, I say! My suffering goes beyond all measure!

TALTHYBIUS: – telling them not to let the son of such a hero grow to manhood –

ANDROMACHE: If only his eloquence would condemn his own children to death!

TALTHYBIUS: – but that they must fling him from the ramparts of Troy. [ANDROMACHE *seizes her son* ASTYANAX *and clutches him to her.*] Accept that this must be so and all will recognize your good sense. Do not hold on to him. Submit to the pain of your suffering as befits your rank and do not pretend to strength when you are so weak. Nowhere is there anyone for you to turn to. You must consider your situation: your city
730   and your husband are no more; you are at the mercy of others, and we are capable of doing battle with a single woman. Because of this you must curb your desire to resist and avoid doing anything that would bring shame or ill will upon you. I do not want you hurling curses at the Greeks. If you say any of the things that make the army angry, this boy will go unburied and unpitied. Keep your own counsel, accept your fate with dignity and you will not leave his corpse unburied; also, you yourself will find the Greeks more gracious.

740   ANDROMACHE: My precious boy, honoured as no other child, you will be killed by your enemies and will leave your mother in misery. Your father's prowess has brought no advantage to you. Oh what bitter fortune was in my bridal ceremony, in the marriage that brought me once to Hector's halls, not to bear a son for Greeks to butcher, but one to rule over Asia's

fertile plains! Are you crying, my boy? Do you realize what
is to happen to you? Why have your hands grabbed hold of
me? Why do you cling to my dress like some little bird   750
burying itself in my wings? Hector will not come, he will not
seize his famous spear and rise up from the ground to save
your life, nor will your father's kinsmen or the strength of
Phrygia. You will fall pitifully from on high, hurled by merciless
hands, and with broken neck breathe your last.

O my precious baby,[35] that your mother loves to hold in
her arms! How sweet the smell of your skin! All for nothing
then did this breast suckle you in your baby clothes! Wasted
were the pains I endured, wasted the labour that racked me
at your birth! Now greet your mother, no other time will   760
you have, embrace the one who gave you birth, fold your
arms around my neck and let your lips touch mine. [*In a sudden
spasm of anger:*] You Greeks, inventors of cruelties unworthy
of civilized men, why are you killing this child? What is his
crime? Daughter of Tyndareus,[36] never were you born from
Zeus; I say you were sired by many fathers, first by the Spirit
of Vengeance, then by Envy, by Murder, by Death and all
the foul things nurtured by the earth. I am quite certain that
Zeus is not your father, for death is what you bring to Greeks 770
and Trojans in their thousands. I curse you! Those lovely eyes
of yours have plunged the famous plain of Troy into hideous
ruin. [*The soldiers close in on* ASTYANAX.] Oh, take him, carry
him away, fling him to his death, if this is your will! Make a
banquet of his flesh![37] The gods have destroyed me and I am
powerless to save my son from death. Cover my wretched
body and throw me into a ship; it is a splendid wedding I shall
celebrate, the bride who has lost her own son!

CHORUS-LEADER: Unhappy Troy, countless are the lives you
have lost, all because of a single woman and her loathsome   780
marriage!

TALTHYBIUS: *Come my boy, leave your poor mother's loving embraces
and make your way to the lofty summit of your ancestral towers where
it is decreed that you shall meet your end.* [*To the soldiers:*] *Seize*

him! [ANDROMACHE's *cart is now pulled away from the scene towards the Greek camp.*] *What is needed for jobs of this kind is a herald untouched by pity, a man more disposed to cruelty in his heart than I am.* [TALTHYBIUS *and his party leave with* ASTYANAX.]

790 HECABE: *My child, son of my luckless son, we are being robbed of you against all justice, your mother and I. What has happened to me? What service can I render you, poor dear? See here, I beat my head and strike at my breasts – this is my tribute to you; they still recognize me as their mistress. Oh, I weep for Troy, I weep for you! What woe have we been spared? What stands between us and immediate, utter ruin for all?* [*She falls to the ground in despair.*]

CHORUS [Strophe]: *Telamon, king of bee-haunted Salamis,*[38] *on that sea-girt island lying across from the sacred hill you established your*
800 *home, there where Athena revealed the first shoots of the silvery olive, to be a heavenly crown and glory to shining Athens. From there you set forth, set forth sharing in deeds of renown with Alcmena's archer son*[39] *as companion, to sack Ilium, our town of Ilium, in days gone by.*

[Antistrophe:] *That was the time when, pining for his lost mares,*
810 *that hero brought from Greece the first flower of her manhood. By Simois' fair-flowing stream he shipped his seafaring oars and, making fast his cables from the stern, fetched from the ship his unerring bow and arrows that were to bring death to Laomedon. With a crimson blast of flame he razed Phoebus' true-planed walls of stone and laid waste the land of Troy. Twice in two onslaughts the murderous spear*
820 *brought down the sons of Dardanus around their battlements.*

[Strophe:] *All for nothing, then, son of Laomedon, do you step delicately amidst the goblets of gold and have the task of filling the cups of Zeus,*[40] *most noble service. The city that gave you birth is consumed by fire and the seashores wail, like a mother-bird screaming*
830 *for her young, here for husbands, here for children, here for aged mothers. Gone are they now, your fresh pools for bathing, and the wide spaces where you ran to take exercise. Yet beside the throne of Zeus you keep your face, fresh in its charms, in lovely serenity; but*
840 *the land of Priam has been destroyed by the spears of the Greeks.*

[Antistrophe:] *Eros, Eros, who came of old to Dardanus' halls
and stirred the hearts of the dwellers in heaven, how high you exalted
Troy in those days when you made her one in marriage with the gods!
But no more will I speak of what brought shame to Zeus.*[41] *The light
of Dawn*[42] *with her white wings, that light so loved by mortals, looked
grimly on as our land, looked on as our city's towers were laid in* 850
*ruin. Yet in her bedchamber she had a husband from this land to give
her children, one who was carried off in a chariot of gold, drawn by
four stars. Great were the hopes in his native land. But gone is the
love the gods once had for Troy.*

[MENELAUS *enters with attendants.*][43]

MENELAUS: How lovely shines the sun's brilliance this day on 860
which I will take possession of my wife! It was not, as men
think, for a woman's sake that I came to Troy, but to punish
the man who abused my hospitality by stealing my wife from
my house. Now he has got his deserts, thanks to the gods, he
and his country, subdued by the spears of the Greeks. But I
am here to bring back the Spartan woman (it pains me to use
her name, the wife who once was mine), since here in these 870
prisoners' quarters she is numbered with the other women of
Troy. She is the army's gift to me – the men who laboured
with their spears to win her – either to kill her or, should I
wish to show mercy, to have her brought back to the land
of Argos.

I have decided to spare Helen a death at Troy; I will bring
her over the sea in my ship to the land of Greece and then
give her there in recompense to those whose loved ones died
at Troy; they will kill her.

Come, you men, enter the tents and fetch her out! Drag 880
her here by that murderous hair of hers! With the next favourable wind we'll take her to Greece. [*His attendants go into the
tent.*]

HECABE [*raising her hands in prayer*]: O you who give the earth
support[44] and are by it supported, whoever you are, power
beyond our knowledge, Zeus, be you stern law of nature or
intelligence in man, to you I make my prayers; for you direct

in the way of justice all mortal affairs, moving with noiseless tread.

MENELAUS: What's this? You have a novel way of praying to the gods!

890 HECABE: I approve of your decision to kill your wife, Menelaus. But do not look at her, or she will fill you with longing and make you her prisoner. She ensnares men's eyes, captures cities, sets homes on fire; she possesses such enchantment. I know her, as do you and all her victims.

[*Enter Menelaus' men, escorting* HELEN *richly dressed.*]

HELEN: Menelaus, this action of yours strikes a most alarming note, having your servants use force to bring me out here in front of these tents. I suspect you hate me now, but I still wish to put the question: am I to live or not? What have you and 900 the Greeks decided?

MENELAUS: There was no need to count votes; the whole army gave you to me to kill as I was the victim of your crimes.

HELEN: Then can I make a reply to this and argue that, if I die, my death will be unjust?

MENELAUS: I have come here to end your life, not to have a debate.

HECABE: Let her speak, Menelaus, so she may die having had this right, and give me the task of putting the case against her.[45] You know nothing of the suffering she caused in Troy. The whole indictment succinctly put will be her executioner; 910 no loophole will be left for her.

MENELAUS: This concession you ask for will take up time. But if she wishes to speak, she may. Be assured, however, I will let her do this in deference to what *you* have said, not out of any regard for her.

HELEN [*to* MENELAUS]: Perhaps you will refuse to meet my points, whether you think them well made or not, since you look on me as an enemy. I will reply to the charges I imagine you will bring against me and put forward counter-arguments.

Firstly, it was this woman who gave birth to all these 920 troubles when she gave birth to Paris. Secondly, it was the

old king who destroyed both Troy and me when he failed to
kill the baby boy who was then called Alexandros, that torch
in her dream that would light so grim a fire. Let me tell you
how events unfolded after this beginning.

He it was who judged the three goddesses, that threefold
group. Pallas' gift to Alexandros was that he would overthrow
Greece as general in command of a Trojan army. Hera
promised that, should he prefer her, Paris' empire would
extend over Asia and the furthest ends of Europe. The Cyprian
spoke admiringly of my beauty and promised I would be his,
if she outstripped the goddesses by her fair looks. Consider   930
the next step in the process. The goddesses are defeated by
the Cyprian and to this extent my marriage benefited Greece:
you are not under the sway of foreigners as a result of conflict
or yielding to one man's power.

But what was good fortune for Greece was ruin for me:
sold for my beauty and now vilified by the very ones who
should have placed a crown upon my head. You will say I
have not yet met the point before us, how it was that I stole
away in secret from your house. The man who was this
woman's evil spirit, whether Alexandros or Paris[46] is the name
you wish to give him, had a powerful goddess at his side when
he came. This was the man you left behind in your home,   940
you worst of husbands, and sailed away from Sparta to the
land of Crete. So much for that matter. Next I will put a
question not to you but to myself. Why was it that I left your
house to go away, quite in my right mind, with a stranger,
betraying my country and home? Punish the goddess and
show yourself stronger than Zeus, who rules over the rest of
the gods but is that lady's slave; the blame is not mine.[47]   950

This point may give you a plausible argument against me:
when Alexandros died and passed below the earth, no goddess
then controlled my heart's desires and my duty was to leave
that house and return to the ships of the Greeks. This was just
what I was eager to do. My witnesses are the guards on the
towers, the men who kept watch from the walls, who often

discovered me secretly using a rope to lower myself from the
960 battlements to the ground. How then my husband would it
still be right for me to die, how right for you to wield the
sword, when that man married me by force, and, instead of a
victor's prize, my days in Troy have brought me bitter servitude? You may want to be stronger than the gods, but, if you
do, it is a foolish wish.

CHORUS-LEADER: Majesty, destroy this woman's persuasive
words and protect your children, protect your homeland, for
she speaks with fair words from a foul heart; now *that* inspires
fear.

HECABE: First I will come to the defence of the goddesses and
970 show that there is no justice in what she says. I do not believe
that Hera and virgin Athena were guilty of such folly that the
one was ever prepared to sell off Argos to the barbarian, or
that Pallas would deliver Athens into slavery under Phrygians.
It was not high spirits or pride in their looks that made them
come to Ida; what could have inspired the goddess Hera with
such a passion for beauty? Did she crave a finer husband than
Zeus? Was Athena hunting for some god to take as her husband,
she who shunned the marriage-bed and begged her father to
980 let her stay a virgin? Do not represent the gods as witless to
lend colour to your own wickedness; you will have trouble
convincing men of sense,[48] I think.

It was with the Cyprian at his side, you said (and here you
made yourself look ridiculous), that my son came to the house
of Menelaus. Could she not have remained quietly in heaven
and brought you and the city of Amyclae besides to Ilium?
My son was handsome beyond all other men; when you saw
him your mind *became* the goddess.[49] All the indiscretions of
mortals pass for Aphrodite and it is appropriate that the god-
990 dess's name begins with folly.[50] You saw him resplendent in
his foreign costume and gold and you went out of your mind.
For, living in modest circumstances as you were in Greece,
you hoped that, once you had shaken off the dust of Sparta,

you would enjoy a riot of extravagance in the city of the Phrygians that flowed with gold. Menelaus' palace gave little scope for the life of luxury you wanted to revel in.

So much for that idea. Force was used by my son, you say, when he took you away. Why then was this not noticed by any of the Spartans? Did you scream for assistance from Castor or his brother? They were still there, young and strong, as 1000 yet not raised to the stars. When you came to Troy, with the Greeks hot on your trail, and the deadly clash of spears began, any news of Menelaus' success you greeted with, 'My brave Menelaus!', hoping to vex my son[51] with the thought he had a powerful rival for your love. But if ever Fortune favoured the Trojans, Menelaus was forgotten. You kept an eye on chance and studied how to follow in her footsteps, but virtue held no such attractions for you.

Then you describe how you were so reluctant to stay that you used a rope to lower yourself in secret from the battlements. Were you discovered anywhere tying a noose 1010 for your neck or sharpening a sword, the course of action a woman of honour would have taken if she yearned for the husband she once had? And yet how often I urged you to act: 'Leave here, my daughter! My sons will find new brides; I will smuggle you out safely to the ships of the Greeks. Bring this fighting between the Greeks and ourselves to an end!' But this was not at all to your taste. You were playing the great lady in the house of Alexandros and wanted foreign 1020 servants to bow low before you. This was what mattered to you.

And after all this you come out here, you abominable creature, tricked out in these fine clothes, and look your husband in the eye, under the same sky! You should have come out humbly in tattered clothes, quaking with fear, your head shaven, with a modest bearing rather than a shameless air, in view of your past crimes.

Menelaus, so that you may know how I mean to end my

speech, crown Greece as your good name requires by killing
1030   this woman and establish this law for the rest of womankind:
the penalty for betraying one's husband is death.

CHORUS-LEADER: Menelaus, punish your wife as your forefathers and house would approve. Show yourself noble in
your enemies' eyes and prevent your fellow-Greeks from
charging you with unmanliness.

MENELAUS: We have arrived at the same conclusion, you and
I, that this woman of her own choice left my house to share
a stranger's bed. She introduced the Cyprian into her speech
merely to flatter herself. [*To* HELEN:] Off with you now to
the place of stoning! I want you to die and pay in an instant
1040   for the years of suffering endured by the Greeks; I want you
to learn not to bring disgrace upon me!

HELEN [*throwing herself in front of him and clasping his knees*]: No,
I beg you, do not make me guilty of the madness of the
goddesses and kill me! Show some understanding!

HECABE: Do not betray the men she killed, your comrades-in-
arms! I entreat you in their name, in their children's name!

MENELAUS: Enough, old woman. I pay her no attention. [*To
his servants:*] Away with her, take her off to the ship that will
carry her over the sea!

HECABE: Do not let her board the same ship as you!

MENELAUS: Why ever not? Does she weigh more than she used
1050   to?[52]

HECABE: There is no lover who does not love for ever.

MENELAUS: That depends on how the lovers view matters. But
I will do as you wish: she will board a different ship from
mine; for there is actually sense in what you say. And once
she gets to Argos she will meet a foul end as befits so foul a
creature and make all women curb their lustful instincts. This
is no easy task, but just the same her execution will strike fear
into their wanton hearts, even if their shamelessness exceeds
hers. [MENELAUS *and attendants leave with* HELEN.]

1060 CHORUS [Strophe]: *Have you then betrayed us to the Greeks, o Zeus,*

*abandoning your temple in Ilium with its altar and incense, the
burning cakes, and scent of myrrh rising into the air, forsaking holy
Pergamum and the ivy-clad glens of Ida washed by torrents of melted
snow, Ida whose heights are struck by the first shafts of dawn, the
place of holiness that is filled with the sun's light?*   1070

[Antistrophe:] *Gone are the sacrifices held in your honour, the
tuneful sound of dancers singing, the gods' festivals celebrated in the
long hours of the night; the gilded statues of the Trojans and their
holy cakes,*[53] *twelve in number. I wonder, o King, I wonder if, as
you sit on your ethereal throne in heaven, you take account of these
things, when my city has perished in fire, wasted by the blazing surge
of the flames.*   1080

[Strophe:] *O my love, o husband mine, in death you wander,
without burial, without the water that purifies; but I shall speed across
the seas on the wings of some ship, onward to Argos where the horses
graze and men dwell in walls of stone that reach to the sky, the
masonry of Cyclopes. Children cluster at the city's gates, weeping
and crying aloud, aloud, as they cling to their mothers' necks:*   1090
*'Mother, help! Alone, yes all alone I am taken from your sight by
the Greeks, taken to some dark ship; across the sea its oars will carry
me, to Salamis loved by the gods, or to the Isthmian height that looks
down on the two seas, the gates to Pelops' realm.'*

[Antistrophe:] *When Menelaus' ship is in mid-ocean, may a*   1100
*flaming bolt of lightning, hurled from those holy hands, strike it
midway between its banks of oars, since he takes me away from Ilium,
my country, to tearful slavery in Greece, while the daughter of Zeus
possesses the mirrors of gold that maidens delight in. May he never
reach his Spartan homeland and the palace of his forefathers; may*   1110
*he never see the city of Pitana and the bronze gates of the goddess's
home, now that he has captured the woman whose sinful marriage
brought shame on noble Greece and pitiful suffering to the streams of
Simois.*

[TALTHYBIUS *enters with men who are carrying the corpse of*
ASTYANAX *on his father's shield.*]
Oh, no! Fresh woes assail our land, following hard on woes not yet

1120 *old! Wretched wives of the Trojans, you see Astyanax before you,*
a corpse, carried by the Greeks who killed him, hurling him pitilessly
like a quoit from the battlements.

TALTHYBIUS: Hecabe, one ship is left and stands ready with her
oars to take the rest of the spoils of Achilles' son to the shores
of Phthia. Neoptolemus himself has set sail on hearing of fresh
misfortunes that have affected Peleus; he has been driven from
his land by Acastus, they say, the son of Pelias. This outweighed
any desire he had to stay and he is gone, taking Andromache
1130 with him. She brought many tears to my eyes when she
took her leave, as she wept for her homeland and made her
farewells to Hector's tomb. She asked Neoptolemus to give
burial to this corpse, your Hector's son who died when he
was thrown from the ramparts. She also begged him not to
take to Peleus' home this bronze-backed shield, the terror of
the Greeks, with which the boy's father used to protect his
ribs, not to place it in the same bedchamber where she would
1140 receive her new husband, but to let it serve for the boy's
burial in place of a coffin of cedar-wood or stone. She begged
that the dead body be given into your arms, so that you might
wrap it in cloths and cover it with garlands, as your strength
and circumstances permitted. For she has gone, prevented by
her master's urgency from giving her child proper burial.
When you have dressed the corpse, we shall raise a mound of
earth over it and put to sea.

You must now lose no time in carrying out the task
1150 appointed. One piece of work I have spared you; when I
crossed Scamander's stream here, I bathed the corpse and
washed out the wounds. Well, I'll go now to dig a trench for
his grave. If we share these duties between us, you and I, we'll
save on time and start our voyage home all the more quickly.

[TALTHYBIUS' *men move forward towards* HECABE, *carrying*
the shield. Exit TALTHYBIUS.]

HECABE: Put down upon the ground Hector's rimmed shield,
a painful sight that gives no pleasure to my eyes. O you Greeks,
who take more pride in deeds of war than possession of

intelligence, what fear of this boy made you spill blood in this unprecedented fashion? Was it that he might one day restore 1160 fallen Troy? Then you are not warriors at all, it seems; even when Hector was rampaging over the battlefield with a horde of Trojans behind him, our men fell in great numbers; but now that Troy is taken and the Trojans dead, a child, a tiny boy made you afraid. I despise fear that has no rational basis.

O my darling boy, how cruelly death came to you! If you had died in your city's defence, a married man in your prime, having tasted the joys of kingship that make men rival the gods, then happiness would have been yours, if there is any happiness in such things. But as it is, my child, you have no 1170 knowledge of seeing or discovering these pleasures in your mind; they were yours to inherit, but you had no use of them. Poor boy, how cruelly your own ancestral walls, defences Loxias built, have mangled you and shorn from your head those curls your mother cherished so lovingly, showering them with kisses! Now your bones are crushed and from your bloody head Death grins out (let me not hide the horror). O hands so precious, so like your father's, now you dangle before me splayed out at the wrist! O mouth I loved, with all those brave oaths you uttered, you are silenced now! You deceived 1180 me then when you dived into my dress and said, 'Grandma, I'll cut a big curl from my hair for you and bring crowds of my friends to your grave and give you a loving send-off.' But it is not you who will bury me, younger though you are, but I you – an old woman without city or children, burying a wretched corpse. Oh, when I think back, all those hugs we had, all the times I fed you and let you sleep beside me, all wasted! What could a poet write about you one day on your tomb? 'This boy was once killed by Greeks because they were afraid of him.' The epitaph is a disgrace to Greece! Well, 1190 deprived you may be of your father's privileges, but still you shall have his bronze-backed shield to serve as a coffin.

O shield that kept safe my Hector's fine strong arms, you have lost the great warrior who looked after you. How sweet they are, the marks that lie on your handle and on your well-turned rim the line of sweat that used to drip from Hector's brow as, chin on shield, he laboured hard and long in the fight! [*To the women inside the tents:*] Fetch it out, bring out such clothing as we can muster to dress this poor corpse! The god has not given us the fortune to make a fine show. What I have is yours to take. Foolish the man who delights in his good fortune, supposing that it will never leave him. For it is Fortune's way to jump now in one direction, now in another, like a man who cannot choose whom to support; and no one owes his happiness to himself alone. [*Servants enter in response to* HECABE'*s call.*]

CHORUS-LEADER: Look, here are women bringing in their hands garments from the Trojan spoils to dress the corpse.

HECABE: My child, your grandmother places on you fine clothes from the store that once was yours; but it is not as victor over your friends in riding or archery that I adorn you, customs that the Trojans respect in moderation. Now Helen, abhorred by the gods, has robbed you of what is yours, destroying your life besides and plunging into ruin all your house.

CHORUS [*no longer able to suppress their grief*]: *Ah, you have touched, you have touched my heart! O great prince of Troy, I have lost you now!*

HECABE: I dress you now in the Trojan finery that you should have put on at your wedding, when you would have taken as your bride the noblest of Asia's daughters. And you, dear shield of Hector, glorious in victory once and mother of trophies beyond number, receive the adornment of this child; though you have not died, you will share death with his corpse. You are far more worthy of honour than the armour of Odysseus,[54] wicked as he is clever.

CHORUS: *Oh, the pity of it! My child, once the earth receives you, bitter tears will be shed over you! Pour out your sighs, mother,* –

HECABE: *Oh my sorrow!*

CHORUS: – *they will be a song for the dead.*

HECABE: *Oh the pain!*

CHORUS: *Yes, pain at sufferings you cannot forget!*

HECABE: With bandages I will tend to your wounds, a sorry doctor indeed, having the name without the power to work a cure. For the rest, your father shall look to your needs among the dead.

CHORUS: *Beat, beat upon your head with steady pounding of your fists! Oh, my sorrow, my sorrow!*

HECABE [*suddenly fixing her eyes on the sky*]: Women, dearest friends! [*She breaks off rapt.*]

CHORUS [*frightened*]: *Speak, Hecabe; what is the meaning of this cry?*

HECABE [*slowly, as if announcing a revelation she has just received*]: So all that concerns the gods, then, is that I and Troy should suffer, city hated beyond all others; wasted, then, are the 1240 sacrifices of oxen that we made. But if the god had not overthrown us, casting below the earth what was above it, we would have faded from memory, with none to celebrate us, and would give no themes for the songs of men hereafter.[55] [*To the women who entered earlier:*] Go on your way, bury the corpse in its miserable grave! He has garlands, such at least as the dead require. I imagine it makes little difference to the dead whether they receive rich gifts for the grave; this is just empty ostentation on the part of the living. [*The funeral* 1250 *procession leaves but* HECABE *does not move.*]

CHORUS: *Oh! Oh! How pitiful she is, the mother who saw her great hopes for your future come to nothing! Great happiness was accounted yours because of your noble birth but a terrible death has ended your life. Ah! Who are these men I see on Troy's heights, brandishing flaming torches in their hands? Some new disaster is going to befall Troy.*

[*Re-enter* TALTHYBIUS *and soldiers with torches.*]

TALTHYBIUS: You company commanders charged with setting 1260 fire to this city of Priam, I have the word for you: no longer keep idle the flame in your hands but fling your firebrands so we may level Ilium's city and sail off home from Troy happy men!

Now, you daughters of Troy, so that my single instruction

may have a double effect, when the army commanders sound the shrill note of the trumpet, the rest of you will go down to the ships of the Greeks to embark, but you, old Hecabe, most unfortunate of women, accompany these men. [*Enter* 1270 ODYSSEUS' *men.*] They have come for you from Odysseus whose slave you now are, sent by the ballot away from your homeland.

HECABE: Oh what misery is mine! This is now the culmination, the final outcome of all my sorrows. I am leaving my native land and my city is consumed by fire. Come old feet, make haste, though it is hard; I wish to bid farewell to my long-suffering city. O Troy, once you held pride of place among the peoples of Asia, but soon you will be stripped of your famous name. They are putting you to the torch and leading us away now from your land to be slaves. O you gods! Yet 1280 why do I invoke the gods? Even before this they were deaf to our appeals. Come, let me run upon the pyre; I could not meet a nobler end than perishing in the flames together with my country.

TALTHYBIUS: Poor lady, your misfortunes are driving you out of your senses. [*To* ODYSSEUS' *men:*] Bestir yourselves, enough of your delaying! You must escort Odysseus' prize to him and deliver her into his hands.

[*The play concludes with a lament sung by* HECABE *and the* CHORUS.]

HECABE [Strophe]: *Oh no, no, no! Son of Cronus, Phrygia's Lord, Father of our race, do you see how we are treated here, these sufferings* 1290 *unworthy of Dardanus' race?*

CHORUS: *He sees them; but Troy, great city that is no city, has perished and exists no more.*

HECABE [Antistrophe]: *Oh no, no, no! Ilium is on fire, Pergama's buildings and the city's high walls are consumed by flames!*

CHORUS: *Like some smoke on heavenly wing the land that the spear* 1300 *has levelled fades away into nothingness.*

HECABE [Strophe]: *O land that nursed my children!*

CHORUS: *Ah! Ah!*

216

HECABE: *O my children, hear me, listen to your mother's voice!*

CHORUS: *It is the dead you call upon with your lamentation.*

HECABE [*kneeling on the ground*]: *Yes, upon them, as I lay my aged limbs on the ground and beat the earth with both fists.*

CHORUS [*following her lead*]: *Look, each one of us kneels on the ground as we call upon our wretched husbands in the world below.*

[ODYSSEUS' *men try again to move them on.*]

HECABE: *We are led off, dragged away —*

CHORUS: *Sorrow, sorrow is in your cry!*   1310

HECABE: *— to houses where we will live the life of slaves.*

CHORUS: *Away from the land of our birth.*

HECABE: *Oh the pain! Priam, Priam, without burial you perished, without the support of loved ones, yet you know nothing of the ruin that has settled on me!*

CHORUS: *Yes, for his eyes were sealed by dark death, a holy god, but how unholy the slaying!*

HECABE [Antistrophe]: *O dwellings of the gods, city that I love, —*

CHORUS: *Ah! Ah!*

HECABE: *— the deadly flames, the thrusting spears are upon you!*

CHORUS: *Soon you will crash to the soil of your homeland and lose your name for ever.*

HECABE: *Winging up to the sky, the dust like smoke shall take from*   1320
me the sight of my home.

CHORUS: *And the country's name shall vanish from men's minds. Cities rise and pass away; wretched Troy is no more.*

[*Loud crashing noises are heard in the distance, mingled with the blare of trumpets.*]

HECABE: *Did you notice, did you hear?*

CHORUS: *Yes, the citadel has crashed in ruin.*

HECABE: *A quaking everywhere, a quaking . . .*

CHORUS: *. . . engulfs the city.*

HECABE: *Ah! Trembling, trembling limbs, support my steps! Onward to your new life, to the day of slavery!*   1330

CHORUS: *Ah! City of sorrow! But even so, direct your steps to the ships of the Greeks.*

[*Slowly the women leave the orchestra under guard.*]

NOTES

ANDROMACHE

Setting and situation: Andromache takes up position outside the house of Neoptolemus, at a shrine of the goddess Thetis, and a statue of the goddess is also visible (lines 161–2, 246, 260). The situation is that of a suppliant drama, where a helpless victim, usually a woman, awaits the arrival of a rescuer. This is a favourite plot-type of Euripides: cf. e.g. *Heracles* and *Helen*, and of course *Suppliant Women* itself.

1 *Thebe*: not the city of Thebes in Boeotia, but a town in the Troad from which Andromache came. It was sacked by Achilles, who killed her father and brothers. Andromache's origin is mentioned frequently in the *Iliad*: see esp. Book 6, 413–30.

2 *shared the home of Peleus*: Peleus, a mortal, married Thetis, a sea-goddess. At first his marriage marked him out as one of the most fortunate of men, but Thetis abandoned him and returned to the sea. At the end of the play, however, the two are reunited and she bestows divinity on her husband.

3 *have borne him a child*: this child is never named in the play, but was called Molossus. He unites the two royal families, that of Troy and the family of Achilles. He is to be the founder of the royal house of Molossia (NW Greece), towards which Athens was well disposed when Euripides' play was first produced.

4 *Menelaus*: Menelaus is seldom sympathetically treated in Euripides. In the *Trojan Women* he is slow witted and easily spellbound by Helen's charms; in *Helen* he is bombastic and self-important; in this play, as in *Orestes*, he is an unscrupulous villain. Although Homer presents him more attractively, there are already suggestions in the *Odyssey* that he is less quick on the uptake than Helen. The much more negative treatment in Euripides must be connected with the wars between Athens and Sparta.

5 *whom the god had killed*: Apollo was a pro-Trojan god, and guided Paris' arrow so as to bring about Achilles' death. There was a tradition that Neoptolemus died

at Delphi, though versions varied as to why he went there. Euripides seems to have elaborated on earlier accounts, particularly in involving Orestes and in making this Neoptolemus' *second* visit to the god.

6 *schemes; you're a woman*: in conventional (male) opinion, women regularly use deception and are more cunning, though less strong physically, than men. Euripides constantly exploits this concept (e.g. *Medea*, *Ion*).

7 *[sings an elegiac lament]*: this passage of elegiac couplets is a unique metrical occurrence in tragedy. The passage would have been sung to the accompaniment of an *aulos* (an instrument like an oboe). The language is reminiscent of Homer. See further D. L. Page, 'The Elegiacs in Euripides' *Andromache*', in *Greek Poetry and Life: Essays presented to Gilbert Murray* (Oxford 1936), pp. 206–23.

8 *this gorgeous diadem of gold*: the rich finery of Hermione, the legitimate wife, is a visual contrast with the slave-garb of the downtrodden concubine, Andromache. The clothing also serves to characterize Hermione: her pride and hauteur lead her to show off her rich possessions. Similar use is made of fine dress for Helen in the *Trojan Women* (1022–6).

9 *Asiatic women*: Hermione's hostility leads her to insult Andromache's origins, drawing on the rich vein of anti-barbarian rhetoric which had been mined by orators and poets since the Persian wars. See also 168–78; E. Hall, *Inventing the Barbarian* (Oxford 1989), esp. pp. 188–90.

10 *I will not accept conviction*: like other details in this preamble, the legalistic phrasing here indicates that an *agon* ('formal debate-scene') is in progress. As often in these scenes, the expression of opposing views leads only to further antagonism; here, a contest of words passes into threats and action.

11 *I nurtured your bastards at my own breast*: Andromache's self-presentation as a virtuous wife reaches unexpected extremes here. Various illegitimate offspring of Priam are mentioned in the *Iliad*, but none are attributed to Hector (some are mentioned by the historian Hellanicus, but Euripides probably pre-dates his work). Euripides has extended the father's practice to the son; it is not clear whether this is meant to shock, titillate or simply intensify the rhetorical force of Andromache's speech.

12 *no less than Greeks*: while rhetorical contrasts between Greek and barbarian ways are commonplace in tragedy, other forms of argument (influenced by philosophic and ethnographic writings) looked for common ground between cultures and explored the bases of different but equally valid value systems. Euripides allows his characters to question the superiority of Greek customs; the same willingness to question can be seen in the work of the historian Herodotus.

13 *the hateful contest of beauty*: this passage refers to the 'Judgement of Paris'.

Paris, while minding herds on Mount Ida outside Troy, was visited by the three goddesses, Hera, Athena and Aphrodite, escorted by the messenger-god Hermes. He was asked to decide which of them was the most beautiful; each goddess promised different rewards. Paris chose Aphrodite as the winner and his reward was the beautiful Helen. The hatred of Athena and Hera towards Troy originated with this episode. Euripides frequently refers to the scene as the fateful origin of the Trojan war. For a full study, see T. C. W. Stinton, *Collected Papers on Greek Tragedy*, pp. 17–75.

14 *to put the infant to the sword*: in the usual version Hecabe dreamed when she was pregnant with Paris that her son would be a firebrand that would consume all Troy. In this passage, Cassandra, who had the power of prophecy, foretells the disasters Paris would bring about. As a result, Paris was exposed on the hillside, but survived and later returned to Troy.

15 *not fit . . . to be Troy's conqueror*: as mentioned above, Menelaus' status is regularly belittled in Euripides. In a later scene of this play Peleus will subject him to more systematic abuse.

16 *the wretched city of the Phrygians*: the argument is that, just as Menelaus thought it worth fighting a war and destroying Troy for a woman (Helen), so now he may think it worth further conflict to please another woman (Hermione, Helen's daughter).

17 *Seize her, you men*: Menelaus outrageously violates his oath: this would be thought shocking even in the time of the Peloponnesian war, during which trickery and dubious tactics of this kind may have become more common (cf. Thucydides ii, 5, 5–7; iii, 34, 82.7).

18 *Inhabitants of Sparta . . .*: this is one passage in the play in which it would be hard to deny contemporary resonances. An ancient commentator on these lines remarked: 'Euripides uses Andromache as a mouthpiece to revile the Spartans because of the war that was in progress at the time'. Similar complaints of Spartan unreliability can be found in Aristophanes (e.g. *Acharnians* 308, *Lysistrata* 629, 1269–70), and find support in Thucydides (e.g. iv, 80; v, 18.7).

19 *CHILD*: a speaking part is provided for a child-actor (as also in *Alcestis* and *Medea*), intensifying the pathos. There are no parallels in the surviving plays of Aeschylus or Sophocles.

20 *PELEUS*: old men are often weak or ineffectual in tragedy, e.g. the blind prophet Tiresias, or the aged Cadmus in the *Bacchae*. But here Peleus asserts his heroic stature and gains control of the situation.

21 *come towards me!*: it is a popular fallacy in modern criticism that violence cannot take place on the Greek stage. Scenes of this kind, involving some kind of tussle or fisticuffs, are reasonably common. See M. Kaimio, *Physical Contact in Greek Tragedy* (Hèlsinki 1988), ch. 6.

22 *with cowards for ancestors*: Peleus' invective, which deploys many techniques of courtroom rhetoric, begins with a slur on Menelaus' ancestry. The various crimes or treacherous deeds of Pelops (who won a chariot race and his bride by sabotaging his opponent's vehicle) and Atreus (who killed his brother's children and served them up to him at dinner) would have come to the audience's mind.

23 *No Spartan girl . . .*: in Sparta the freedom allowed to women was extreme by strict Athenian standards; in particular, they were allowed to participate along with young men in gymnastic training. The boys ran naked, the girls wore not much more. Prurient exaggeration of the consequences was a commonplace.

24 *your brother, urging him . . . throat be slit*: the Greek fleet, once assembled at Aulis, was unable to set sail because of opposing winds. The prophet Calchas declared that Agamemnon's daughter Iphigenia must be sacrificed in order to win a safe passage to Troy. According to Peleus, Menelaus, eager to recover Helen, prevailed on Agamemnon to perform this atrocity. The situation is dramatized in full in Euripides' later play *Iphigenia at Aulis*.

25 *one glimpse of her breasts*: the scene in which Menelaus finally confronted his wife figured in a lost epic poem, the *Little Iliad* (cf. also Aristophanes, *Lysistrata* 155–6). He was about to kill her, but was softened by the sight of her bared breasts. The episode clearly underlies the scene between Menelaus and Helen in the *Trojan Women* (860–1059).

26 *than a true-born son*: the problems of a bastard son are hinted at in Sophocles' *Ajax* (the inferior Teucer) and in Euripides' *Hippolytus* (Hippolytus himself). See D. Ogden, *Greek Bastardy* (Oxford 1996), chs. 5–6, for the relation between mythical tragedy and Athenian reality.

27 *the trouble Helen caused . . . work of the gods*: it is common for characters in epic and tragedy to blame their misdeeds on divine intervention, but normally this does not absolve them of responsibility. Hence Menelaus' case is weak here (like Helen's paradoxical self-defence in the *Trojan Women*, 914–65, esp. 946–50).

28 *Phocus*: Peleus had killed his half-brother Phocus, and was sent into exile for this. The story is referred to in early epic and in Pindar.

29 *there is a certain city*: we have heard nothing about this problem before, and it is overwhelmingly likely that Euripides means us to think that Menelaus is simply inventing an excuse to depart in order to save face. Possible historical allusions (i.e. echoes of Spartan difficulties in the Peloponnese at the time of production) have also been suggested, but these are purely speculative in the absence of a firm date for *Andromache*; they also weaken the effect of negative characterization of Menelaus.

30 *[Epode]*: the chorus, impressed by Peleus' achievements in the present, recall the tales told of his youth: he took part in the battle between the Lapiths and the barbarously drunken Centaurs; he joined Jason on the *Argo* in the quest for the Golden Fleece (the 'Clashing Rocks' were one of the supernatural obstacles they faced on that journey); and he accompanied Heracles, son of Zeus, on the first Greek campaign against Troy (the generation before the great Trojan war).

31 *now she's having second thoughts*: the change of mind on Hermione's part leads on to a very different presentation of her when she appears on stage. Although not impossible, the change in characterization is certainly startling, but typical of Euripides. It accompanies a change in the direction of the plot: Andromache's dilemma gives way to the question of Neoptolemus' fate. For discussion of this kind of shift in Euripidean plots see M. Heath, *The Poetics of Greek Tragedy*, ch. 2, esp. pp. 92–5; also relevant is W. G. Arnott, 'Euripides and the unexpected', in McAuslan–Walcot (ed.), *Greek Tragedy*, pp. 138–52.

32 *suppliant . . . statue*: that Hermione is now driven to contemplate taking refuge as a suppliant emphasizes still more the reversal of situation; she herself now resembles the helpless Andromache at the opening of the play.

33 *first of ships*: this refers to the Argo, according to some legends the first ship ever built. The 'dusky cliffs' referred to are the Clashing Rocks, on the way into the Black Sea (see n. 30 above).

34 *[Enter ORESTES]*: again we see Euripides' fondness for introducing unexpected developments. We may have expected Neoptolemus, or the reappearance of Peleus or Menelaus. Orestes comes as a greater surprise.

35 *journeying to . . . Dodona*: as with the parting protestation of Menelaus, it is hard to think that this is a genuine claim. Orestes subsequently admits that he knew all about the situation in Neoptolemus' household.

36 *visits of wearisome women*: the bad influence of visiting women is also deplored in *Hippolytus* (384). It seems to be a misogynistic commonplace; Hermione adopts the rhetoric of male disapproval in order to represent her own virtuous outlook to her male addressee.

37 *goddesses whose faces drip blood*: the Furies, or Erinyes, terrifying powers who dwell below the earth and punish evildoers. They are associated with crimes within the family, and have pursued Orestes because he has slain his mother (cf. *Electra* 1252ff., where the Heavenly Twins foretell this pursuit).

38 *Such is the net of death . . .*: at this point, the full extent of Orestes' advance planning is revealed: not only has he already intended to carry Hermione away with him, but he has taken steps to ensure that Neoptolemus will not follow to recover her. These lines prepare us for the narrative of Neoptolemus' death at Delphi.

39 *Phoebus, who raised up . . . fair crown of walls*: Apollo and Poseidon worked as hired labourers for the Trojan King Laomedon and constructed the mighty walls of Troy, which were subsequently destroyed (cf. *Trojan Women* 4–7; *Iliad* Book 21, 441–57). The distinction between the first sack of Troy, by Heracles and other heroes, and the second and final destruction after the ten years of war, is blurred here.

40 *war-dance . . . that leap that won him fame at Troy*: the 'Pyrrhic dance' is referred to: it involved violent movement mimicking the actions of men in combat. There is a pun on Neoptolemus' other name 'Pyrrhus' (not used in this play, but going back to the early epic called the *Cypria*).

41 *How then can he be wise?*: for doubts about the wisdom of Apollo's actions or prophecies, cf. *Electra* 971, 1246. On passages of this kind, see further J. Mikalson, *Honor thy Gods*, pp. 136–9. On the attitude to Delphi, see the Preface to this play.

42 *by the banks of Simois!*: the implication is that death in open battle at Troy would have been more glorious, less humiliating, than death as a result of this treacherous assault. Similar laments are voiced about Agamemnon in Aeschylus' *Libation-Bearers*.

43 *destroyed by a bolt of lightning*: this may be an ironic echo of 846, where Hermione, prior to the arrival of Orestes, herself wished for death by this means.

44 *before your children*: the natural sequence of events is for the older generation to die before the younger. Here (as in war and other crises), the normal pattern is disrupted and the old man must live on in desolation.

45 *bless you at your wedding*: the marriage of Peleus and Thetis was attended by all or most of the divine family; for this reason it was often seen as a symbolic occasion of supreme human prosperity (cf. Pindar, *Pythian* 3, 86–105, a passage which goes on to spell out the misery which followed). Humanity cannot rise permanently to the level of the divine.

46 *Peleus, it is I, Thetis*: the epiphany of a divine figure has special force here where the goddess is the human being's former wife, and when the occasion is the death of their grandson.

47 *Helenus*: not previously mentioned in the play, Helenus is a seer and a son of Priam, who appears in the *Iliad*. This is the earliest place which mentions his marriage to Andromache, which may well be Euripides' own invention.

48 *following in his line as king of Molossia*: on the descendants of Molossus, see n. 3.

49 *Leuce's shore within the sea that travellers fear*: Leuce, the 'White Island', is, like Elysium, a never-never land where the dead can live again; it was given a firmer geographical location in early Greek literature, and Euripides follows this tradition by referring to the 'sea that travellers fear', i.e. the Black Sea. Achilles was worshipped by Greeks living in this area.

50 *Many are the forms . . . today*: these closing choral lines also appear in identical or closely similar form at the end of *Alcestis*, *Medea*, *Helen* and *Bacchae*. It has often been suggested that they are editorial insertions in some cases, but a choral comment is normal at the end of a Greek tragedy, and the sentiments, though conventional, are appropriate enough in each case. For discussion, see D. H. Roberts, *Classical Quarterly* 37 (1987), pp. 51–64.

HECABE

1 *GHOST OF POLYDORUS*: it is common practice in Euripides for the first speaker to give a fairly detailed account of the events so far. A supernatural figure like a god has an advantage here, as he knows things that the human characters do not. Similarly Polydorus' ghost is able to describe how he died before any of those in the Greek camp know of the fact.

2 *guest-friend*: the relationship between host and guest had a special sanctity in Greek society, imposing obligations on both sides. Polymestor's crime is therefore even more shocking than it would be otherwise.

3 *not capable of . . . wielding a spear*: in the *Iliad*, Polydorus is present and fighting at Troy where he is killed by Achilles. Euripides has altered the myth to increase the pathos. The character Polymestor may well be his invention.

4 *his tomb*: it is mysterious why Achilles' tomb should be in Thrace; in the usual legend he was buried at Troy, and in the *Trojan Women* Polyxena has been sacrificed to him there (40).

5 *a welcome sacrifice*: the barbarity of human sacrifice was unknown in Greece in historic times, but haunts the myths. In the *Iliad*, Achilles himself sacrificed a number of Trojan youths on the pyre of Patroclus, to honour his dead friend.

6 *I will have all that I wish*: the Greeks, like most societies, attached great importance to formal burial: according to one belief, it was impossible for the soul to enter the realm of Hades until the body had been given the proper rites. The significance of this issue is clear from other plays as well, e.g. Sophocles' *Ajax* and *Antigone*, or Euripides' *Suppliant Women* (see esp. 301–13 and 524–63). It is noteworthy that Polydorus himself does not seek revenge on Polymestor: contrast Hecabe later.

7 *the prophet-maid, Bacchus' follower*: Cassandra. Although her inspiration comes from Apollo, she is associated with Bacchus because he is regarded as a source of madness and wild or ecstatic states.

8 *Laertes' son, that glib flatterer of the mob*: as usual in tragedy, Odysseus is presented unfavourably. Here he is described as a regular demagogue, one who gets his way with the masses by flattering them.

9 *son of Achilles*: Neoptolemus.

10 *great contest*: the phrase anticipates the debate which follows, using the word *agon*, almost a technical term for a rhetorical exchange.

11 *came to spy on Troy*: a version of this story is narrated by Helen in Book 4 of Homer's *Odyssey*; there, she is the key figure and preserves Odysseus' safety. This version, which involves the queen of Troy helping an enemy spy, is much less probable, and may well have been invented by Euripides so as to give Hecabe a stronger argument to use.

12 *in your supplication*: supplication is common in Greek drama: it involves prostrating oneself and entreating another person for mercy or help of some kind. Physical contact and ritual forms of appeal reinforce the pressure on the other person to yield. To reject a suppliant is sometimes said to be an offence against Zeus, but such rejection is common when, as here, the person appealed to will gain no tangible advantage by concession.

13 *I will go with you*: Polyxena's resolve provides a foil to Hecabe's despairing misery. We are meant to admire her nobility (later further emphasized in the messenger speech describing her death); at the same time there is an intense feeling of waste as her death becomes inevitable.

14 *the first palm that ever grew*: Leto, mother of Apollo and Artemis, wandered through the world in her pregnancy, and finally gave birth to them on Delos, where she clung to a palm tree during her birth-pangs. The story is told in full in the Homeric *Hymn to Apollo*.

15 *the saffron robe of Athena*: the daughters of good families in Athens prepared a magnificent robe to be offered to the city's patron goddess at her festival, the Great Panathenaea, held every four years. The subject matter of the embroidered pictures was conventionally the slaying of the monstrous Giants, or Titans, who attempted rebellion against Zeus; in this battle Athena had played a major part. In fact the chorus, being captive foreigners, would not be permitted to work on this sacred garment.

16 *home in Hades*: this seems to mean that Troy itself is a place of death and horror now, like Hades. Alternatively, the chorus may mean that they have been spared death by captivity.

17 *your young heifer*: young men and especially women were commonly compared to animals (e.g. in love poetry), and the comparison here need not be dismissive. Also, a heifer would be a natural victim in a sacrifice; Polyxena now occupies that role.

18 *exposed her breasts . . . like a statue in its beauty*: comparisons with the visual arts are quite common in Euripides, though painting is more frequent than statuary. Possibly the poet was thinking of actual representations of this scene in art. Polyxena's action in baring her breasts shows her virginal purity, and the response of the Greek soldiers is suitably respectful.

19 *O my daughter*: Hecabe addresses the dead Polyxena even though she is not present. This device, known as 'apostrophe', may seem artificial but in a formal genre like tragedy is often a sign of deep emotion.

20 *when Paris first . . . on Ida's slopes*: a reference to the preparation of a fleet to journey to Greece and carry off Helen. The chorus look back to the origins of the war which caused their present suffering.

21 *a herdsman on Ida*: again this is Paris, who adjudicated on the question whether Hera, Athena or Aphrodite was the most beautiful of goddesses. He chose the third, who bribed him with the offer of the most beautiful of all mortal women (Helen) as his wife. See also n. 13 on *Andromache*.

22 *what shall I do?*: Hecabe's extended hesitation marks the importance of the appeal she is about to make, as well as keeping Agamemnon (and to some extent the audience) in suspense. The idea of falling at Agamemnon's knees points to a supplication scene. Hecabe had already fallen at Odysseus' feet and begged him to be generous earlier in the play, but without success (275–8). Now she appeals to Agamemnon for a darker purpose, and is successful.

23 *Fortune herself*: Fortune (Greek *Tyche*), like many other abstractions, was personified and deified in Greek mythology, and references to her become more frequent in the late fifth and fourth centuries BC. She is particularly prominent in the New Comedy of Menander. See the entry in the *Oxford Classical Dictionary* under 'Tyche'.

24 *the gods are strong . . .*: the passage is paradoxical. Two conceptions seem to be combined: the gods as a source for human morality (imposed by divine decree), and the idea that human belief in the gods is actually brought about by convention or custom (the Greek word *nomos*, translated here as 'law', covers these other concepts as well). In a play in which divine concern for human virtue and vice seems conspicuously absent, this ambiguity about the gods is appropriate, as well as echoing contemporary debates in typically Euripidean fashion.

25 *stand back as a painter would*: as in the earlier description of Polyxena's sacrifice (see n. 18), the reference to a visual portrayal of the scene may be a reminiscence of scenes on vases. Nevertheless, this self-objectification by characters is found elsewhere in Euripides (e.g. *Hippolytus* 1078–9), and contributes to the odd mixture of intense emotionality and more detached intellectual response to crisis which distinguishes his plays.

26 *persuasion*: in fifth-century BC Athens there were indeed teachers who imparted this art for pay: the sophists, such as Protagoras and Gorgias. But the audience is meant to see that Hecabe has all the resources of rhetoric at her disposal already, even without such teaching; and yet at this stage her eloquence does not help her.

27 *the one the Trojans call Cassandra*: this speech has been much discussed, and some critics have condemned Hecabe for using her daughter as a bargaining-counter; some have even regarded her virtually as a bawd. This is hardly fair: Hecabe is bound to use every argument at her disposal, and Cassandra is already in Agamemnon's power.

28 *I wish I possessed a tongue in all my parts*: the notion is far-fetched, but characters in Greek tragedy when facing desperate situations often make impossible wishes of this kind: cf. *Alcestis* 357, where Admetus wishes he had the voice of Orpheus to go down to the underworld and plead for Alcestis' life.

29 *overpowered Aegyptus' sons*: the Danaids, or daughters of Danaus, forced to marry the sons of Aegyptus against their will, killed them on their wedding night. Only one of the fifty daughters spared her bridegroom.

30 *emptied Lemnos altogether of menfolk*: because their wives were afflicted with an unpleasant body odour, the men of Lemnos imported concubines to take their place, whereupon the women of Lemnos murdered all their menfolk. Like the Danaid story, this atrocity becomes a symbol of the murderous potential of women (cf. Aeschylus, *Libation-Bearers* 631–2).

31 *At midnight my end began . . .*: the chorus recall the night on which Troy was taken. The Greek fleet had departed, and all the Trojans thought they had abandoned the war. A massive Wooden Horse was left on the shore, containing the pick of the Greek leaders. The Trojans foolishly dragged the horse into the city and dedicated it in Athena's temple. Once night came the Greeks emerged and began the slaughter described in the stanzas which follow. (Cf. the chorus on the same subject in *Trojan Women* 511–67.)

32 *like some girl of Sparta*: as is mentioned in *Andromache* 595–601, Spartan girls participated with the young men in gymnastic exercises, a practice regarded as surprising and potentially immoral by other Greeks. (See *Andromache*, n. 23.)

33 *How worthy of you!*: Hecabe is of course exploiting the ambiguities of language: she means that Polymestor's shameless lie corresponds to the viciousness of his character as she now knows it to be. Polymestor takes it as a sincere compliment. Irony of this type is frequent in Greek tragedy.

34 *My eyes . . .*: the situation, with a chorus on stage overhearing agonized cries from within, echoes the climax of Aeschylus' *Agamemnon*, the archetypal scene of this kind. But here Polymestor will not be slain outright, but blinded. It is possible that when he reappears he wears a mask painted to represent his bleeding eyes.

35 *state your case . . . come to a fair judgement*: as often, the legal terminology prepares the audience for a set-piece debate: Agamemnon will act as 'judge', but we have already seen that he is a prejudiced authority.

36 *speech . . . actions*: despite the eloquence of the characters, skill at speech-making is often criticized or regarded with suspicion in tragedy, and this is paralleled in other genres of the period. For a valuable discussion see S. Halliwell, 'Between Public and Private: Tragedy and Athenian Experience of Rhetoric' in *Greek Tragedy and the Historian*, ed. C. B. R. Pelling (Oxford 1997), pp. 121–41.

37 *This is unthinkable*: the enmity between Greek and barbarian, less obviously inevitable in Homer, is exaggerated in tragedy, no doubt under the influence of the Graeco-Persian wars. But although here both 'barbarians', Polymestor and Hecabe, have acted savagely and without much scruple, it is clear that the Greeks do not occupy a loftier moral plane. See generally E. Hall, *Inventing the Barbarian*.

38 *to us Greeks this is disgraceful conduct*: Agamemnon's self-importance deflates his own claims; cf. the attitude of Jason towards Medea in *Medea* (e.g. 525–44).

39 *You will take little pleasure, I think, when the sea-spray . . .*: Polymestor foretells the future fates of Hecabe and Agamemnon: the former will be transformed into a bitch and die at Troy, the latter will be murdered by his wife on his return home. The prophecy makes clear that theirs is a hollow victory, but Agamemnon at least is not prepared to listen to it.

40 *Dionysus*: Dionysus, like Apollo, has prophetic powers. There was an oracle associated with him at Mount Pangaeon in Thrace.

41 *killed by this man's wife . . .*: Clytemnestra will kill Agamemnon for several reasons, among them his liaison with Cassandra, who also dies by her hand.

42 *May our voyage to our homeland be a happy one!*: like the next phrase, this line carries heavy irony. The audience knows that the Greek fleet will meet with storms which will wreck many of their ships and drive others off course (cf. the prologue of the *Trojan Women*, where Athena and Poseidon agree on this); some, such as Menelaus, will not return home for years. The situation in Agamemnon's own household has already been mentioned, but he blindly ignores this warning.

SUPPLIANT WOMEN

1 *SUPPLIANT WOMEN*: the ritual act of supplication involves both submission (kneeling and pleading) to one who is in a position of greater power, and putting moral and religious pressure on them to do as you want them to do. It imposes an obligation, but can be resisted by the hard-hearted or by those who feel that their interests lie elsewhere (as Theseus at first thinks in this play). Supplication is attested in historical times, but its impact seems to have weakened in the late fifth century BC; despite or because of this, it is frequently dramatized in tragedy.

2 *[surrounded by the CHORUS]*: it is quite unusual in Euripidean tragedy to have the chorus on stage from the beginning of the play (it may have been more common in Aeschylus' time). The tableau created emphasizes the emotional pressure which the chorus are applying to Aethra, and the importance of their suffering for the overall effect of the play.

3 *his share in the kingdom of Oedipus*: after Oedipus blinded himself and withdrew from the kingship (as dramatized in Sophocles' *Oedipus the King*), his two sons Eteocles and Polynices decided to share rule of Thebes. They would each rule in turn for a year. Eteocles took the first turn, but at the end of one year he refused to yield power to his brother; hence Polynices sought military support from other states, and the war of the Seven against Thebes ended with the two brothers killing each other in hand-to-hand combat.

4 *flouting the laws of the gods*: the dead should be given due honour, as Greeks and most societies believe; it is therefore natural to suppose that the gods also insist that the dead should have their due. To deny a corpse burial is both an inhumane and an impious act. The principle is explicit in Homer and the issue of burial is prominent in many tragedies (e.g. Sophocles' *Antigone*, where again divine authority is invoked).

5 *by means of debate or armed force*: cf. line 347, where Theseus mentions the same alternatives. In the end, force will indeed be necessary. This is in contrast with Aeschylus' version of the same legend in his lost play the *Eleusinians*, in which we know persuasion prevailed.

6 *where the fruitful ears of corn were first seen*: the legend had it that a man of Eleusis, Triptolemus, was the first to sow and plough corn under the instruction of the goddess Demeter. Eleusis was throughout antiquity a sacred site of special importance, and Demeter's Mysteries there were among the most revered ceremonies in the Greek world.

7 *the Maid and Demeter*: Demeter and her daughter Persephone were regularly worshipped together. Persephone, according to myth, was the wife of Hades, lord of the dead and an awesome figure. After she was abducted by Hades, her absence caused Demeter to bring about world-wide famine; eventually it was agreed that Persephone would spend part of the year in the underworld (our winter), part on the earth (the summer months). There was some inhibition about referring to her by name: hence 'the Maid'.

8 *I entreat you, old woman*: the chorus's first words emphasize their role as suppliants. The desperate devotion and the deeply religious appeal are unusual at this stage in a tragedy: normally in their opening song the chorus have more to say about their background and recent events.

9 *the gashes . . . flesh*: in scenes of mourning in Greek drama it is conventional for the mourners to tear their hair and skin, beat their breasts, and perform other acts of self-mutilation: by this means they identify with the suffering of the dead. Though tragedy may exaggerate the violence of everyday practice, there is little doubt that Greek funeral customs were sometimes equally un-restrained. In the play this self-punishment reaches its extreme form in Evadne's suicide.

10 *Less than reverently . . . by necessity*: that is, they have come not as regular worshippers but as intruders at a ceremony already underway; and the errand they come on is associated with death and ill luck.

11 *our servants' hands are heard*: the chorus are accompanied by handmaidens, though it is unlikely that they join in the singing.

12 *sons of the dead*: these form a secondary chorus and they will become more important at the end of the play, when Athena foretells their expedition against Thebes (the war of the Epigoni or 'Successors' of the Seven led by Adrastus and Polynices).

13 *with your head covered by your cloak*: Adrastus conceals his face out of guilt and shame. His prolonged silence and concealment have tantalized the audience since the beginning of the play. Cf. 734, where he breaks silence again after a long period. For some other examples of this technique, see O. Taplin, *Greek Tragedy in Action*, ch. 7: 'Tableaux, Noises and Silences'.

14 *Such is the work of war's cruelty*: the sentence is one of many in the play which has a wider generalizing force beyond the particular situation dramatized. The audience can, if they wish, read this as a message for their own day.

15 *Tydeus*: a hero of Aetolia who becomes one of the Seven against Thebes. His son Diomedes is a prominent and highly sympathetic figure in the *Iliad*, but Tydeus is painted in much darker colours in most accounts.

16 *His father's curse*: Oedipus, enraged at his sons' treatment of him, cursed them and condemned them to lasting rivalry. The versions vary in different writers, but here it seems clear that Polynices voluntarily left Thebes in a short-lived attempt to avert the curse.

17 *wronged the one who left*: see n. 3 above.

18 *the gods' blessing*: according to traditional Greek belief, no major undertaking should be attempted without consulting the gods or at least seeking their goodwill through sacrifice: see e.g. J. Mikalson, *Athenian Popular Religion*, ch. 6 on the forms of divination. Advanced intellectual thinking sometimes questioned these beliefs, but this had little impact on general practice.

19 *Amphiaraus*: a prophet, and the only one of the Seven who gets a consistently good press. He foresaw the disastrous outcome, but his warnings did not prevail. In the end he was swallowed up in the earth during the attack on Thebes. An oracular shrine of Amphiaraus existed in classical times.

20 *My troops were young*: youth and hot-headedness go together, or so the Greeks generally believed. See further line 232; Thucydides ii, 8.1, 20.2 and vi, 12, 15.

21 *Sparta is ruthless and given to duplicity*: this gratuitous insult obviously springs from Athenian anti-Spartan feeling in wartime. Cf. the more extended denunciations of Sparta in *Andromache* 445 (n. 18).

22 *This is a question . . .*: although it is alien to modern realistic drama, the practice of opening a speech with extended generalizations which do not immediately lead to the main argument is common in Greek tragedy; audiences obviously relished these moral disquisitions. Theseus' account of divine benevolence and references to early man's development towards civilization owe something to contemporary thinkers such as Protagoras: see W. K. C. Guthrie, *History of Greek Philosophy* vol. 3 (Cambridge 1969), pp. 18−19, 60−83; E. R. Dodds, *The Ancient Concept of Progress and Other Essays* (Oxford 1973), ch. 1. But Theseus' high-minded rationalism leads him to refuse the suppliants' request; it is his mother Aethra who has a more tragic and compassionate attitude to life.

23 *gave your daughters to strangers*: this may seem the least of Adrastus' blunders to modern readers, but it was clear from his first encounter with them that Tydeus and Polynices were violent and dangerous men; moreover, a law proposed by Pericles required both parents to be Athenians if their offspring were to inherit the right to Athenian citizenship. Athenian ideology, it is implied, should have been a model for Argos.

24 *three divisions in society . . .*: the political analysis here anticipates the more sustained discussion between the herald and Theseus in the next scene.

25 *this same ancestral blood*: a similar appeal to kinship is made in the supplication in Euripides' *Children of Heracles* (207ff.). Arguments of this kind are frequent in Greek diplomacy: see e.g. Herodotus vii, 150, ix, 106; S. Hornblower, *A Commentary on Thucydides*, vol. 2 (Oxford 1996), pp. 61−83.

26 *put a stop to these tears . . .*: as the following words suggest, he is not just calming her distress but trying to avert improper action on holy ground. Grief and mourning, like pollution, are inappropriate in a temple or shrine.

27 *by birth*: at line 472 the herald also says that they have no business involving themselves with Argive affairs. But contrast the argument from kinship at 264 (see n. 25 above).

28 *Then I will not stay silent*: Aethra's speech is important not only because it changes Theseus' mind, thus affecting the whole course of action hereafter, but also because it sets out a positive case for war in a just cause. The emphasis on Athenian glory and on divine law highlights the two motives which impel Theseus to agree. Few Athenians would have denied the validity of these arguments, though Euripides makes plain enough later in the play that war also brings destruction. In those later scenes, however, the Argives and Thebans are the ones who suffer.

29 *the established laws of all Greece*: although Greek states were fiercely independent and competitive, the suggestion here is that certain central principles transcend different constitutional or legal systems. The right to burial, already cited as a law backed by the gods, is one of these; Theseus uses the same argument at 526 and 671.

30 *tackling a wild boar*: Theseus in his youth killed a ravaging wild boar (or sow) in the region between Megara and Corinth. The Athenians liked to think of Theseus as an Athenian Heracles, and this was one of his 'labours', commemorated in sculpture and literature.

31 *It is in risking danger that it shows its greatness*: this line encapsulates much of the Athenian self-image in the fifth century BC: they liked to see themselves as a daring and energetic people, achieving more than others because they had the courage to run greater risks. The Corinthians' speech in Thucydides i, 70 sums up these qualities from an enemy's viewpoint.

32 *the whole citizen-body . . . power of decision*: according to myth, Theseus is king of Athens, but the drama is being produced under the radical democracy. Consequently he is presented as exceptionally conscientious in his dealings with the people. The portrayal of Theseus may have reminded the audience of the special ascendancy of Pericles, an aristocratic leader who dominated Athenian politics for over a decade until his death in 429 BC.

33 *liberty with equality of franchise*: as part of their effort to associate Theseus with democratic practice, the Athenians anachronistically represented him as the founder of a proto-democratic form of government; cf. e.g. Demosthenes 60, 28, and J. Davie, *Greece & Rome* 29 (1982), pp. 25–34.

34 *governs . . . as monarch?*: the ideological thrust of the scene is immediately made clear: this will be a debate between incompatible political points of view. In the constitutional sphere, as in other respects, Thebes is sometimes viewed in tragedy as an 'anti-Athens': see F. Zeitlin, in *Nothing to Do with Dionysos?*, ed. J. Winkler and F. Zeitlin (Princeton 1990), pp. 130–67. Nevertheless, the debate is not a walkover for Theseus: the herald's criticisms of democracy are not fully answered, and many in the audience might have recognized their partial truth.

35 *Who . . . wishes to address this gathering?*: this echoes the words proclaimed by the herald at assembly meetings: cf. Aristophanes, *Acharnians* 45; Demosthenes 18, 170.

36 *lopped off like stalks*: this alludes to a famous anecdote about the tyrant Thrasybulus, who gave a visitor a lesson in firm government by strolling with him through a cornfield and repeatedly chopping off the taller ears of corn (Herodotus v, 92).

37 *men destroyed by their own arrogance*: the herald's comments seem justified, both by the general verdict in the literary tradition about the Seven (of whom Capaneus in particular was a notorious blasphemer), and by Theseus' stern assessment in the earlier scene with Adrastus. But we later see that there is another side to the story, and that the champions possessed outstanding qualities which the Athenians can admire and imitate (see Adrastus' 'funeral oration', 857–917). Even here the herald's argument is weaker as regards the virtuous prophet Amphiaraus.

38 *Silence, Adrastus!*: his aggressiveness may surprise us, but the dramatic interruption is presumably meant to show how vigorously Theseus has taken up the cause of the Seven and how the herald's arrogance has angered him.

39 *interfere . . . in the business of others*: the phrase (and the vocabulary in the Greek) echoes contemporary criticisms of Athenian imperialist activity. What the Athenians think of as necessary intervention may look like selfish aggression to those at the receiving end. Modern analogies are innumerable.

40 *sown*: Cadmus was said to have sown the teeth of a monstrous snake he had slain; from these teeth grew up armed warriors, the first citizens of Thebes. The myth explains the military prowess of the Thebans. At 579, Theseus turns it against them by implying that the progeny of a snake will be sluggish or cowardly; and see 'army of men sprung from the dragon's teeth' at 703–4.

41 *not to taint my fortunes with your own*: Adrastus' misfortunes so far suggest that he may be a jinx if taken on the new expedition.

42 *Callichorus' stream*: one of the sacred springs of Eleusis, where the chorus remain at present. They imagine themselves travelling to the site of the battle. The 'towers' are obviously those of Thebes.

43 *city of twin streams*: the rivers Ismenus and Dirce, near which Thebes stood.

44 *heifer-maid, our ancient mother*: Io was a priestess of Hera whom Zeus wooed or raped; her son by Zeus was the ancestor of the family of Danaus, and so was taken to be ancestress of the Argives in general. Io was for part of her life transformed into the form of a heifer, either as a punishment by the jealous Hera, or as a precaution by Zeus to conceal her from Hera.

45 *the club from Epidaurus*: Theseus took this club or mace from a villainous robber Periphetes; the slaying of this man is another of Theseus' 'civilizing' labours.

46 *[breaking his silence]*: Adrastus has not spoken since silenced by Theseus earlier. His speech here comes as a surprise, for he speaks with new authority and insight. Repentance and reflection on the meaning of Theseus' success mean that he is now able to voice a number of moral principles which, even if we do not regard them as the poet's 'message', are clearly to be taken seriously.

47 *[Five of the seven dead captains]*: the two absentees are Amphiaraus and Polynices. The former was swallowed up by the earth, the latter is probably absent because his mother Jocasta is not to be thought of as among the chorus (indeed, according to Sophocles' version of the myth she would be dead by now).

48 *You mothers, cry out*: choral reflections in an ode pass into formal lamentation conducted in sung exchanges with Adrastus.

49 *and now Adrastus, I ask you . . .*: this request from Theseus leads into the 'funeral oration' of Adrastus for the five dead men present; Theseus then caps this with comments on the other two members of the Seven. The lyric poet Pindar mentions Adrastus giving an oration for the Seven at Thebes. The speech Adrastus makes is remarkable for its rehabilitation of the dead men, of whom so many criticisms have been made. Here they are seen not as monstrous aggressors but as exemplary citizens. The interpretation of the scene is much disputed; see C. Collard, *Bulletin of the Institute of Classical Studies* 19 (1972), pp. 39–53.

50 *separately, as a sacred corpse*: death by lightning was regarded with superstitious awe. Such victims had to be buried separately, and the ground where they lay became taboo.

51 *Seven mothers*: the figure is conventional for the whole group of women involved. It need not imply that all the mothers are present: see n. 47 above.

52 *songs that golden-haired Apollo refuses to hear*: that is, funeral laments or dirges, the very opposite of the song associated with Apollo, the life-affirming paean.

53 *[Enter EVADNE]*: Capaneus has been mentioned several times, but we have not been led to expect his wife's appearance, still less the dramatic suicide which follows. After much of the play has concentrated on the political and moral aspects of the war, we now see what the death of the Seven means to a named individual (the grief of the collective chorus is rather different in its effect).

The scene is highly emotional and Evadne's singing and movement would be frantic. Suicide of a surviving partner is found elsewhere in Euripides (e.g. the lost *Laodamia*), but it looks as though the death of Evadne in these circumstances is his own invention; the shock for the audience is all the greater. The staging is hard to reconstruct, but presumably the actor playing Evadne jumped from the roof of the stage-building on to a pyre heaped up behind it.

54 *with a Bacchante's wild haste*: frenzy and manic distress are easily associated with Bacchic inspiration. Euripides no doubt echoes Andromache's distress on hearing the lament for Hector's death in the *Iliad*: she too is described as running like a mad woman to the walls.

55 *Kindle the wedding torch . . .*: like Cassandra in the *Trojan Women*, Evadne uses the language of the marriage ceremony in a distorted or macabre way. She will be wedded anew to Capaneus, in death. Metaphorical links between marriage and death are common in tragedy: see R. Seaford, *Journal of Hellenic Studies* 107 (1987), pp. 106–30.

56 *[SONS of the dead]*: as already mentioned in n. 12, the sons have been present throughout, in attendance on the mothers of the Seven. Their glorious yet destructive future now comes into view, first in the boys' expression of their desire for vengeance, and then especially in the prophetic words of Athena. The combination of maternal tenderness with the prospect of future violence makes for a complex effect: the sons are already beginning to follow in their fathers' footsteps, but the prospect of further bloodshed distresses the chorus.

57 *from one generation to the next*: this glance towards the future paves the way for the more explicit instructions given by Athena, who lays down the terms of an Athens–Argos alliance. Connections with an actual historical treaty in Euripides' day should be viewed with caution, given our uncertainty as to the exact date of the play. See G. Zuntz, *The Political Plays of Euripides*, pp. 88–93, and C. Collard, *Suppliants*, vol. 1, pp. 10–11.

ELECTRA

1 *FARMER*: this figure, who is never named, seems to be a Euripidean invention. Traditionally Aegisthus and Clytemnestra kept Electra unmarried (her name itself etymologically refers to this condition: *a + lektron*, 'no marriage bed'), and she resentfully weeps at this in Aeschylus and Sophocles. In the end she will be wedded to Pylades, as prophesied at the end of the play (1249, 1284–7). The farmer, therefore, is not necessary for the plot but makes an important contribution to the different atmosphere of Euripides' play.

2 *his father's old tutor*: this man appears later in the play and identifies Orestes

(487–584). The dramatists' freedom of choice can be seen by comparing the different role of the old tutor in Sophocles' *Electra*, in which he accompanies Orestes and Pylades to Argos and helps them in their mission.

3 *nobility is undermined by poverty*: this speech, like others in the play, hints at the contradictions between Athenian democratic ideology and traditional respect for aristocratic birth and status, as represented in myth by the monarchic families of tragedy. In the *Odyssey*, the swineherd Eumaeus is similarly of aristocratic origin, but has been kidnapped and sold into slavery; his noble birth 'explains' his honourable behaviour.

4 *second-class offspring in our own home*: the following exchange serves to characterize Electra and the farmer: where she is intense and self-pitying, he is more good-humoured and patient. Her determination to make the worst of her situation is also illustrated by her reactions to the chorus's overtures.

5 *PYLADES*: Pylades is merely a loyal presence throughout the play: he has no speeches to make. The same applies in Sophocles' *Electra*. In Aeschylus' *Libation-Bearers* he appears to be a mute character but at the climax of the play, before the killing of his mother, makes one crucial speech urging Orestes to strike. In both Sophocles and Euripides the attention shifts to the influence of Electra.

6 *without any man's knowledge*: this suggests that Orestes is taking a particularly cautious line (as later, when he is surprisingly slow to reveal his identity and confide in Electra): he is not the bold warrior whom Electra seems to anticipate (524–6).

7 *see a woman, a servant*: Orestes' mistake is natural because of the humble dress that Electra wears.

8 *[a song of mourning]*: the singing by Electra and chorus continues until 213, where both revert to spoken verse and turn to less emotional concerns.

9 *a drinker of milk who roams the mountains*: a herdsman who lives off the milk and meat provided by his cattle.

10 *Hera's temple*: Argos (with which nearby Mycenae is often equated in tragedy) held Hera in special reverence; conversely, in the *Iliad* she speaks of Sparta, Argos and Mycenae as the cities dearest to her (Book 4, 52–3).

11 *a greater right to touch*: like Orestes' previous line, this form of words leads us to expect a revelation of his identity; but instead, he holds back further. This technique of 'retardation', used frequently in the *Odyssey* and elsewhere in tragedy, was clearly popular with Greek audiences.

12 *from city to city, not living under any one set of laws*: as this line makes clear, 'Greece', whether in the classical or the mythical era, was not a unified nation (though some features of Greek society, e.g. language and religion, did create a sense of common identity). Different *poleis* ('states') were often self-governing and certainly preserved their independent traditions and customs. See further the entry in the *Oxford Classical Dictionary* on 'nationalism'.

13 *a close secret*: considering that the chorus have been visible from the start, Orestes' concern is belated by realistic standards. We are dealing here with a convention of tragedy: the chorus is normally aligned with one major character (here Electra), and can be sworn to secrecy.

14 *If only I could slit my mother's throat*: this horrifying pronouncement continues the negative characterization of Electra, a tendency not significantly diminished by the fact that this is a regular style of prayer in Greek poetry, especially tragedy.

15 *No man . . . awareness*: these interesting reflections on the relation between intelligence, education and compassion are typically Euripidean, and reflect both his philosophic interests (see General Introduction) and the general tendency of the Greeks to view morality in intellectual terms. In context, the lines preserve Orestes' disguise, explaining why he has expressed himself so warmly.

16 *I too want to be told now*: since the chorus evidently know Electra well, this is a slightly artificial cue for a set-piece speech by Electra on her miserable condition. We have already heard her misery and resentment in the earlier lyrics with the chorus; now she restates her woes in iambic lines.

17 *gowns fastened with clasps of gold*: the stress on Clytemnestra's luxurious dress is confirmed later when she appears in person (998–1003). Electra's hatred arises partly from her own poverty and lack of such attire.

18 *These are the insults*: in Aeschylus' trilogy, Aegisthus was an unattractive figure, less authoritative than Clytemnestra. In this speech Euripides characterizes him as a grotesque and hysterical maniac. The later description of his courteous hospitality therefore takes us by surprise: can Electra's account be true?

19 *and no doubt you've told them the rest*: there seems to be cynical humour here, though it goes too far to see the relation of Electra and her husband as anticipating modern kitchen-sink drama (as B. M. W. Knox comes near to suggesting in *Word and Action*, pp. 251–5).

20 *Oh, how true it is*: on the textual issues in this speech see 'Note on the Text', and S. Goldhill's article cited there. Orestes' moralizing reflections are of a kind which tragic audiences in the fifth and fourth centuries clearly enjoyed; they also take up themes which were debated by the sophists and their pupils (e.g. the relation of morality to birth and environment, 'nature versus culture'). Yet it is notable that the aristocratic Orestes, even in disguise, speaks not a word to the farmer: is this a satirical touch, suggesting the limitations of his own 'nobility'?

The passages omitted from the translation, as being probably interpolated, are lines 373–9 and 386–90. Since there is much disagreement about their status, and since this example was specifically discussed in the 'Note on the Text', we give a version of them here. The first follows on from Orestes' reflections on the presence of virtue and intelligence in a poor man.

[. . . in one of slender means.] How then can any man take these matters and evaluate them correctly? By wealth? He will be employing a vile judge in that case. Or should he prefer those who are impoverished? But poverty brings with it a disease, teaching a man to be bad through necessity. Well, should one have recourse to arms? But who could bear witness as to who is a good man while facing up to a spear? It is best to leave all this alone, abandoning things to chance.

The second passage follows on from Orestes' comment on the well-born.

[. . . how he behaves to others!] For men of this sort are the ones who manage well their cities and their homes; whereas empty-headed sacks of flesh are just gilded parasites in the assembly. And even when it comes to battle, the strong man's right arm doesn't resist the spear more effectively than the weak man's; it all depends on natural capacity and courage.

21 *Trojan Simois*: the Simois was one of the rivers of the Trojan plain. The whole ode evokes in highly poetic and colourful terms the splendour of the Greeks' expedition as it set forth from Aulis to Troy: the glory of the war is supremely exemplified in the heroic Achilles, son of a goddess. As the final epode brings out, this forms the background to Agamemnon's sordid death; there is also a contrast with the shadier and much less glorious actions of Orestes.

22 *Hephaestus' anvil*: this refers to the forging of armour for Achilles by the smith of the gods. As presented in the *Iliad*, this only happened in the ninth year of the war, after his original armour had been lost; but the version described here, in which he receives it as the expedition sets out, may be older and is certainly represented in pre-Euripidean vase-painting.

23 *a Centaur father*: Chiron, the wise Centaur, acted as a tutor for the youthful Achilles, as for other heroes.

24 *Perseus*: an earlier hero, most famous for his slaying of the monstrous Gorgon Medusa, whose hideous face turned men to stone. There are several references to this exploit in the play, and it may be that Perseus' killing of Medusa is being compared and contrasted with Orestes' slaying of his mother.

25 *that made Hector blanch and run*: the reference is to Hector's final encounter with Achilles, in which he panics and runs from his assailant. This is described in Book 22 of Homer's *Iliad* (though, as mentioned in n. 22, the shield there is a new one).

26 *the lioness that breathes fire*: the Chimaera, another monstrous opponent of a hero, slain by Bellerophon on the winged horse Pegasus ('Pirene's steed' because he created the famous spring at Pirene, near Corinth, with a blow of his hoof). The Chimaera was part lion, part goat, part snake.

27 *Compare a lock of that hair with your own*: this suggestion introduces a sequence which seems to echo the recognition scene in Aeschylus' *Libation-Bearers* (174–211). There, Electra herself observes the equivalent signs and draws the conclusion that her brother is near. On her more sceptical attitude here, see General Introduction, p. xxii. Some critics have thought this section of *Electra* to be an interpolation by another hand, but this device of alluding to his great predecessor, but with a touch of parody, is entirely characteristic of the poet.

28 *nobility is rarely a guarantee of worth*: this striking one-liner continues the themes articulated in Orestes' speech. Inevitably the audience begins to wonder how far Orestes does in fact represent an ideal of nobility.

29 *A scar along his eyebrow*: like the 'parody' of Aeschylus, this speech makes use of a distinguished literary source. In Homer's *Odyssey* the hero is identified by his old nurse, who observes a scar which he received in a boar-hunt in his youth (Book 19, 392–475). Here the youthful adventure is more trivial!

30 *[I . . . father]*: these words represent the probable meaning of a line that seems to have dropped out of the text in centuries of transmission.

31 *Mother's death shall be* my *responsibility*: Electra's blood-curdling line follows a long silence since her enthusiastic welcome of her brother. Silences of this kind are often meaningful in tragedy (cf. Cassandra in Aeschylus' *Agamemnon*), and her intervention is all the more effective.

32 *Ten days . . . for purification*: the mother was thought to be in a state of pollution or unclean for the first few days after giving birth. A sacrifice on the tenth day, usually performed by others who had been present, brought this period of uncleanness to an end (see 1133).

33 *[raise their arms together in prayer]*: this short invocation again pays tribute to Aeschylus' *Libation-Bearers*, in which Orestes and Electra, together with the chorus, invoke Agamemnon at great length in lyrics. The abridged version here is chanted only, and is cut off without much ceremony by the old man.

34 *trampling me in the dust*: Electra's determination to gain revenge is a 'masculine' characteristic, aligning her with heroic figures such as Sophocles' Ajax. In this she re-enacts her mother's career: Aeschylus had made much of Clytemnestra's 'man-minded heart' (*Agamemnon* 11 and often elsewhere).

35 *The tale still lives . . .*: the myth allusively outlined in this choral ode is a complex one. A golden lamb, a divine artefact, gave its possessor the right to the throne of Mycenae. The two brothers Atreus and Thyestes (fathers of

Agamemnon and Aegisthus respectively) both desired the kingship. Thyestes seduced Aerope, his brother's wife, and thus gained possession of the lamb; in the most common version, this was followed by the horrific revenge of Atreus, who killed Thyestes' sons and served them up, disguised amid other meat, to their father at dinner. Usually it is said that Zeus reversed the course of the sun as a symbolic gesture at this hideous crime; but Atreus nevertheless regained his throne. Here the change of the sun's course is an acknowledgement of Atreus' sovereignty. The changes and emphases Euripides has introduced have been variously interpreted. The reserve which the chorus express about the more incredible aspects of the myths can be paralleled elsewhere in his plays (cf. General Introduction, pp. xxix–xxx).

36 *These tales . . . benefit the worship of the gods*: this is not necessarily a sceptical or a cynical remark by the poet speaking through the chorus, although the line has been read that way in the past. The idea that religious devotion can be reinforced by false or unlikely tales, provided they are believed by the majority, is not unusual, and indeed finds much support in history.

37 *the glorious brothers*: Clytemnestra was the sister of Castor and Pollux, now deified as the Heavenly Twins; they will appear to resolve the situation at the end of the play.

38 *his messengers should have come*: a messenger promptly arrives, almost on cue; there may be a mischievous allusion to the conventions of the genre.

39 *sacred parts . . . examining them*: in ancient society the inner organs, especially the livers, of sacrificial animals were scrutinized for abnormal features and for their general condition as a form of divination. This is constant practice even in historical times.

40 *what should I say . . . ?*: Electra embarks on a full-scale denunciation of Aegisthus, with all the weapons of the rhetorical art. This is in line with her comments on him earlier in the play (326–31), but in conflict with the more agreeable conduct the messenger has described. The contradiction is disquieting, and never reconciled.

41 *'The man isn't master in that marriage'*: the 'man-minded' Clytemnestra of Aeschylus is updated, with more acerbic social comment of the kind recognizable from Athenian society and our own; cf. K. J. Dover, *Greek Popular Morality* (Oxford 1974), pp. 96–8.

42 *your behaviour towards women*: this is not a traditional item in the catalogue of Aegisthus' crimes; it has been imported from the rhetorical repertoire (particularly the abuse of tyrants: cf. *Suppliant Women* 450–55).

43 *Wait!*: Orestes' hesitation as the prospect of matricide comes nearer gives an opportunity for a further contrast between his irresolution and Electra's hate-filled dedication. Aeschylus' Orestes felt fewer doubts before the killing.

44 *go on to set the same trap for her . . .*: this line draws attention to the reworking of the *Oresteia* which continues in the rest of the scene. Just as Agamemnon returned from Troy ceremoniously, and was lured into the house to his death by Clytemnestra's lying speeches, so Clytemnestra will now arrive richly attired, and will meet a similar deception from Electra. The farmer's hovel replaces the royal palace.

45 *the daughter I lost*: Iphigenia, whom Agamemnon was forced to sacrifice at Aulis so that the Greek fleet could sail for Troy. In Aeschylus too this crime was a major factor in Clytemnestra's killing of her husband; but in both authors the relative importance of this motive and her passion for Aegisthus remains uncertain.

46 *if he had been seeking . . . I could have forgiven him*: these alternative scenarios are common in tragedy: the *Children of Heracles*, the *Phoenician Women*, and the lost *Erechtheus* all present narratives in which a noble young man or woman must die that a city may be saved.

47 *a crazy woman in tow*: she refers to the inspired prophetess Cassandra, Agamemnon's captive concubine.

48 *Castor*: both Helen and Clytemnestra were sisters of Castor and Pollux. Electra probably mentions Castor in particular because he was her former suitor (see 312–13).

49 *sacrifice . . . to the gods*: the irony is obvious: Clytemnestra herself will be the sacrificial victim (as Agamemnon was before in Aeschylus' presentation).

50 *[corpses . . . are revealed]*: according to the conventions of the Greek theatre, the bodies are wheeled out from within the stage building on a platform, which the Greeks called the *ekkuklema* ('rolling-out machine'). This is a device to show indoor events on an open-air stage. Again the exposure of the corpses imitates Aeschylus' production.

51 *[. . .]*: in the exchange which follows, the text in the manuscripts is badly preserved and several words are uncertain; in at least two places a few words have dropped out of the text.

52 *Phoebus, Phoebus . . .*: it is common for mortals to reproach the gods or complain of divine injustice; Euripides strikingly transfers this discontent to these lesser divinities (formerly mortal). The negative presentation of Apollo is also found elsewhere in Euripides (cf. *Andromache* and *Ion*).

53 *The terrible Spirits of Destruction*: he means the Furies, or Erinyes, who will persecute Orestes as a matricide. They also appeared in the third play of Aeschylus' *Oresteia* trilogy (in the *Eumenides* he showed them hunting down Orestes by the smell of the blood on his hands), the events of which are rapidly summarized in what follows.

54 *a hill of Ares*: the Areopagus, in central Athens, was the site of an ancient and prestigious lawcourt of that name, which had special authority in homicide cases. The myths of its origin vary: in Aeschylus, Orestes was the first person tried by that court, but here it has an older pedigree.

55 *Helen never went to Troy*: this version originated with the lyric poet Stesichorus (sixth century BC), and was probably revived by Euripides himself (though there is a partial parallel in a passage of Herodotus 2, 112–20). He mentions it only briefly here, but uses it as the basic premiss of his *Helen*. The story that Helen was a phantom all along has an obvious consequence: the Trojan war and all the suffering it brought was pointless after all.

56 *both maid and married woman*: Electra was married to the farmer (who has dropped out of the play by now), but as the marriage was not consummated she can still be a 'maid', and he, as is said just below, is Orestes' brother-in-law only in name.

57 *does not pollute you*: contact, even verbal, with sinners brings pollution, which the gods will not permit. Hence they will converse with the chorus but not with Orestes (yet they concede a few lines later that they can speak to Electra). The slight inconsistencies of their behaviour reinforce the dissatisfaction which a human audience must feel about their high-sounding responses to questions.

58 *these hell-hounds*: this refers to the Furies, who are normally represented as women with snake-like hair, but who resemble hounds in the frenzy of enthusiasm with which they pursue their quarry.

59 *the Sicilian sea*: for many years critics took these lines to refer to the famous Athenian expedition to Sicily in 415–13, and made deductions accordingly about the date of the play. But the reference is vague and may not be linked to historical events at all. See G. Zuntz, *The Political Plays of Euripides*, pp. 63–71.

60 *share his voyage with those who commit perjury*: one guilty man aboard a ship may lead to the sinking of the whole vessel: the principle is cited elsewhere in poetry (cf. the exchange between Athena and Poseidon at the start of the *Trojan Women*), and even in fifth-century BC oratory (e.g. Antiphon 5, 82).

TROJAN WOMEN

1 *the city of my Phrygians*: in the *Iliad* we are told that Apollo and Poseidon built the defensive walls of Troy for King Laomedon. In that poem, however, Poseidon is on the side of the Greeks, because Laomedon defrauded them of their pay. Greek mythology readily accommodates variations of this kind.

2 *a horse teeming with men-at-arms*: the Greeks pretended to leave Troy and sail home; they left behind the Wooden Horse, a gigantic hollow structure in which a team of warriors was concealed. The Trojans foolishly pulled the Horse into Troy to dedicate it to Athena. During the night that followed, the Greek heroes emerged, opened the gates to their returning comrades and proceeded to loot Troy and kill the Trojans.

3 *ruin on the Phrygians*: the hatred of Hera and Athena towards Troy originated with the choice by Paris of Aphrodite as the most beautiful of goddesses; see n. 13 on *Andromache* on the Judgement of Paris. The episode is referred to in the debate between Helen and Hecabe in this play (903–1033, esp. 924–37 and 969–82).

4 *Helen*: she will appear later in the play, characterized as a subtle and charming deceiver. Greek writers varied greatly in their presentation of Helen, and Euripides himself was to make her a much more sympathetic character in his *Helen*.

5 *Cassandra*: Apollo wooed her and gave her the gift of prophecy, but she then rejected his advances. He could not remove the gift, but nullified it by decreeing that nobody would believe her prophecies. This punishment is seen in action when she appears.

6 *common interest to us both*: the formality of this exchange is natural in the dignified genre of tragedy, but also suits the cold-blooded manner of negotiation between the divinities, neither of whom shows much concern for their human inferiors.

7 *Ajax dragged Cassandra off by force*: this is the lesser Ajax, son of Oileus. During the sack of Troy he attempted to drag Cassandra from sanctuary in Athena's temple and rape her; and his crime will bring others to grief in the storm planned by Athena.

8 *their journey home*: both the *Odyssey* and Aeschylus' *Agamemnon* describe storms which dispersed the Greek fleet on the homeward journey. Many ships were sunk, while others were driven far off course. Some of the heroes, including Odysseus and Menelaus, did not return to their homes for years.

9 *in time to come*: these generalizing lines might be applied by Athenian spectators to their own imperial activities, perhaps specifically to the sack of Melos (see Preface). It is pointless to speculate whether Euripides meant them to be applied in this way.

10 *twisted cables, Egypt's crop*: the cables are woven from papyrus reed (*byblos*).

11 *the land of Theseus*: the chorus pray they may be sent, even in slavery, to Athens; they would prefer this to Sparta because Helen will be living there again. Naturally this would appeal to an Athenian audience, hostile towards Sparta; but there is a quirky effect in introducing praise from such a remote foreign source.

12 *Crathis*: the River Crathis flows into the Tarentine Gulf close to the Athenian colony of Thurii, in the 'foot' of Italy.

13 *Spartan wife*: Clytemnestra.

14 *to serve at the tomb of Achilles*: Talthybius speaks ambiguously to spare Hecabe the full pain. In fact Polyxena has already been sacrificed to the ghost of Achilles, as Hecabe learns later. Contrast the rather different handling of the same event in *Hecabe* (218–37ff.), where Hecabe hears of this plan in detail before it happens.

15 *a foul, treacherous master*: the description of Odysseus is from a hostile source, but fits with the way he is generally presented in Euripides' work. The likeable rogue and cautious planner of the *Odyssey* is often presented as a more ruthless and scheming figure in later literature: see W. B. Stanford's excellent study, *The Ulysses Theme* (2nd edn, Oxford 1963).

16 *Raise up the torch!*: the scene involving Cassandra is discussed in the Preface to this play. It is partly modelled on the scene in Aeschylus' *Agamemnon* in which Cassandra foretells Agamemnon's death and her own to an unbelieving chorus. Here, however, the paradoxical rhetoric with which she argues her case is a typically Euripidean addition. New also is the emphasis on the celebration of a 'wedding'.

17 *O Hymen, lord Hymenaeus!*: 'Hymen' and 'Hymenaeus' are ritual cries uttered at weddings and seem to invoke a shadowy divinity of marriage, about whom there is little fixed tradition.

18 *evan! evoe!!*: these are ecstatic or celebratory cries, found also in worship of Dionysus.

19 *Hephaestus*: the use of this name does not seem to mean much more than that he embodies fire and so is present in torch-lit processions.

20 *I will kill him*: Cassandra means that her presence as concubine will enrage Clytemnestra, and so she will bring about Agamemnon's death.

21 *more fortunate than the Greeks*: this argument seems perverse to all those present, though the audience, having witnessed the pact between Athena and Poseidon, understand that the Greek victory is in part a hollow one. Sophists of the late fifth century BC often argued implausible or paradoxical cases to show their rhetorical prowess, and their works have influenced Euripides: cf. e.g. *Heracles* 151–64, where the evil Lycus argues that Heracles was a coward; also, in a papyrus fragment of the *Cretans*, Pasiphae argues that it is her husband's fault, not hers, that she has had sex with a bull.

22 *destroyed what he held most dear*: this refers to Iphigenia, sacrificed at Aulis for a fair wind.

23 *Not one . . . at his tomb*: the posthumous rites will not be performed by relatives because the Greek warriors are buried in foreign soil.

24 *a decent woman*: Penelope, the wife of Odysseus, is a model of fidelity and domestic virtue throughout the tradition.

25 *I will not insult her*: as Polymestor prophesies at the end of the *Hecabe* (1259–67), the queen will be transformed into a bitch, and will never journey to Greece.

26 *troubles past numbering in his home*: this passage includes multiple references to the wanderings of Odysseus as described by Homer. When Odysseus finally reaches his home in Ithaca, he finds his wife besieged by suitors and has to fight to regain his house and kingdom.

27 *mystic emblems, farewell*: as in Aeschylus' *Agamemnon* (1264–8), Cassandra renounces her prophetic apparel because she sees that her power of foresight will do her no good; she is going to die unbelieved, and the god will not help her.

28 *O you gods!*: throughout the play, Hecabe and the chorus regularly declare that the gods have abandoned Troy despite the many sacrifices the Trojans have offered, and despite the dynastic links between Trojans and gods. We have already seen that this is so from the prologue. On the general concept of divine powers abandoning a city, see R. Parker, 'Gods cruel and kind', in *Greek Tragedy and the Historian*, ed. C. B. R. Pelling.

29 *my poor Polyxena*: Hecabe is still unaware of her daughter's death; Andromache will soon disillusion her.

30 *our Trojan maid, daughter of Zeus*: Athena is meant. In the *Iliad* too she is held in high honour in Troy, but ignores their appeal for aid (Book 6, 305–11).

31 *the mountain maid*: Artemis.

32 *your son cheated death*: this refers to the story which formed the basis of the first play of the trilogy, *Alexandros*. For this, see the Preface to *Trojan Women*. Alexandros (Paris) was exposed at birth, but survived and later returned to Troy, with disastrous consequences.

33 *the dark riddle Talthybius gave me*: Talthybius had used ambiguous language in an effort to spare Hecabe the bad news (264).

34 *Your daughter*: Polyxena.

35 *O my precious baby . . .*: the tenderness of these lines can be compared with the words of Medea as she longs to spare her children (*Medea* 1071–5). Although Greek tragedy deals with a remote mythical world, the emotions which the dramatists arouse in scenes of this kind are universal.

36 *Daughter of Tyndareus*: Helen. Although Helen was in fact the child of Zeus and Leda, she was nominally 'daughter' of Tyndareus, Leda's mortal husband.

37 *Make a banquet of his flesh*: this line reminds the audience of other tragic myths in which children are indeed treated in this way (e.g. Tantalus and Pelops; Atreus and Thyestes' children). The fact that such events are familiar in the tragic genre makes the suggestion less artificial.

38 *Telamon . . .*: this ode begins by describing the first sack of Troy during the reign of King Laomedon by Greek heroes of an earlier generation, Telamon and Heracles. Heracles had rescued Laomedon's daughter from a sea-monster, but was denied the reward of a team of mares which he had been promised; hence 'pining for his lost mares' (809–10).

39 *Alcmena's archer son*: Heracles, son of Zeus and Alcmena, famed for his skill with the bow.

40 *son of Laomedon . . . cups of Zeus*: the son of Laomedon was Ganymede, whose beauty was such that Zeus himself fell in love with him and carried him off to Olympus to be his immortal cupbearer. The chorus go on to contrast the serenity of Ganymede's existence with the disasters that have befallen Troy, the home he left behind. The ode implies criticism of the gods, who owe much to Troy and yet have abandoned her.

41 *what brought shame to Zeus*: the point is that (despite 'marriage' in the previous sentence) Zeus' liaison with Ganymede was adulterous.

42 *The light of Dawn*: this refers to another erotic link between Olympus and Troy: the goddess Dawn carried off the Trojan youth Tithonus to be her husband. The usual version was that she gained him immortality but neglected to ensure that he would remain youthful, and so he gradually became older and more wizened. This aspect is ignored here, as the disappointment would spoil the contrast between the joys of the gods and the miseries of Troy.

43 *[MENELAUS enters . . .]*: the scene which follows provides a more intellectual and argumentative interest occurring between scenes of harrowing grief. The debate between Helen and Hecabe shows the playwright's rhetorical virtuosity, but also shows how little words can influence events. Hecabe has the better of the argument, yet Helen will in the end evade punishment and return to a comfortable life in Sparta.

44 *O you who give the earth support . . .*: on Hecabe's prayer, see General Introduction, p. xxviii. The prayer combines various conceptions and terminologies from philosophic thinkers of Euripides' own time.

45 *putting the case against her*: it is natural that Hecabe should want an opportunity to denounce Helen (in the *Iliad*, Helen complains that all the women of Troy detest her); but the quasi-legal language paves the way for a typical Euripidean *agon* or 'contest of speeches', as in a lawcourt.

46 *Alexandros or Paris*: Priam and Hecabe named their child Alexandros, but when he was exposed and rescued by herdsmen they brought him up under the other name. Here the use of the alternatives has an extra point: it is common in prayer to cite various names for a god, and Helen does so here, half jokingly, as part of her suggestion that he was a kind of evil spirit brought into being by Hecabe.

47 *the blame is not mine*: the question of Helen's responsibility for her actions is already obscure in the *Iliad*: was she abducted or did she leave willingly? Did she leave with Paris because she wanted to or because Aphrodite forced her? More recently the sophist Gorgias had composed a paradoxical defence of Helen, which still survives, including the argument that if she was in love, she was not responsible because love is a god and irresistible. Euripides seems to have read the work by Gorgias and adapted its arguments.

48 *convincing men of sense*: the argument Hecabe presents against the story of the 'Judgement' is surprising, since Euripides makes frequent reference to it and it may have been mentioned in *Alexandros*. Perhaps the poet is deliberately drawing attention to the implausibilities and inconsistencies of the myths. The problem is discussed by T. C. W. Stinton, *Collected Papers on Greek Tragedy*, pp. 46 and 248–50.

49 *your mind became the goddess*: again Euripides allows his characters to speak with the intellectual sophistication of his contemporaries: the theory implied here is that 'gods' are really allegorical representations of human passions.

50 *the goddess's name begins with folly*: the word for 'folly' used here is *aphrosyne*; Hecabe means that one could derive the name Aphrodite from this word.

51 *hoping to vex my son*: cf. the *Iliad*, Book 3, where Helen wishes to return to Menelaus and praises him while mocking Paris' inadequacy on the battlefield.

52 *Does she weigh more than she used to?*: this extraordinary line seems to bring the scene close to comedy. Menelaus, a self-important figure and a cuckold, makes a foolishly frivolous joke, despite the seriousness of the issue. Helen's future success in manipulating this dull-witted companion is easily imagined.

53 *holy cakes*: flat, circular cakes, known as 'moon-cakes', were sometimes used as a form of bloodless sacrifice; see further, *Oxford Classical Dictionary*, entry for 'cakes'.

54 *armour of Odysseus*: the crafty and deceptive Odysseus is mentioned as the opposite of the manly warrior Hector. The line may allude to the divine armour of Achilles, which Odysseus inherited after the hero's death.

55 *songs of men hereafter*: as in various passages of Homer, the speaker anticipates a time when the events she is experiencing will be the subject of song. The reference is vague and does not necessarily refer to the Euripidean drama itself. Passages of this type are unusual in Greek tragedy, though more frequent in Shakespeare (see A. Barton, *Shakespeare and the Idea of the Play* (London 1962); D. Bain, *Actors and Audience* (Oxford 1977), chs. 11 and 12).

BIBLIOGRAPHY

Texts

The standard Greek text, which forms the basis for this translation, is the new Oxford Classical Text edited by J. Diggle (3 volumes, 1984–94); this supersedes the much-used edition by G. Murray in the same series. The edition is arranged chronologically. *Andromache* and *Hecabe* are printed in volume 1, the other three plays in this Penguin edition in volume 2.

Those wishing to consult the plays in Greek will find the best guidance in the following annotated editions:
Andromache: ed. P. T. Stevens (Oxford, 1971); ed. M. Lloyd (Warminster 1994).
Hecuba: ed. C. Collard (Warminster 1991).
Suppliants: ed. C. Collard (2 vols., Groningen 1975: very detailed).
Electra: ed. J. D. Denniston (Oxford 1939); ed. M. J. Cropp (Warminster 1988).
Trojan Women: ed. K. H. Lee (London 1976); ed. S. A. Barlow (Warminster 1986).

Other translations

The Loeb Classical Library, which publishes bilingual editions of most classical authors, is currently bringing out an edition of Euripides by David Kovacs, arranged chronologically: two volumes have appeared, and more are imminent. This edition replaces an older and wholly unsatisfactory edition by A. S. Way. Those who need to consider the detail of the Greek text should note that Kovacs presents his own text, which often differs from Diggle's.

Other translations available include those by various hands in the series edited by D. Grene and R. Lattimore, *The Complete Greek Tragedies* (Chicago 1941–58). Otherwise, complete versions of Euripides are hard to find, though the major plays are often translated individually or in smaller selections.

General works on Greek tragedy

Goldhill, S., *Reading Greek Tragedy* (Cambridge 1986).

Hall, E., *Inventing the Barbarian: Greek Self-definition through Tragedy* (Oxford 1992).

Heath, M., *The Poetics of Greek Tragedy* (London 1987).

Jones, J., *On Aristotle and Greek Tragedy* (London 1962).

Knox, B. M. W., *Word and Action: Essays on the Ancient Theater* (Baltimore 1979).

Lesky, A., *Greek Tragedy* (Eng. tr., London 1954).

Pelling, C. B. R., *Greek Tragedy and the Historian* (Oxford 1997).

Taplin, O., *Greek Tragedy in Action* (London 1978).

Taplin, O., *The Stagecraft of Aeschylus* (Oxford 1977): despite the title, relevant to all the tragedians.

Vernant, J.-P. and Vidal-Naquet, P., *Myth and Tragedy in Ancient Greece* (New York 1988; amalgamates two earlier collections of essays).

Vickers, B., *Towards Greek Tragedy* (London 1973).

Easterling, P. E. and Knox, B. M. W. (eds.), *The Cambridge History of Classical Literature*, vol. 1 (Cambridge 1985), includes expert essays on the Greek theatre and on each of the three tragedians (Knox covers Euripides); these chapters, together with those on satyric drama and comedy, are reissued in paperback as *Greek Drama*, eds. Easterling and Knox (Cambridge 1989).

Useful collections of work include:

Easterling, P. E. (ed.), *The Cambridge Companion to Greek Tragedy* (Cambridge 1997).

McAuslan, I. and Walcot, P. (eds.), *Greek Tragedy* (*Greece & Rome Studies* 2, Oxford 1993).

Segal, E. (ed.), *Oxford Readings in Greek Tragedy* (Oxford 1983).

Silk, M. (ed.), *Tragedy and the Tragic* (Oxford 1996).

The Greek theatre

Csapo, E. and Slater, W. J., *The Context of Ancient Drama* (Michigan 1995): this excellent source-book translates and discusses many ancient texts relevant to theatrical conditions in the Greek and Roman world.

Green, J. R., *Theatre in Ancient Greek Society* (London 1994).

Green, R. and Handley, E., *Images of the Greek Theatre* (London 1995).

Pickard-Cambridge, A. W., *The Dramatic Festivals of Athens* (2nd edn revised by J. Gould and D. M. Lewis, Oxford 1968; reissued 1988).

Simon, E., *The Ancient Theatre* (Eng. tr., Methuen, London and New York 1982).

Historical and cultural background

Andrewes, A., *Greek Society* (London 1971); originally published as *The Greeks* (London 1967).

Davies, J. K., *Democracy and Classical Greece* (London 1978; revised and expanded 1993).

Mills, S., *Theseus, Tragedy and the Athenian Empire* (Oxford 1997).

Religion and thought

Bremmer, J. M., *Greek Religion* (*Greece & Rome New Surveys* 24, Oxford 1994).

Burkert, W., *Greek Religion* (Eng. tr., Oxford 1985).

Dodds, E. R., *The Greeks and the Irrational* (Berkeley 1951).

Mikalson, J., *Athenian Popular Religion* (Chapel Hill 1983).

Mikalson, J., *Honor thy Gods: Popular Religion in Greek Tragedy* (Chapel Hill and London 1991): helpful, but perhaps emphasizes too strongly the gap between literature and the realities of cult and worship.

Studies of Euripides in general

Barlow, S. A., *The Imagery of Euripides* (London 1971).

Collard, C., *Euripides* (*Greece & Rome New Surveys* 14, Oxford 1981): an excellent short account with many examples and full bibliographical guidance.

Conacher, D. J., *Euripidean Drama: Myth, Theme and Structure* (Toronto and London 1967).

Michelini, A. M., *Euripides and the Tragic Tradition* (Madison, Wisconsin and London 1987): valuable chapters on the history of interpretation; also contains detailed 'readings' of four plays, including *Hecabe* and *Electra*.

Murray, G., *Euripides and his Age* (London 1913).

Discussions of plays in this volume

ANDROMACHE

Kovacs, D., *The* Andromache *of Euripides: an interpretation* (*American Classical Studies* 6, Chico, Calif. 1980).

Storey, I. C., 'Domestic disharmony in Euripides' *Andromache*', in *Greece & Rome* 36 (1989), pp. 16–27; reprinted in McAuslan and Walcot, *Greek Tragedy* (op. cit.), pp. 180–92.

HECABE

Daitz, S. G., 'Concepts of freedom and slavery in Euripides' *Hecuba*', *Hermes* 99 (1971), pp. 217–26.

Heath, M., '*Iure principem locum tenet*: Euripides' *Hecuba*', *Bulletin of the Institute of Classical Studies* 34 (1987), pp. 40–68.

Michelini, A. M., *Euripides and the Tragic Tradition* (op. cit.), pp. 131–180.

Mossman, J., *Wild Justice: A Study of Euripides'* Hecuba (Oxford 1995).

Nussbaum, M., *The Fragility of Goodness* (Cambridge 1986), pp. 395–421.

SUPPLIANT WOMEN

Collard, C., 'The Funeral Oration in Euripides' *Suppliants*', *Bulletin of the Institute of Classical Studies* 19 (1972), pp. 39–53.

Gamble, R. H., 'Euripides' *Suppliant Women*: decision and ambivalence', *Hermes* 98 (1970), pp. 385–404.

Macleod, C. W., 'Thucydides and Tragedy' in his *Collected Essays* (Oxford 1983), pp. 140–58 (esp. pp. 147–152).

Zuntz, G., *The Political Plays of Euripides* (Manchester 1955), chs. 1–3.

ELECTRA

Arnott, W. G., 'Double the vision: a reading of Euripides' *Electra*', in *Greece & Rome* 28 (1981), pp. 179–91; reprinted in McAuslan and Walcot, *Greek Tragedy* (op. cit.), pp. 204–217.

Goldhill, S., *Reading Greek Tragedy* (op. cit.), pp. 245–59.

Lloyd, M., 'Realism and character in Euripides' *Electra*', *Phoenix* 40 (1986), pp. 1–19.

Michelini, A. M., *Euripides and the Tragic Tradition* (op. cit.), pp. 181–228.

Vickers, B., *Towards Greek Tragedy* (op. cit.), ch. 10 (esp. pp. 558–66).

TROJAN WOMEN

Croally, N. T., *The Trojan Women and the Function of Tragedy* (Cambridge 1994).

Scodel, R., *The Trojan Trilogy of Euripides* (Göttingen 1980).

Special aspects

de Jong, I. J. F., *Narrative in Drama: the Art of the Euripidean Messenger-speech* (*Mnemosyne Supplement* 116, Leiden 1991).

Diggle, J., *Studies in the Text of Euripides* (Oxford 1982) and *Euripidea* (Oxford 1994): detailed discussions of many textual problems by the editor of the standard text.

Halleran, M. R., *Stagecraft in Euripides* (London and Sydney 1985).

Kovacs, D., *Euripidea* (*Mnemosyne Supplement* 132, Leiden 1994): includes detailed catalogue of ancient texts which refer to Euripides, and discusses problems of the text of the first few plays.

Kovacs, D., *Euripidea altera* (*Mnemosyne Supplement* 161, Leiden 1996): continues the textual discussions where the previous item left off.

Lloyd, M., *The* Agon *in Euripides* (Oxford 1992).

Stinton, T. C. W., 'Euripides and the Judgement of Paris', *Journal of Hellenic Studies: Supplementary Paper* 11 (1965); reprinted in Stinton, *Collected Papers on Greek Tragedy* (Oxford 1990), pp. 17–75.

General reference works

Hornblower, S. and Spawforth, A. (eds.), *The Oxford Classical Dictionary* (3rd edn, Oxford 1996): detailed and authoritative.

Howatson, M., *The Oxford Companion to Classical Literature* (Oxford 1989): useful particularly for summaries of myths.

GLOSSARY OF MYTHOLOGICAL
AND GEOGRAPHICAL NAMES

Information given here is not normally reproduced in the notes to specific passages.

ACASTUS son of Pelias of Iolcus.

ACHAEA a region in the N. Peloponnese, south of the Corinthian Gulf.

ACHILLES son of the hero Peleus and the sea-nymph Thetis; greatest of the Greek heroes who fought at Troy; clad in armour forged by Hephaestus, he killed the Trojan champion Hector, but died in battle later, slain by Paris' arrow. Father of Neoptolemus.

ADRASTUS king of Argos. He offered friendship and the hands of his daughters to two exiled heroes, Tydeus and Polynices, and then led an army against Thebes in an effort to reinstate Polynices, who had been ousted from the throne by his brother Eteocles.

AEACUS Greek hero of an earlier generation than the Trojan war: father of Peleus and grandfather of Achilles.

AEGEAN the part of the Mediterranean Sea separating Greece from Asia Minor.

AEGEUS son of Pandion and king of Athens; father of Theseus.

AEGIALEUS son of Adrastus of Argos, and one of the Epigoni or Successors of the Seven against Thebes; this group of sons march successfully against Thebes in their turn. Aegialeus is the only one of them slain in that expedition.

AEGISTHUS son of Thyestes and lover of Clytemnestra, with whom he conspired to murder her husband Agamemnon.

AEGYPTUS brother of Danaus. His sons sought to marry Danaus' daughters against their will; when forced into this marriage, the women slaughtered their new husbands (with one exception) on their wedding night.

AETHRA wife of Aegeus and mother of Theseus.

AETOLIA a region in central Greece bordering on the Corinthian Gulf.

AGAMEMNON king of Argos and Mycenae, leader of the Greek expedition against Troy. Father of Iphigenia, Orestes and Electra (also, in some versions, of Chrysothemis). Killed by his wife Clytemnestra.

AJAX there were two heroes of this name. The one mentioned in this volume is the 'lesser' Ajax, son of Oileus; chiefly famous for attempting to abduct and rape Cassandra at the sack of Troy. He was punished with death on the homeward journey.

ALCMENA wife of Amphitryon and mother (by Zeus) of Heracles, mightiest of the Greek heroes.

ALEXANDROS see 'Paris'.

ALPHEUS a river originating in Arcadia in the Peloponnese and passing by the great cult-site of Zeus at Olympia; flows into the Ionian Sea.

AMMON an Egyptian deity whose oracle in the Libyan desert was famous among the Greeks, who often identified the god there with their own Zeus.

AMPHIARAUS one of the Seven against Thebes, and the only one who, being a prophet, foresaw the failure of the expedition and argued against it. He was forced to join it by a promise to his wife. In the end he was miraculously swallowed up by the earth.

AMPHION son of Zeus and Antiope; a marvellous singer and player of music, whose songs enchanted wild beasts and even moved the stones forming the walls of Thebes, which he ruled jointly with his twin brother Zethus.

AMYCLAE a village near Sparta, part of the domain of Menelaus.

ANDROMACHE wife of the Trojan prince Hector and mother of Astyanax; with her husband and child both dead, she travelled as a slave to Greece and lived as a concubine of Neoptolemus, by whom she had a son. After Neoptolemus' death she married Helenus, another exiled Trojan.

APHRODITE daughter of Zeus; goddess of love and desire.

APIDANUS a river in Thessaly, in N. Greece.

APOLLO son of Zeus and Leto, brother of Artemis; one of the most powerful and dignified of the Olympian gods. He was famous for his good looks, his prowess as an archer, his musical gifts, and above all his power of prophesying the future through his oracles, of which that at Delphi was the most famous.

ARCADIA a mountainous region in the central Peloponnese.

ARES god of war, usually regarded as a cruel and threatening figure.

ARGOLID the region around Argos in the Peloponnese, also embracing e.g. Tiryns and Nemea.

ARGOS city in N. Peloponnese, often conflated in tragedy with the older site nearby, Mycenae.

ARTEMIS daughter of Zeus and Leto; sister of Apollo, and like him an archer; virgin goddess, associated with hunting and wild animals.

ASIA   in Euripides a fairly vague term for the lands east of Greece, from the Hellespont as far as India.

ASOPUS   a river near the border between Attica and Boeotia, running south of Thebes.

ASTYANAX   infant son of Hector and Andromache, killed by the Greeks after the taking of Troy. He was flung from the battlements, in case he grew up to fight a war of revenge.

ATALANTA   a beautiful young woman who resisted marriage until won by Hippomenes, who defeated her in a race. Their son was the attractive Parthenopaeus, one of the Seven against Thebes.

ATHENA   daughter of Zeus; virginal goddess of wisdom and patroness of Athens.

ATHENS   the main settlement in Attica, in central Greece.

ATREUS   former king of Argos and Mycenae, father of Agamemnon and Menelaus.

AULIS   a Greek town in Boeotia, opposite Euboea; the place where the great fleet of Greek forces assembled to set out for Troy. Because of unfavourable winds, Agamemnon was forced to sacrifice his daughter Iphigenia before they could leave there.

BACCHANTE   a follower (usually female) of Bacchus, inspired with irrational ecstasy, often wild and violent in action.

BACCHUS   another name for Dionysus, god of wine and associated with other wild and sensuous pleasures.

CADMUS   son of Agenor from Tyre; founder of Thebes after he had slain a monstrous dragon guarding the site. He sowed the dragon's teeth, from which sprang forth warriors, the first men of Thebes.

CALLICHORUS   one of the sacred springs of Eleusis in Attica.

CAPANEUS   one of the Seven against Thebes, notorious for his sacrilegious boasting, for which he was struck down by Zeus' thunderbolt. In Euripides' version his wife Evadne kills herself on his pyre.

CAPHAREIUM   a promontory to the SE end of Euboea.

CARTHAGE   city in N. Africa (modern Tunisia), founded by Phoenicians.

CASSANDRA   daughter of Priam and Hecabe; priestess of Apollo, who tried to seduce or rape her, but she resisted. She had the power of prophecy (in some versions the gift of Apollo), but it was fated that she would never be believed.

CASTOR   like his brother Pollux (or Polydeuces), a son of Zeus by Leda; brother of Helen and Clytemnestra. In some stories only one of them was immortal, but they are normally paired as the Dioscuri or Heavenly Twins, elevated after death to divine status and placed among the stars (the constellation Gemini, 'the Twins'). They were thought to watch over sailors at sea.

CECROPIA a poetic term for Athens: see 'Cecrops'.

CECROPS early mythical king of Athens, allegedly half man, half snake.

CENTAURS mythical creatures, half horse, half man. They were ambiguous in other ways: some (particularly the wise Chiron, tutor of Achilles) were kind and benevolent to men, while others were dangerous or potentially violent. This violent side was notoriously revealed when the Centaurs got drunk at the marriage of Pirithous and Hippodamia; a pitched battle ensued (the battle of the Lapiths and Centaurs).

CHARYBDIS a deadly whirlpool, sometimes personified as a sea-monster. This was one of the perils faced by Odysseus in his wanderings.

CHERSONESE part of Thrace; a large promontory in the NE Aegean Sea; modern Gallipoli.

CIRCE an immortal enchantress who had the power to transform men into animals (esp. pigs); she succeeded in doing this to some of Odysseus' crew on his journey home, but the hero himself escaped and won her friendship.

CISSEUS father of Hecabe.

CITHAERON western part of the mountain range separating N. Attica from Boeotia.

CLASHING ROCKS one of the supernatural obstacles faced by Jason on his quest for the Golden Fleece – massive rocks which moved in the water to smash any ship passing between them. They were vaguely located in the Bosphorus area. He succeeded in passing this barrier, apparently with Medea's aid on the return journey.

CLYTEMNESTRA wife of Agamemnon, whom she murdered on his return from Troy, partly because of his treatment of Iphigenia, her daughter. Also mother of Orestes and Electra.

CRATHIS a river in S. Italy, flowing into the Gulf of Tarentum.

CREON one of the royal family of Thebes, brother of Jocasta. After the deaths of Oedipus' sons, he assumed the kingship.

CRONUS father of Zeus and mightiest of the previous generation of immortal Titans, whom Zeus and other gods overthrew.

CYCLOPS (plural Cyclopes) a one-eyed giant, hostile to men. The most famous Cyclops was Polyphemus in Homer's *Odyssey*, who trapped Odysseus and his men on their wanderings, and ate many of them before the hero managed to devise an escape.

CYPRIAN, THE (or 'CYPRIS') Aphrodite, goddess of love, who was born from the sea off Cyprus.

DANAUS father of the fifty girls known as the Danaids, and more generally conceived as the ancestor of the Danaans (which is sometimes a general title for Greeks but often more specifically means Argives).

DARDANUS first founder and king of Troy; hence the Trojans are sometimes called 'Dardanians'.

DAWN goddess personifying this natural phenomenon, conceived as young and beautiful; fell in love with the Trojan Tithonus (and in other stories Cephalus).

DELOS an island (one of the Cyclades), in the middle of the Aegean sea; birthplace of Apollo and Artemis and a major cult-centre.

DELPHI a town in the mountainous region of Phocis, location of the temple and oracular shrine of Apollo.

DEMETER goddess of fertility in nature, presiding over the crops and other products of the earth; mother of Persephone.

DIOMEDES son of Tydeus, and one of the Epigoni or 'Successors' who eventually sacked Thebes. He also participated in and survived the Trojan war.

DIONYSUS son of Zeus by Semele; god of wine and other natural forces; often seen as a wild and irrational deity, bringer of madness.

DIOSCURI ('sons of Zeus') Castor and Pollux, the Heavenly Twins; see 'Castor'.

DIRCE a wicked queen of Thebes, killed by Amphion and Zethus. After her death her name was associated with a stream near Thebes.

DODONA a sanctuary of Zeus in Epirus in N. Greece; one of the oldest Greek oracular shrines.

DORIANS one of the sub-groups of Greeks, often opposed to the Ionians. Sparta and Argos were Dorian states, Athens Ionian.

DORIAN LAND the Peloponnese, supposedly conquered in the Dorian invasion in very early times (12th century BC). The Doric dialect was used e.g. by the Spartans.

ECHO a personification of the natural effect of an echo.

EDONIANS(s) the name of a tribe of western Thrace.

ELECTRA daughter of Agamemnon and Clytemnestra; sister of Orestes, whom she supports in the murder of their mother.

ELECTRAN GATE one of the seven gates of Thebes, facing SE towards Mt Cithaeron.

ELEUSIS a major town in Attica, NW of Athens near the sea. Traditionally this was where Persephone, who had been abducted by Hades, was reunited with her mother Demeter. In historical times the Mystery-rites of Demeter and Persephone were celebrated here, and the town was famous throughout Greece for this reason.

ELEUTHERAE a small settlement in Attica, N. of Eleusis towards the border with Boeotia.

EPEIUS a Greek craftsman who, aided by Athena's inspiration, constructed the Wooden Horse.

EPIDAURUS a small state in the NE Peloponnese, south of the Isthmus.

EPIGONI ('Offspring') the sons of the Seven against Thebes who succeeded in sacking Thebes where their fathers had failed.

ERECHTHEUS a mythical early king of Athens. Hence the Athenians are sometimes called Erechtheids or 'sons of Erechtheus'.

EROS the personification of Love in boy's form, conceived as son and constant companion of Aphrodite (his father varies in different versions, but sometimes he is referred to as son of Zeus). The more familiar name 'Cupid' is Latin in origin.

ETEOCLES son of Oedipus and Jocasta; brother of Polynices, with whom at first he agreed to share power at Thebes; after one year of supremacy he refused to surrender power and so provoked war. He finally fell in single combat with his brother, who also died.

ETEOCLUS an Argive, one of the Seven against Thebes. Not to be confused with the more important Eteocles.

ETNA volcanic mountain in Sicily.

EUBOEA large island off the coast of Attica and Boeotia.

EUROTAS chief river of Laconia, the district around Sparta.

EVADNE wife of the Argive warrior Capaneus. After his death in the expedition against Thebes, she killed herself on his pyre.

FORTUNE personification of random chance or change of circumstances; as is natural in tragedy, more often mentioned in contexts of misfortune or disaster.

FURY a daemonic and dangerous creature who was thought to persecute evil-doers in life and after death; hence any horrific and avenging figure, especially female.

GORGON a type of hideous female monster with snakes for hair, so horrible that to look at one outright would turn a man to stone. The most famous Gorgon, Medusa, was slain by Perseus, who chopped off her head by looking not at her, but at her reflection in his shield.

HADES (a) one of the three most powerful Olympians, the others being Zeus and Poseidon. They divided up the universe, and Hades drew the underworld as his domain; (b) the underworld itself.

HALIRRHOTHIUS a son of Poseidon, who was killed by Ares for raping his daughter Alcippe. As a result Ares was obliged to stand trial at the Areopagus in Athens with the rest of the gods as his judges.

HECABE (Latinized as 'Hecuba') queen of Troy and wife (subsequently widow) of Priam; mother of Hector, Paris, Polyxena, Cassandra and others.

HECATE a sinister goddess associated with darkness, witchcraft and ghosts.

HECTOR son of Priam and Hecabe; husband of Andromache and father of Astyanax; the most valiant of Trojan warriors, killed in single combat by Achilles. After his death Troy was doomed.

HELEN daughter of Zeus and the mortal woman Leda; wife of Menelaus and mother of Hermione. She was carried away or seduced by the Trojan, Paris. The Trojan war was fought to get her back. She eventually returned to Sparta and lived with her husband.

HELENUS son of Priam and Hecabe; a prince of Troy who had prophetic powers. He survived the Trojan war and eventually married Andromache and became king in part of Epirus.

HEPHAESTUS son of Zeus and Hera; god of fire and of the arts of craftsmanship, especially metalwork, but lame and often treated disparagingly by his fellow divinities.

HERA queen of the gods and consort of Zeus; presides over marriage; often associated with Argos, one of her favourite cities.

HERACLES son of Zeus and Alcmena; greatest of the Greek heroes, famous for his many victories over monsters and barbaric peoples; enslaved by Eurystheus and compelled to perform twelve labours; after his death, deified and married to Hebe.

HERMES son of Zeus and the nymph Maia; messenger of the gods.

HERMIONE daughter of Menelaus and Helen; at first betrothed to Orestes, but subsequently married reluctantly to Neoptolemus, with whom she lived discontentedly until his death released her.

HIPPOMEDON an Argive, one of the Seven against Thebes.

HYADES 'the rainy ones', nymphs associated with water and rain. Like the Pleiades, they were imagined as goddesses enshrined in the stars and influencing the earth's weather.

HYMEN, HYMENAEUS perhaps originally a celebratory cry at wedding ceremonies, but often taken as the name of a god presiding over such events.

IDA a range of mountains in the Troad, where Paris the Trojan was exposed and raised by shepherds.

ILIUM another name for Troy.

INACHUS a river to the east of Argos.

IONIAN SEA the part of the Mediterranean separating mainland Greece from Italy.

IPHIGENIA daughter of Agamemnon and Clytemnestra. Her father was forced to sacrifice her in order to gain favourable winds for the Greek fleet; see 'Aulis'.

IPHIS an Argive, father of Evadne (according to Euripides' version; the legends differ).

ISMENUS a river to the east of Thebes.

ISTHMIAN COUNTRY see 'Isthmus'.

ISTHMUS the narrow stretch of land connecting central Greece with the Peloponnese.

ITHACA an island off western Greece, part of the kingdom of Odysseus.

LACONIA region in the S. Peloponnese, the centre of Sparta's dominions.

LAERTES former king of Ithaca and father of Odysseus.

LAOMEDON former king of Troy and father of Priam. Notoriously bad at keeping his promises, even to the gods. His failure to honour these debts led to the first sacking of Troy by Heracles.

LAPITHS a people occupying N. Thessaly, ruled by Pirithous; see also 'Centaurs'.

LEMNOS an island in the N. Aegean Sea. There was a story that the women of the island killed all their menfolk for taking concubines.

LETO a goddess or Titaness who bore Apollo and Artemis to Zeus on the island of Delos.

LEUCE an island of uncertain location where the privileged dead heroes were imagined to live on; among these was Achilles.

LIBYA part of N. Africa, sometimes loosely used to refer to the whole continent other than Egypt.

LIGURIA a region in N. Italy, extending along the coast from Genoa to what is now Southern France.

LOXIAS a title of Apollo, perhaps meaning 'crooked' or 'slanting', with reference to his ambiguous oracles.

LYCAEUS a mountain in Arcadia in the Peloponnese, a major sanctuary of Zeus.

MAIA a nymph, mother of Hermes by Zeus.

MAID, THE Persephone, consort of Hades. Although she had a kinder face, as daughter of Demeter and bringer of fertility, she is often regarded with awe, and 'the Maid' is a way of avoiding use of her name.

MENELAUS son of Atreus and brother of Agamemnon; king of Sparta; husband of Helen. The Trojan war was fought by the Greeks on his behalf, to recover her.

MOLOSSIA a region in Epirus, in NW Greece.

MUSES, THE nine in number, goddesses of the arts and especially poetry; daughters of Memory.

MYCENAE in very ancient times, a great centre of power and wealth in the Peloponnese. By Euripides' time it was eclipsed and indeed destroyed by Argos, with which in some passages it is virtually identified.

MYCONOS a small island in the Aegean, near Delos.

NAUPLIA town in the Peloponnese near Argos, serving as its port.

NEOPTOLEMUS son of Achilles by Deidameia; after his father's death, he came to Troy and played a leading part in the final stages of the war. In Euripides' version, he was murdered by the Delphians as a result of a plot laid by Orestes.

NEREIDS sea-nymphs, daughters of Nereus. Often associated with Thetis, mother of Achilles.

NEREUS a sea-divinity, often conceived as part man and part fish. He had the gift of prophecy.

NILE the chief river of Egypt and one of the great rivers of the world. In ancient times, as in modern, the question of its source was one which fascinated travellers and poets.

NYMPHS a generic term for a wide range of minor female deities associated with features of the natural world, notably rivers, trees and hills.

ODYSSEUS one of the chief leaders of the Greeks at Troy; son of Laertes, king of Ithaca, husband of Penelope. He was the favourite of Athena, and a cunning deviser of plans; often he was represented as too clever for his own good, and even as an immoral schemer.

OEDIPUS king of Thebes; son of Laius and Jocasta; by a terrible trick of fate he killed his father and married his mother, by whom he fathered four children, including the rival sons Eteocles and Polynices.

OICLES father of the Argive prophet Amphaiaraus.

OLYMPIA in the W. Peloponnese, the chief sanctuary of Zeus in mainland Greece, and location of the Olympic games.

OLYMPUS a mountain in N. Greece, on the borders of Macedonia and Thessaly. Because of its majestic height, it was considered the home of the gods, though the name is sometimes used more loosely, to describe a remote heavenly realm.

ORESTES son of Agamemnon and Clytemnestra, brother of Electra. After growing up in Phocis near Delphi, he returned to Argos to avenge his father's death.

ORION a gigantic hunter, who pursued the Pleiades, a group of nymphs; both pursuer and pursued were transformed into constellations.

OSSA a mountain in Thessaly, in NE Greece.

PALLAS another name for the goddess Athena.

PAN son of Hermes; half goat, half man, this lesser deity is a figure of the wild and is often thought to induce frenzy and fits of madness (hence 'panic').

PANDION early mythical king of Athens, grandson or great-grandson of Erechtheus.

PARALUS an Athenian commander who joins with Theseus in the expedition against Argos.

PARIS Alexandros, son of Priam and Hecabe. By abducting Helen, he caused the Trojan war and the destruction of his city. Paris was the name given to him by the shepherds who rescued him when he was exposed in infancy.

PARNASSUS a mountain north of Delphi, sacred to Apollo and the Muses.

PARTHENOPAEUS son of Atalanta; one of the Seven against Thebes. His name means 'maiden-boy', and alludes to his feminine good looks.

PELASGIA a term loosely used to refer to the area occupied by the original pre-Greek inhabitants of the Greek mainland; hence 'Greece' generally.

PELEUS son of Aeacus, king of Phthia, in Thessaly; a hero of the generation before the Trojan war; married to the sea-nymph Thetis, he became the father of Achilles.

PELION a mountain in Thessaly, in NE Greece.

PELOPS land of Pelops = Peloponnese.

PENEUS the chief river of Thessaly in NE Greece.

PERGAMUM or PERGAMA a name given to the inner citadel of Troy; more loosely, taken as referring to Troy itself.

PERSEPHONE daughter of Demeter, and often associated with her in cult. Abducted by Hades, she was eventually obliged to spend part of the year on earth and part in the underworld with her husband.

PERSEUS one of the great heroes of Greek myth, slayer of the Gorgon, Medusa. He was a forebear of the even greater hero Heracles.

PHARSALUS a town in Thessaly in NE Greece.

PHASIS a river flowing into the eastern extremity of the Black Sea, near Colchis.

PHOCIS the larger territory surrounding Delphi, to the west of Boeotia.

PHOCUS half-brother of the heroes Telamon and Peleus. They killed him and were consequently exiled by Aeacus, the father of all three.

PHOEBUS see 'Apollo'.

PHORBAS an Athenian captain, supporter of Theseus. In some versions he was said to have been Theseus' tutor.

PHRYGIA area in W. Asia Minor; often used more loosely to refer to Asia and the 'barbarian' territories generally. Hence 'Phrygians' often = 'Trojans'.

PHTHIA region in Thessaly, the kingdom of Achilles' son Neoptolemus.

PIRENE famous fountain at Corinth, allegedly created by the magical horse Pegasus ('Pirene's steed').

PITANA a township in Spartan territory.

PITTHEUS father of Theseus' mother Aethra, and former king of Trozen.

PLEIADES seven daughters of the Titan Atlas and of Pleione. They were pursued by Orion and turned into a constellation. They are associated with the marking of the seasons for farming activity.

POLLUX (Greek form is 'Polydeuces') one of the Dioscuri or Heavenly Twins; see 'Castor'.

POLYDORUS youngest son of Priam and Hecabe; sent into safekeeping in Thrace but murdered by Polymestor.

POLYMESTOR king of Thrace and treacherous ally of the Trojans.

POLYNICES brother of Eteocles and son of Oedipus and Jocasta; see 'Eteocles'.

POLYXENA daughter of Priam and Hecabe; sacrificed by the Greeks to appease the ghost of Achilles.

POSEIDON god of the sea and also of other threatening natural forces such as earthquakes.

PRIAM king of Troy, husband of Hecabe. He was the father of many children, especially Hector, Alexandros (also called Paris), Polyxena, Cassandra. At the sack of Troy he was killed by Neoptolemus.

PROTEUS like Nereus, an immortal sea-god and prophet. He had the power to change into any shape, hence the term 'protean'.

PYLADES son of Strophius, king of Phocis, and close friend of Orestes, who was brought up in Strophius' court. He accompanied Orestes in disguise to Argos, joined him in the killing of Aegisthus and Clytemnestra, and subsequently married Electra.

PYTHIAN associated with Apollo, whose oracle was at Delphi, sometimes called Pytho.

PYTHO another name for Delphi. The story was that Apollo had killed a huge snake (python), who had possessed the shrine before him. Hence Apollo bore the title 'Pythian'. The Pythian Games were held at Delphi.

SALAMIS an island off the SW coast of Attica; home of Telamon, father of the greater Ajax.

SCAMANDER one of the rivers of the plain of Troy.

SCYROS an island SE of Euboea, one of the Cyclades. Achilles took refuge there before the Trojan war and wooed the princess Deidameia; their son Neoptolemus was born there.

SEVEN AGAINST THEBES the gathering of heroic champions assembled by Polynices in order to attack Thebes at the head of the Argive army.

SEPIAS a cape in S. Magnesia, in NW Greece. It was there that Peleus had first encountered Thetis and won her as his bride.

SICILY large island south of Italy. Colonized by Greek settlers in the 8th and 7th centuries BC, and regarded in Euripides' time as a part of the Greek world.

SIMOIS a river of the plain of Troy.

SIREN the Sirens were a group of female creatures, part human and part bird, dwelling on a remote island, who entranced passing sailors with their song, luring them to their deaths.

SIRIUS the dog star.

SPARTA chief city of Laconia, kingdom of Menelaus and Helen; in historical times one of the dominant cities of the Peloponnese and regularly opposed to Athens. This antagonism is often projected back into the mythical period.

SPHINX a monstrous female creature which threatened Thebes and devoured her citizens until Oedipus, by solving her riddle, brought about her death.

STROPHIUS king of Phocis and ally of Agamemnon; father of Pylades.

TALTHYBIUS herald of the Greek army at Troy and particularly of Agamemnon.

TANAUS a river south of Argos in the Peloponnese.

TANTALUS son of Zeus and father of Pelops; ancestor of Atreus, Agamemnon and Menelaus. He was a great sinner who was punished in the underworld after death; the misfortunes of the house of Agamemnon are sometimes traced back to his actions.

TELAMON son of Aeacus, brother of Peleus and father of the greater Ajax; king of the island of Salamis, and one of the heroes of the generation before the Trojan war.

THEBE a town in the Troad, home of Andromache. She left it to come to Troy as Hector's wife. Subsequently Achilles sacked the town and killed her father and brothers.

THEBES chief city of Boeotia, north of Athens.

THESEUS son of Aegeus and Aethra; most famous of the mythical kings of Athens.

THESSALY region of NE Greece.

THETIDEUM a shrine sacred to the goddess Thetis.

THETIS a goddess of the sea, who married Peleus and bore him the hero Achilles. She abandoned Peleus and returned to the sea, but never entirely forgot her mortal connections.

THRACE a region to the extreme NE of the Greek mainland, beyond Macedonia; southern Greeks regarded it as primitive and savage.

THYESTES son of Pelops and brother of Atreus; father of Aegisthus, whose usurpation of Agamemnon's throne was partly a form of revenge for the crime of Atreus, who had killed Thyestes' other sons and served them up to their unsuspecting father for dinner.

TITANS an earlier race of immortals overthrown and replaced by Zeus and his fellow Olympians.

TROY city in Asia Minor, ruled by Priam and his family. In earlier times its kings included Dardanus and Laomedon. Its citadel was known as Pergama or Pergamum. The Greeks destroyed it at the end of the ten-year Trojan war.

TYDEUS one of the Seven against Thebes who died in battle there; father of Diomedes, who was one of the more successful Epigoni.

TYNDAREUS father of Helen and Clytemnestra, Castor and Pollux (some of these had Zeus as their real father, particularly Helen, but terms such as 'daughter of Tyndareus' are still used in a loose way).

ZEUS the most powerful of the Olympian gods and head of the family of immortals; father of Apollo, Athena and many other lesser gods, as well as of mortals such as Heracles.

READ MORE IN PENGUIN

In every corner of the world, on every subject under the sun, Penguin represents quality and variety – the very best in publishing today.

For complete information about books available from Penguin – including Puffins, Penguin Classics and Arkana – and how to order them, write to us at the appropriate address below. Please note that for copyright reasons the selection of books varies from country to country.

In the United Kingdom: Please write to *Dept. EP, Penguin Books Ltd, Bath Road, Harmondsworth, West Drayton, Middlesex UB7 0DA*

In the United States: Please write to *Consumer Sales, Penguin Putnam Inc., P.O. Box 12289 Dept. B, Newark, New Jersey 07101-5289*. VISA and MasterCard holders call 1-800-788-6262 to order Penguin titles

In Canada: Please write to *Penguin Books Canada Ltd, 10 Alcorn Avenue, Suite 300, Toronto, Ontario M4V 3B2*

In Australia: Please write to *Penguin Books Australia Ltd, P.O. Box 257, Ringwood, Victoria 3134*

In New Zealand: Please write to *Penguin Books (NZ) Ltd, Private Bag 102902, North Shore Mail Centre, Auckland 10*

In India: Please write to *Penguin Books India Pvt Ltd, 11 Community Centre, Panchsheel Park, New Delhi 110017*

In the Netherlands: Please write to *Penguin Books Netherlands bv, Postbus 3507, NL-1001 AH Amsterdam*

In Germany: Please write to *Penguin Books Deutschland GmbH, Metzlerstrasse 26, 60594 Frankfurt am Main*

In Spain: Please write to *Penguin Books S. A., Bravo Murillo 19, 1° B, 28015 Madrid*

In Italy: Please write to *Penguin Italia s.r.l., Via Benedetto Croce 2, 20094 Corsico, Milano*

In France: Please write to *Penguin France, Le Carré Wilson, 62 rue Benjamin Baillaud, 31500 Toulouse*

In Japan: Please write to *Penguin Books Japan Ltd, Kaneko Building, 2-3-25 Koraku, Bunkyo-Ku, Tokyo 112*

In South Africa: Please write to *Penguin Books South Africa (Pty) Ltd, Private Bag X14, Parkview, 2122 Johannesburg*

READ MORE IN PENGUIN

A CHOICE OF CLASSICS

Aeschylus	**The Oresteian Trilogy**
	Prometheus Bound/The Suppliants/Seven against Thebes/The Persians
Aesop	**Fables**
Ammianus Marcellinus	**The Later Roman Empire (AD 354–378)**
Apollonius of Rhodes	**The Voyage of Argo**
Apuleius	**The Golden Ass**
Aristophanes	**The Knights/Peace/The Birds/The Assemblywomen/Wealth**
	Lysistrata/The Acharnians/The Clouds
	The Wasps/The Poet and the Women/ The Frogs
Aristotle	**The Art of Rhetoric**
	The Athenian Constitution
	De Anima
	Ethics
	Poetics
Arrian	**The Campaigns of Alexander**
Marcus Aurelius	**Meditations**
Boethius	**The Consolation of Philosophy**
Caesar	**The Civil War**
	The Conquest of Gaul
Catullus	**Poems**
Cicero	**Murder Trials**
	The Nature of the Gods
	On the Good Life
	Selected Letters
	Selected Political Speeches
	Selected Works
Euripides	**Alcestis/Iphigenia in Tauris/Hippolytus**
	The Bacchae/Ion/The Women of Troy/ Helen
	Medea/Hecabe/Electra/Heracles
	Orestes and Other Plays

READ MORE IN PENGUIN

A CHOICE OF CLASSICS

Hesiod/Theognis	**Theogony/Works and Days/Elegies**
Hippocrates	**Hippocratic Writings**
Homer	**The Iliad**
	The Odyssey
Horace	**Complete Odes and Epodes**
Horace/Persius	**Satires and Epistles**
Juvenal	**The Sixteen Satires**
Livy	**The Early History of Rome**
	Rome and Italy
	Rome and the Mediterranean
	The War with Hannibal
Lucretius	**On the Nature of the Universe**
Martial	**Epigrams**
Ovid	**The Erotic Poems**
	Heroides
	Metamorphoses
	The Poems of Exile
Pausanias	**Guide to Greece** (in two volumes)
Petronius/Seneca	**The Satyricon/The Apocolocyntosis**
Pindar	**The Odes**
Plato	**Early Socratic Dialogues**
	Gorgias
	The Last Days of Socrates (Euthyphro/ The Apology/Crito/Phaedo)
	The Laws
	Phaedrus and **Letters VII and VIII**
	Philebus
	Protagoras/Meno
	The Republic
	The Symposium
	Theaetetus
	Timaeus/Critias

A CHOICE OF CLASSICS

Plautus	**The Pot of Gold and Other Plays**
	The Rope and Other Plays
Pliny	**The Letters of the Younger Pliny**
Pliny the Elder	**Natural History**
Plotinus	**The Enneads**
Plutarch	**The Age of Alexander** (Nine Greek Lives)
	The Fall of the Roman Republic (Six Lives)
	The Makers of Rome (Nine Lives)
	Plutarch on Sparta
	The Rise and Fall of Athens (Nine Greek Lives)
Polybius	**The Rise of the Roman Empire**
Procopius	**The Secret History**
Propertius	**The Poems**
Quintus Curtius Rufus	**The History of Alexander**
Sallust	**The Jugurthine War/The Conspiracy of Cataline**
Seneca	**Four Tragedies/Octavia**
	Letters from a Stoic
Sophocles	**Electra/Women of Trachis/Philoctetes/Ajax**
	The Theban Plays
Suetonius	**The Twelve Caesars**
Tacitus	**The Agricola/The Germania**
	The Annals of Imperial Rome
	The Histories
Terence	**The Comedies (The Girl from Andros/The Self-Tormentor/The Eunuch/Phormio/The Mother-in-Law/The Brothers)**
Thucydides	**History of the Peloponnesian War**
Virgil	**The Aeneid**
	The Eclogues
	The Georgics
Xenophon	**Conversations of Socrates**
	A History of My Times
	The Persian Expedition